Fishing FOR DUMMIES®

2ND EDITION

by Peter Kaminsky
with new material by Greg Schwipps

Wiley Publishing, Inc.

Fishing For Dummies®, 2nd Edition

Published by
Wiley Publishing, Inc.
111 River St.
Hoboken, NJ 07030-5774
www.wiley.com

About the Authors

Peter Kaminsky caught his first fish, a 30-pound grouper, on a party boat in the Florida Keys. It was the first time he went fishing, and that grouper won $45 for the big fish of the day. Kaminsky was hooked. He was Managing Editor of *National Lampoon* at the time. Soon after, he began to write for *Outdoor Life, Field & Stream,* and *Sports Afield.* In 1985, he began his regular contributions to *The New York Times* "Outdoors" column. Kaminsky also wrote "The Underground Gourmet" in *New York* magazine and is a frequent contributor on food and dining in *Food & Wine* magazine. He has written numerous books on cooking and fishing. His current book is Culinary Intelligence. As a television producer, Kaminsky is a creator and executive producer of The Mark Twain Prize for American Humor and The Gershwin Prize for Popular Song. Kaminsky is a graduate of Princeton University and lives in Brooklyn.

Greg Schwipps fished the farm ponds around his home in Milan, Indiana, as soon as he could walk to them. He later earned an MFA at Southern Illinois University at Carbondale, and he now teaches creative writing at DePauw University in Greencastle, Indiana. His work has appeared in outdoor magazines such as *Outdoor Indiana, Indiana Game & Fish,* and *In-Fisherman.* In 2010, his first novel, *What This River Keeps,* won the Eugene and Marilyn Glick Indiana Authors Award in the Emerging Writer category. He lives with his wife, Alissa, and their two dogs in Wilbur, Indiana, and fishes the White and Ohio rivers. www.gregschwipps.com

Dedication

From Peter: For Lucian and Honeybunch.

From Greg: For my dad and grandfather, who made the time to take me fishing.

Authors' Acknowledgments

From Peter: There are many people to thank, but first an anonymous thank you to all the anglers — men and women who have shared their knowledge, companionship, and often their tackle with me over the years. I would especially like to acknowledge the late Gene Calogiero (forgive me, Gene, I'm just guessing at the spelling, and you're not around to correct me anymore), who first taught me how to tie flies and fish the Esopus Creek; Nick Lyons for his generous counsel and support as I tried to learn how to write about this wonderful sport; John Culler for buying my first fishing piece in *Outdoor Life;* Duncan Barnes for years of putting up with my aging-hippy-writer's ways; Susan Adams for making a home for me at *The New York Times* (and Joe Vecchione for getting me started there); Tom Akstens for being an exemplar of a passionate and joyful angler; a debt beyond measure to the unsung Everglades guide Jack Allen, the most complete angler I know, who, by his example, has taught me that one can make a life out of angling, not rich in money, but face it, for most of us, the money isn't going to happen anyway, so we might as well enjoy the fishing.

From Greg: I should thank first the fine folks at Wiley who welcomed me into the 2nd Edition of *Fishing For Dummies:* Lindsay Lefevere for presenting the opportunity, and Sarah Faulkner and Elizabeth Rea for expertly shepherding me through the writing process. Thanks to copy editor Susan Hobbs, and to technical reviewer Jeff Knapp for his great insights. The fine angler Mikey Hemkens helped out, as well. Any writer would be lucky to have such a team. Thanks, too, to Lucia Watson, the super-chef who graciously shared some recipes with us, and a tip of the fishing cap to Doug Stange; he's a great fisherman and friend at *In-Fisherman* from way back.

I fish most often with my brothers, Tim and Ron, and our cousin, Ben. There are many lighthearted references to their prowess throughout this book. They're not quite as inept as I make them seem, but as always, I had fun making jokes about them in print. We fish most often for catfish, a long-neglected and maligned fish — may they continue to find their rightful place in anglers' good graces everywhere. (Right, Dr. Pepper?) Finally, thanks to my fishing partner, Alissa, who is a fine angler and a pretty danged good wife.

Publisher's Acknowledgments

We're proud of this book; please send us your comments at http://dummies.custhelp.com. For other comments, please contact our Customer Care Department within the U.S. at 877-762-2974, outside the U.S. at 317-572-3993, or fax 317-572-4002.

Some of the people who helped bring this book to market include the following:

Acquisitions, Editorial, and Media Development

Project Editor: Elizabeth Rea

Executive Editor: Lindsay Lefevere

Copy Editor: Susan Hobbs

Assistant Editor: David Lutton

Technical Editor: Jeff Knapp

Editorial Manager: Michelle Hacker

Editorial Assistant: Rachelle S. Amick

Art Coordinator: Alicia B. South

Recipe Tester: Emily Nolan

Nutritional Analyst: Patricia Santelli

Cover Photos: ©iStockphoto.com/ Lawrence Sawyer; ©iStockphoto.com/ Lisa Thornberg

Cartoons: Rich Tennant (www.the5thwave.com)

Composition Services

Project Coordinator: Katherine Crocker

Layout and Graphics: Melanee Habig, Clint Lahnen, Joyce Haughey, Corrie Socolovitch

Proofreader: Tricia Liebig

Indexer: Glassman Indexing Services

Illustrators: Ron Hildebrand, Joseph R. Tomelleri

Special Help: Sarah Faulkner, Jennifer Tebbe

Publishing and Editorial for Consumer Dummies

   Diane Graves Steele, Vice President and Publisher, Consumer Dummies

   Kristin Ferguson-Wagstaffe, Product Development Director, Consumer Dummies

   Ensley Eikenburg, Associate Publisher, Travel

   Kelly Regan, Editorial Director, Travel

Publishing for Technology Dummies

   Andy Cummings, Vice President and Publisher, Dummies Technology/General User

Composition Services

   Debbie Stailey, Director of Composition Services

Contents at a Glance

Table of Contents

Introduction

Tens of millions of Americans fish, and they can't all be crazy. Okay, maybe they can be. They're crazy-passionate about fishing and all that the hobby brings with it. They love the scenery, the camaraderie, the silence, the fight of the fish, the photographs of smiling people holding fish. They love to eat fish, or they love to fight the fish only to release it to fight again another day. They love to fish with their kids, grandparents, spouses, and friends. They love to be outdoors, near water. Don't you need a hobby to feel this passionate about?

Practically anyone can fish. Young people can fish with adult supervision, and they learn great lessons about nature and the environment, among other things, while doing it. Seniors can fish, and many retire every year with plans to do just that. With the help of handicap-accessible ramps and piers, and even motorized reels, those with physical disabilities can fish. Fish pay no attention to race, sexual orientation, or religion. Thanks to millions of acres of public waterways, fishing can be enjoyed by the wealthy and not so rich alike. Fishing is one of the most welcoming outdoor activities around.

Fishing isn't predictable, though (which, for some, is another reason to love it). Fishing takes you outdoors, and not just to the well-manicured and maintained golf courses and ski slopes. Although you can fish in brightly lit and public places, you don't have to, and some fishing finds you in some pretty wild places, indeed. You're always fishing near water, of course, some of it deep and fast-flowing, and there are plenty of sharp hooks around. For that reason, it's not a hobby to be taken lightly. You need to know what you're doing, and this book helps you get there.

About This Book

You're holding the 2nd Edition of *Fishing For Dummies,* which features much new and updated material that I (Greg) have added to the original, written by Peter Kaminsky. For example, I've added much of the material about boating, using circle hooks, and the pursuit of such fun quarry as catfish. That's why throughout this book you'll see "we" used often, or an "I" followed by one of our names in parentheses.

Just as your fishing gear and skills will evolve as you gain experience, the information in this book moves logically from more basic to advanced topics. You don't have to start here and keep reading in order to make sense of anything you find. This isn't a textbook — if a particular topic on the table of contents piques your interest, turn right to it; within every chapter we define terms and point you in the direction of any additional information that might help you located in another chapter.

Like all *For Dummies* books, this one aims to give you the information you need — say, to choose workable fishing gear, hook and land a fish, and know what to do with it once you land it — without burying you in obtuse language and terminology. You find here instead a casual and fun introduction to multi-species angling that we hope answers all your questions and encourages you to spend more time fishing.

Conventions Used in This Book

We use the following conventions throughout the text to make things consistent and easy to understand:

- ✔ New terms appear in *italic* and are closely followed by an easy-to-understand definition.
- ✔ **Bold** highlights the action parts of numbered steps and key words in bullet lists.

What You're Not to Read

We intend for this book to be a pleasant and practical read so that you can quickly find and absorb the fishing material you seek. However, we sometimes can't help going a little bit deeper or relaying information that expands on the basics. You might find this information interesting, but you don't need it to understand what you came to that section to find.

When you see a Technical Stuff icon or a sidebar (a gray-shaded box of text), know that the information next to the icon or in the box is optional. You can lead a full and happy fishing life without giving it a glance. (But here's a chance to make your fishing life even fuller and happier!)

Foolish Assumptions

Before we could write this book, we had to make some assumptions about who you, the reader, might be. We assume that you

- Have either fished before or want to start
- Want to have fun while fishing
- Are curious to know more about fish
- Desire to develop skills to fish in a variety of places
- Would like to know how to catch more than one kind of fish
- Seek to better understand the gear available
- Crave new information about fishing but don't have endless time to devote to the hobby

How This Book Is Organized

The upcoming sections give you a sense of our coverage of fishing. You might notice that the parts of this book follow a natural progression from getting ready to fish, to actually fishing, to dealing with fish that have been caught. You might want to start at the beginning, as you acquire some gear, or maybe you're ready to get a fish in the hand. Either way, don't be shy about casting into the book at whatever part intrigues you.

Part 1: Before the Bite

Fishing trips can be spontaneous and fun, but a little preparation goes a long way. Here, you find information about how to prepare for a fishing trip. We offer advice on how to dress, explore the water once you find it, and we even show illustrations of the fish swimming there! We also want you to stay safe while fishing, so we present a chapter on safety.

Part II: Gearing Up Without Going Overboard

You need some equipment to go fishing, starting with a rod and reel. But there's a lot of gear out there, and some of it costs quite a bit. This part explains what you need, what you don't need, and what you can wait to acquire later. We cover everything from circle hooks, just beginning to catch on in freshwater applications, to fishing from boats.

Part III: The End of Your Line: Enticing Fish with Bait, Lures, and Flies

The rod and reel matter, but the fish sees only what you present on the end of your line. This part walks you through your options, from completely natural livebait to synthetic lures. Livebait can be presented in different ways; not every lure should be retrieved the same way, and not every fly imitates every insect. This chapter helps you decide what to use, and when.

Part IV: Now You're Fishing

This part is where the water meets the hook. We tell you how to rig your line to present your offering naturally, and how to make effective casts. Then we help you land the fish that can't resist your mad skills. This part helps you tie on the hook, hook the fish, and then release the fish (if you choose) back into the water.

Part V: After the Catch

If you catch a fish that you intend to release, but want a decent photograph of it before it swims free, this part gives you advice on how to do that. If you decide to keep some fish to eat, we tell you how to clean and cook the fish. Recipes included here will help turn your fillets into wonderful, tasty meals.

Part VI: The Part of Tens

This part provides two "Top Ten" lists (with a nod to fellow Hoosier David Letterman): ten things you can do to get young people involved in fishing, and ten things we wish someone had told us when we started fishing.

Icons Used in This Book

One of the great things about a *For Dummies* book is the interactive icons used to highlight or illustrate a point. Here are the icons we've used throughout this book to draw your attention:

Some points are worth hammering home. When we reference a concept that we've discussed elsewhere or that is particularly important to your fishing experience, we use this icon.

We try to keep the information in this book light, but when we can't resist delving deeply into a technique or piece of equipment, we use this icon to let you know that the information is skippable.

This icon sits next to any information that saves you time, money, or frustration in your quest for better fishing.

Some actions can hurt the fish, your equipment, or you. We mark those with this dangerous-looking icon.

Where to Go From Here

We've organized this book so that you can either read it start to finish or dip into it here and there to find whatever specific information meets your needs. If you think you're ready to pick out a new rod and reel, turn to Chapter 7 for advice on how to choose a good one. If you'd rather get tips on how to evaluate a lake you've never fished before, check out Chapter 3. If you're pretty sure your first fish will deserve a spot on the wall, check out what we say about fiberglass replicas in Chapter 19. If you prefer traditional angling and traditional reading, turn the page and read this sucker straight through.

Enjoy *Fishing For Dummies,* 2nd Edition, and go fishing!

Part I
Before the Bite

The 5th Wave   By Rich Tennant

"Of course, if you're fishing for anything heavier than a 2-year-old, you'll need a different rod."

In this part . . .

The chapters in this part introduce you to the concept of fishing and many of the species of fish — both freshwater and saltwater — you'll attempt to catch. Covering both the basics, such as simple fish anatomy, to more complex principles, like how to evaluate fishing water you've never seen before, this part provides a lot of what you need to know before you begin fishing. A prepared angler is a successful one, and this part gets you ready.

Chapter 1

Getting Hooked on Fishing

· ·

· ·

*E*veryone knows someone who fishes. After all, more than 50 million anglers walk among us in this country. Maybe you're already an angler. Maybe you're just curious. Maybe you have a son, daughter, grandson, granddaughter, or neighborhood kid who needs a hobby that doesn't involve a screen.

Because I (Greg) have been fishing for almost my entire life, and have been fascinated by fish from my first memories (there's a photo of me wearing nothing but a diaper, holding a big largemouth bass my dad had brought home), people often ask me why I'm so captivated by fishing. Even though I think about fish every single day, it's not an easy question to answer.

But I think I fish for the same reasons so many others do: It's a chance to get outside, to be a small part of something bigger than my own schedule or routine for a while. I fish because I like hanging out in the places where fish live. Fish don't always behave the way I think they should, or follow my plans for them. The weather doesn't either. I like that unpredictability because it forces me to react, to strategize, to ponder. I like angling because I like spending time with fellow anglers. When I have a disappointing fishing trip (and what they say is true — there is no bad day fishing), I can't wait to go again. When I have a great fishing trip, I can't wait to go again.

We hope you can find something in fishing that sustains you, too. In this chapter, we give you an overview of this sport we love, from the motivation to get out there to an idea of where you should go to give it a try. Because there's some gear involved, as well as skill and technique, we introduce you to these topics as well, so that you're prepared to fish successfully.

Why Fish?

Fish are alive, and although the latest studies suggest that they do not feel pain, at least not in a capacity anywhere near the way we do, they do not jump at the chance to be caught. Using your gear and more importantly your mind, you must outmaneuver the fish. This presents an interesting, constantly shifting challenge.

Obviously, fish live in an environment much different from ours. Understand, though, that they're well-suited to that environment. With a few exceptions, they're cold-blooded and possess a good sense of smell. They live in the water (you already knew that), have backbones, and pull oxygen from the water through gills. They are shaped to move efficiently through water (many like torpedoes), using fins to navigate, and most are covered with scales. All fish are also covered with a slimelike mucus that protects them from disease and injury. (This is why you should only handle fish with wet hands — dry hands or a towel will remove this valuable slimecoat.) Fish don't have external ears, but they do have internal ones and are highly sensitive to noise like the thudding of a boat hull. Fish possess a lateral line, running from tail to head, that they use to detect low-frequency vibrations. They use this organ to locate prey and evade predators, while also gathering information about water temperature and current. So fish might not share many characteristics with humans, but they're a more than able opponent when it comes to people trying to outsmart them. They know their surroundings as well as you know your living room. Figure 1-1 shows a typical fish, with some of the traits described here.

Every angler has a particular reason for pursuing the sport, and after a few trips out to the water you're likely to figure out what it is you appreciate and enjoy about it too. From a little one-on-one time with Mother Nature to the calm and peace of the pursuit — not to mention the fact that you can often cook and eat what you catch, and that's not true in many sports — fishing has something for everyone.

For the outdoors

You probably already know this, but fishing is an outdoor activity. So the first reason to take up fishing is that it requires you to go outside. Some of us think that there's something soul-supporting about being outdoors, especially in those places that are natural.

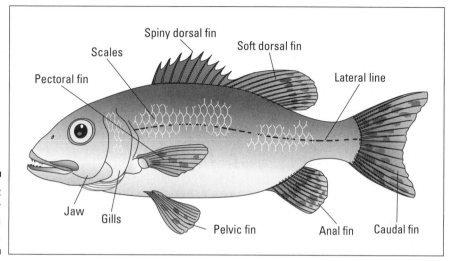

Spiny dorsal fin

Soft dorsal fin

Scales

Lateral line

Pectoral fin

Jaw

Gills

Pelvic fin

Anal fin

Caudal fin

Figure 1-1:
Meet your
average
fish.

For the enjoyment

Take up fishing because you need some time spent quietly by yourself. Or take up fishing because you want to spend quality time with others. Two anglers fishing in a boat, or wading their way quietly upstream, won't be distracted by scrolling news programs, honking cars, or instant messages. Cellphones can be turned off, and Facebook can be ignored for a while. Whether alone or in a small group, fishing quiets the mind.

This is not to suggest that all fishing is quiet! When a monster fish thrashes near the boat, or goes airborne trying to throw the hook, the adrenaline rush the angler feels rivals that of a linebacker after a crushing tackle or a tennis player after serving an ace. It's a physical sensation. (See Chapter 18 to find out how to land that behemoth bass.)

What fishing provides us might be one thing. You, too, will find a way to make fishing work for you. If you crave excitement, fish in a way that offers it. If you seek peaceful, introspective time, fishing can give you that, as well. And no one will make you commit to one kind of fishing all the time. Your fishing can evolve as you do.

For the table

Our ancestors fished for food, and you can, too. Fish are great tasting and good for you, as well. Chapters 20 and 21 tell you how to prepare fish for the table, as we even offer you some proven recipes, allowing you to make wonderful meals of your fresh-caught fish.

Many people today care about where their food comes from, and we like the idea of eating locally grown food. Well, when it comes to sustainability, fishing is tough to beat. Fish are a renewable resource. Selective harvest will ensure that you have plenty of high-quality food available for your lifetime, possibly from a source close to your home. As long as the water quality of your fishing spot remains good, a properly prepared fish can add a healthy option to your menu.

Where Should You Fish?

Chapter 3 discusses this issue in detail, but the best advice we can give you is to fish wherever you can. (Later, we also advise you to fish whenever you can.) Big fish come from both large and small waters. Beautiful places to fish can be found locally. Slip down into a streambed and you'll be surprised how wild your city can be. Many subdivision ponds are stocked, and some of them face very little fishing pressure. Inlets and tidal rivers attract wonderfully large fish at times, too.

Part of the joy and challenge of fishing lies in finding your favorite spots. Fish move seasonally, especially in rivers and oceans, so catching a particular species of fish all year long will often involve moving to follow their migrations. You'll also learn to go to different locales to catch different kinds of fish during certain times of the year.

Fishing freshwater

Not all freshwater fishing is the same, and almost every state offers a wide range of fishing possibilities. Michigan, for example, offers everything from small stream fishing for rainbow trout to Great Lakes fishing for lake trout. Even states far from giant bodies of water boast rivers of varying sizes and both natural and manmade lakes. Your gear, and your approach, will vary quite a bit from place to place, but this too is part of the fun of fishing.

Much freshwater fishing boils down to current: You're fishing in either moving or still water. And there are a lot of fish — and a lot of techniques to fish for them — in both kinds of water. Wherever you live, you are close to good freshwater fishing. Chapter 3 will help you learn how to seek it out.

Fishing saltwater

Saltwater fishing possibilities might not always be local since we don't all live near a coast. When you find saltwater, you find an almost limitless variety of fish. Many of the techniques used in freshwater carry over to saltwater; however, the game changes a bit when you're dealing with the fast, strong fish of the oceans.

For this reason, saltwater fishing can be intimidating. But if you limit your initial forays into saltwater fishing to the inshore waters — places like estuaries, beaches, bays, and marshes — you'll find that even beginners can find plenty of exciting action.

What Are You Fishing For?

I (Greg) once caught a flathead catfish that measured more than 49 inches long from a river that you can wade across in spots. This led my wife to remark, "Why did I ever dip my toes in there?!"

So what are you fishing for? Both salt- and freshwater bodies of water boast a vast range of species, many of which can be taken on rod and reel. Maybe you prefer to catch mostly bluegill and crappie, often taking a mess home to fry. Or maybe you've found great sport by wading flats of big lakes, taking carp on a fly rod.

Your favorite species might change over time, and you can always adjust your gear and tactics to specialize. You might switch seasonally, too. Some fish stop biting when the water reaches 50 degrees in the fall, whereas others bite all winter long. When you get into fishing, we promise you're not going to exhaust the possibilities.

Common freshwater catches

Just as there are many different kinds of habitat for freshwater fish, there are many different kinds of fish populating those habitats. Trout require cooler water. Largemouth bass do well in everything from farm ponds to big reservoirs, and anglers pursue them wherever they swim.

Big rivers hide big fish like catfish, striped bass, and carp, as well as fish like smallmouth bass and white bass. Natural and manmade lakes can be home to any kind of freshwater fish, including walleye, northern pike, and muskies. Bluegill and other panfish like crappies can be found everywhere, as well, from the largest river to retention ponds in subdivisions. Freshwater fish represent a diverse collection of gamefish, and each one of them brings something different to the angler.

For complete coverage of freshwater fish, turn to Chapter 4.

Common saltwater catches

The sky's the limit, or in the case of saltwater fishing, the sea's the limit. Even fishing inshore waters, anglers can catch everything from tarpon to flounder. Anglers fishing the northeast coast can expect flounder and cod to congregate in bays and river mouths. Striped bass and bluefish fall for lures from surfcasters, as will weakfish and seatrout.

Farther south, red drum (redfish), tarpon, and bonefish excite anglers as they cruise the shallow flats of bays. These fish can be taken on traditional gear or fly-fishing tackle. Snook fight like the saltwater version of the largemouth bass, and sharks cruise off many coasts. With saltwater fishing, you don't really know what you're going to catch next, which is part of its great allure.

For the lowdown on the range of saltwater fish available to you, check out Chapter 5.

What Do You Need to Fish?

Commercial fishermen — those fishing to gather fish or shellfish for food — often use devices like nets, traps, or long lines with multiple hooks to take fish. This book deals with sportfishing, which is fishing with a rod and reel. So, just as you need a few clubs to golf, you need a rod and reel to fish in the traditional sportfishing manner.

Beyond the rod and reel, your needs are few. You need a hook to snare the fish's mouth, and a line to get that hook from the rod to the water. You can keep your fishing simple. But, just as a golfer probably acquires more than a couple of clubs, anglers tend to gather the equipment that makes the pursuit of their favorite fish more successful and pleasurable.

The important thing to remember is that fishing does not have to be an expensive hobby. Unlike golf, you seldom have to pay to fish in this country (after you have the required license). However, if you are someone who likes to fish with nice equipment and the latest technology, well, all that awaits you, too. Anglers with deep pockets and a matching desire can fish from large, spacious boats boasting cutting-edge electronics and an arsenal of rods and reels.

One of your first choices when you begin fishing is to decide what kind of gear you intend to use. The four basic kinds are spincast, spinning, baitcasting, and flycasting. Figure 1-2 shows the four kinds of rods and reels, and Chapter 7 covers them in much more detail.

Figure 1-2:
Spincast (a),
spinning (b),
baitcast (c),
and flycast-
ing (d) gear.

a   b   c   d

Picking up fishing essentials

Basically, to begin fishing, you need a rod and reel spooled with line and a handful of *terminal tackle* — things like sinkers and hooks (covered completely in Chapter 9). Even someone who possesses one hook can probably find a garden worm somewhere and catch a fish.

Most likely, you'll want some kind of tackle carrier to carry your terminal tackle, and other *lures* (artificial, manmade baits) and flies. This could be as simple as a plastic tackle box or a fishing vest with pockets.

The right clothes will keep you comfortable and safe, as well. Anglers fishing from boats or near rapid current should wear a life jacket. Waterproof footwear may not be a necessity, but it's pretty close, at times. Sunglasses and a billed hat make life easier while fishing, as well. Figure 1-3 shows two anglers who are pretty much ready for any piscatorial challenge. Chapter 2 tells you much more about how to dress for fishing success.

Adding to your angling arsenal

Cabelas, the giant outdoor retail store, has been selling fishing tackle for nearly 50 years. Bass Pro Shops and Gander Mountain have been around for a long time, too. There are countless local baitshops, and stores like Walmart stock a whole section with fishing equipment.

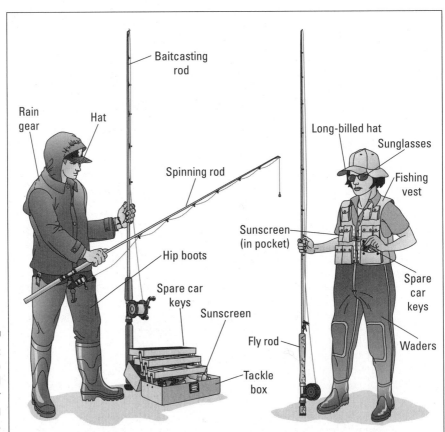

Figure 1-3: Two anglers, well equipped for most fishing trips.

There's no shortage of gear out there. As you get deeper into fishing, you'll see the need to get various pieces of equipment. Anglers who want to start catching striped bass need heavy line and a rod and reel built to handle it. A well-crafted fishing rod can be thing of beauty, so light and supple it feels like an extension of the hand. There's nothing wrong with desiring better gear.

So, while you should start with the basics, feel free to add to that pile of fishing tackle in the corner of your garage. Part of the fun of fishing is seeing how the latest gear can make you a more successful angler.

How Do You Fish?

Fish bite an object because they think it's something to eat, or they strike out of some instinct to do so — they're afraid, or protecting themselves or their young, for example. Fishing, then, requires that you offer something with a hook or hooks attached in hopes of getting a fish to bite it. You can do this by presenting livebait that the fish are used to eating — casting a hooked minnow into a school of crappies, for example. Or you may turn to trickery — using a fly tied to look like a grasshopper to hook a rainbow trout, or using the flash of a wobbling spoon to trigger an attack from a tarpon.

Whatever you use on the end of your line, *presentation* matters. Presentation refers to the methods you use to put your offering in front of the fish. You might cast and retrieve a crankbait past a largemouth bass, or use a river rig to anchor a chunk of cutbait upstream from a feeding channel catfish. Basically, you want to present a bait or lure in a way that looks natural to the fish, and the right presentation should allow you to hook the fish after it strikes.

Casting around: Basic and fly

Because fish are sometimes found some distance from shore, you need to get your bait or lure to them — and this involves the art of *casting*. Casting requires you to use your rod and reel to propel your offering to the target. When using spincast, spinning, or baitcasting equipment, casting requires you to use the flex of the rod to launch the lure outward, and the weight of the lure pulls the line off your reel. When flycasting, you use the (often longer) rod to flex the rod to cast the line, and the (often lighter) lure or fly goes with it.

Like any sport that requires you to do something with your body, casting calls for a certain amount of dexterity and coordination. However, even beginners can learn how to cast effectively. The casting motion (typically involving a swinging, overhead movement) is a simple, natural one. And not every fishing situation calls for perfect casts; many fish are found near shore or around piers or docks, and they require only short, simple casts. To find out how to cast using any of the four kinds of gear, check out Chapter 16.

Finding freshwater fish

Before you can catch a fish, you have to find the fish. That means figuring out where the fish are within a body of water. Understanding *structure* and *cover* helps you do that:

- **Structure** refers to the permanent features that mark a lake or stream — a drop-off, ledge, or a hole is structure. Fish relate to structure and often remain close to it.

- **Cover** consists of things like weedbeds, brushpiles, or floating docks. It matters just as much as structure.

Knowing that fish are often found near cover and structure helps you figure out how to fish for them. When you know where fish are, you can decide how best to approach them. Should you use a topwater lure, drawing a savage surface strike? Or maybe you should present your bait with a bottom rig, waiting for the fish to find and take it.

Different species of fish respond to different presentations, and with experience and the help of this book, you'll improve at both finding the fish and then getting them to bite.

Basic techniques for saltwater fishing

Most presentations involve either still fishing — where a bait or sometimes a lure is cast out and largely left alone until a fish finds it — or by retrieving a lure or bait. Baits and lures can be retrieved in different ways. Some lures are meant to be reeled in quickly, whereas others work better when *jigged* (hopped up and down by lifting and lowering the rod tip). Still other presentations include drifting or trolling baits or lures from a boat.

Fishing saltwater means understanding tides, and how the flow of the rising or falling tides affect gamefish. Because tides tend to congregate baitfish, locating gamefish becomes a matter of finding ambush points where these gatherings of bait become easy prey.

Finding a fishing mentor

Many of us were lucky enough to have a parent or grandparent to teach us how to cast for fish, and more importantly, to make the time to take us fishing. But if that's not the case for you, don't despair. There are plenty of ways to learn how to fish, and many people willing to show you a few shortcuts. We suggest finding someone who fishes for the fish you would like to pursue, and does so in a way that matches your personality. Watch others at boat ramps and baitshops. You might even seek out online fishing forums. Ask questions first to get to know someone, and then see if they extend an offer to take you fishing. Most are happy to share their excitement for the sport. Another option, albeit a costlier one, is to hire a local guide. Observing a guide for a day is a great way to learn about fishing from an expert. As always, don't be afraid to ask questions.

Fish On! Now What?

When a fish strikes your bait, fly or lure, the first thing you have to do is *set the hook.* This refers to the act of imbedding the hook into the mouth of the fish. Many hooksets involve lifting the rod sharply overhead, using the flex of the rod to drive the hook or hooks into the fish's mouth. When using circle hooks, the fish simply swims away until the rod bends deeply toward the fish — then the circle hook rotates around the corner of the fish's mouth and the bend of the rod drives the hook home.

After a fish is hooked, you have to *fight* the fish to the shore or boat, and this means controlling the ensuing struggle enough that the fish cannot wrap the line around a snag or do a number of other things to free itself. This is covered completely in Chapter 18, but you should always strive to keep the rod tip up, using the flex of the rod to maintain a tight line and keep the hook firmly planted in the fish's mouth.

It's not hunting: You can release fish

When a fish is in your net or hand, assuming the fish is legal, you have a choice to make: Do you release the fish, or keep it? (Fish that aren't legal — due to size restrictions, say, or species-specific rules on that body of water — must be unhooked and released immediately.) With practice, you can easily unhook a fish, and most fish, when fought to the bank properly, will zip off unharmed when released back into the water.

If the fight has been particularly long or grueling, the fish might be fully exhausted, in which case the angler might need to *revive* the fish before he or she releases it. Chapter 18 describes how to revive and release an exhausted fish.

Releasing fish ensures that other anglers will have the chance to catch fish, and releasing a trophy is a way to keep the right genes (the kind that make big, healthy fish!) in the pool. Of course, as mentioned in Chapter 19, be sure to get a picture of that award-winning fish before turning it loose.

But fish taste great, and you can keep a few, too

Because a fish's body is made up primarily of muscle, they are great source of protein. With practice, it's possible to clean fish efficiently and with a minimal amount of gore. When properly cleaned, fish can be cooked in many different ways, pleasing even the most discerning palate.

Chapter 21 includes recipes for preparing different kinds of fish in a variety of ways. Most of the recipes come from noted chefs Lucia Watson, owner of Lucia's in Minneapolis, and Peter Kaminsky, a chef and one of the writers of this book. You're sure to find a new favorite dish.

Chapter 2

Gathering What You Need to Fish

- -

In This Chapter

▶ Dressing smarter for fishing

▶ Packing a foul-weather bag

▶ Making waders work for you

▶ Picking the right tackle carrier

▶ Staying legal while fishing

- -

*B*e prepared. That's good advice that the Boy Scouts of America have followed for 100 years now. Some people want their trips to be spontaneous, fun, and unpredictable. Others don't get to go fishing as often as they would like (who does?) and so want every minute they get on the water to be as enjoyable and stress-free as possible. And that means being prepared for the unplanned things that inevitably happen while fishing.

And being ready doesn't mean your fishing expeditions will somehow lack spontaneity or fun. On the contrary — the more prepared you are for a trip, the more energy and time you can dedicate to the important stuff: the fishing. That's the enjoyable part, after all. No one has fun fishing in the rain, cold and hungry, knowing the rainsuit and lunch are back at the house.

This chapter gives you an overview of the basic things you might need before you hit the water. Don't worry — you won't need everything for every trip; the less you have to carry, the better. But we offer advice here for what to wear and what to carry that prepares you for most of your fishing excursions, most of the time. (If you still want to go fishing on every single trip looking like a total rookie, absolutely clueless to what's happening in the world around you, go ahead: Greg's brothers have been doing it for decades, seemingly with no ill effects.)

Dressing for Fishing Success

If you want to take up fishing because you like the idea of impressing other anglers with your latest outfit, you, my friend, are going into the wrong hobby. Or you're going into the right hobby for all the wrong reasons! What you wear while fishing isn't about impressing other anglers. But it should be about comfort and success.

You desire clothes that are comfortable, and you also want them to work for you in all weathers. Hemingway's Santiago says in *The Old Man and the Sea:* "Anyone can be a fisherman in May." And May fishing can be quite pleasant. It can also be cold, rainy, stormy, and downright nasty. And you're not only going to fish in May, are you? You want the right clothes for all seasons and all conditions.

As strange as it sounds, you also need clothes that help you catch fish. You want to wear clothes that don't scare fish by giving away your position, and you need gear that lets you get as close to the fish as you can while being as quiet as possible. But have no fear: We're not talking about getting ready for the prom, here. The clothes you wear while fishing can be inexpensive, old, and ratty. They probably should be. But you should think a little bit about what you're wearing, beyond that lucky feeling you get from your Grateful Dead t-shirt.

Wear layers and always be happy

You don't need to dress better, you need to dress smarter. Wearing layers is the key to adapting to changing weather conditions while fishing. Even on a calm, sunny day, you face big temperature swings on a typical fishing trip. When you start out, possibly before dawn, the day begins dark, chilly, and damp. Four hours later, you find yourself under a blazing sun cooking you with 95 degrees of oven-blast heat.

Of course, the weather can change beyond the normal progression of the sun, as well. Storms blow in, rain starts and stops. Winds pick up and die down. One outfit won't match all of these ever-changing conditions. Even with the latest clothing technology, which really is quite amazing, you need to dress in layers to be comfortable all day or night when fishing.

The basic setup in the following list will serve you in most places, most of the time. Modify it when it's ultra-hot, like in the tropics with no chance of anything remotely cool happening or, at the opposite end of the weather spectrum, when it's cold and going to stay that way, such as Lake Michigan in November. Outside of those extremes, follow this list and you'll be prepared for weather from about 40 degrees F to 90 degrees F, which is the range at which most of us fish:

- **Underwear:** Don a regular old cotton t-shirt and shorts in all but the coolest weather.

- **A long-sleeve cotton turtleneck or t-shirt:** This layer provides an over-all covering of your torso and protects your neck and chest from wind (which you can pretty much always count on if you're in a boat).

- **Long underwear:** Long underwear made of silk or synthetic fabrics that wick away moisture can be light, cheap, and warm. Even if you don't need it while fishing, it takes up little space and you'll be glad you have it when your jeans are wet and you haven't brought spare clothes for the drive home. In cooler weather, long underwear made from merino wool, nylon, polyester, spandex, or fleece will amaze you with its comfort, thinness, and warmth.

- **Hiking or athletic shorts (with pockets):** Have them in your gym bag in the car in case it's a warm day. This means bringing a gym bag with a change of clothes.

- **Jeans or khakis:** There's a reason that people just naturally wear these pants when given a choice. They're comfortable, they break the wind, they keep the sun off, and so on. If you don't like cotton, wear something made of nylon, polyester, or fleece.

- **Long-sleeve cotton shirt (for warmish weather):** When it's hot, we always wear a long-sleeve cotton shirt to keep the sun off. At this stage of the game, we think most of you know that prolonged exposure to the sun is disastrous on unprotected skin. And fishing is a pastime that gives you about as much sun as any human activity. Modern shirts have sun-blocking capabilities built right into the fabric, and advertise the UPF on the label.

- **Long-sleeve wool shirt (for cold weather):** Wool stays warm even when it's wet. For early spring and autumn fishing, you may prefer it to cotton.

- **Fleece pullover:** There are a lot of brand names for that soft, fleecy synthetic material. All are warm, lightweight, and comfortable.

- **Rain jacket:** You can buy very high-tech, very expensive rain jackets that "breathe." That sounds good, but the only thing that we have ever found that keeps you dry in an all-day soaker is a completely impermeable rain jacket. We always have one along when we're on a boat, not just for rain, but also to break the wind when you're making a move from one fishing spot to another. Get one that fits over your fishing vest. Make sure it has a hood. Waist-high is the best length for wading anglers.

If you forget your rain jacket, you can make a poncho out of a lawn-size garbage bag, so it's a good idea to keep a couple in your gym bag or trunk as well. Cut holes for the head and arms and, in a pinch, you're in business. Now, you'll look a little funny, but you'll be dry.

Pack your foul-weather bag

I (Greg) once wrote an article for an *In-Fisherman* magazine publication, and in it I sang the praises of my foul-weather bag. The cartoonist who provided the accompanying illustrations drew a large man hugging his foul-weather bag to his chest, a heart floating over his head. Okay, I can admit it: He got it exactly right. I would gladly wear a t-shirt proclaiming, I (heart) My FWB. And you will, too, once you make your own. Here's how to make a foul-weather bag that will win you over:

✔ Buy a waterproof packsack, available at most tackle shops and from big companies like Cabelas or Bass Pro Shops. The ones I like feature a roll-down top that buckles shut. It doesn't need to be large — about the size of a loaf of bread would do, but mine is about the size of a small office wastebasket. It should be waterproof and submersible.

✔ Stuff it with clothes and gear you might need, should the weather change or an emergency erupt.

✔ In my FWB: rainsuit, knit hat, gloves, fleece pullover, matches, socks. The rainsuit stays near the top because that's what I use most often. The fleece and the hat have kept me warm on many fall and spring nights.

It can be kind of a hassle to drag along the FWB at times, especially if you're traveling on foot and walking a good distance. If you know you're going to be out for only a short time, and the weather has little chance of changing, leave it behind. But when it doubt, bring it along. You'll be glad you had the extra clothing when you get cold or wet, and you'll find that the waterproof bag protects your gear if you don't need it. When the bag is packed, I never need to dry out the clothes or repack it. I just put it aside, and it's ready for the next trip. If I have worn something from the FWB, I simply put it back dry and folded tightly.

I (Greg) carry gloves on every fishing trip, but I don't bring them for the weather. My gloves are those lightweight cloth gloves dipped in a rubberized compound that are ideal for gardening and other outdoor work. As it happens, they work great for handling big fish like catfish with sandpaper mouths. You can buy gloves specifically for fishing, and they're all designed to help you handle fish easier. *Note:* You still don't want to grab a fish by its sides with dry gloves or hands, as this will remove the slimecoat. (Wet your gloves and hands first.) And most of these gloves aren't meant to protect your hands from the teeth of pike or some saltwater species. But they will keep a fish's sandpaper teeth from filing your hands.

Pick a good hat

Are some fishing hats luckier than others? Well, that's up for you (and the fish) to decide. But we do strongly recommend that you wear a hat while fishing. Hats will protect you from the sun or the rain (because you're probably going to see some of one or the other on most trips), and the hat's bill will help shade your eyes to allow you to better watch the water. Your hat, when worn in conjunction with a good pair of polarized sunglasses, will help your eyes cut through the water's glare. (For more on sun protection and sunglasses, see Chapter 6.) This will allow you to see what's happening beneath the water's surface.

A baseball cap works well, as does any brimmed hat, such as a booney hat, which will keep both your face and your neck cool and shaded. Anglers fishing the Caribbean flats developed a long-billed hat, sometimes called a _flats_ hat, which also features a bill in the back to protect your neck from the sun's rays. Some hats now come with ultraviolet protection factor (UPF) ratings, which reflect the sun-blocking capabilities of the fabric, and are ventilated to allow cool breezes to keep your brain from overheating while you ponder fishing strategies.

Because hats tend to blow off when riding in a boat, chin straps are a good idea.

Pull on waders to wander into the fish's world

If you plan on doing any stream wading or surfcasting, you need _waders_. Although you can wade in the warmest months wearing little more than shorts and sneakers, to fish in cooler water, waders offer you warmth and dryness. Essentially, waders are waterproof hipboots meant to cover at least part of your legs and possibly your torso. The first time you wade into a stream wearing waders, you'll marvel at the experience. Standing in the stream almost chest-deep, with the current gently swirling around you, is a little like becoming a fish yourself.

Waders come in a variety of styles, made from a few different kinds of materials. Waders, like tents and boots, are meant to be waterproof. But like tents and boots, waders suffer tears and punctures. Luckily, many times a hole can be patched.

Waders come in several different styles, and are available almost anywhere tackle is sold:

✔ **Boot-foot waders:** This one-piece chest-high outfit has rubber boots attached to the legs of the waders, making it the most convenient design for dressing in a hurry. It is also the only design for surfcasting because sand or pebbles cannot find their way into your boots.

Often, when you buy boot-foot waders, you have to choose between getting felt or lugs on the soles of the boots. When rocks are covered with algae, wet leaves, dead seaweed, or unidentifiable slime, they are very slippery. Felt soles cling and help to counteract the slipperiness. Lugged soles are okay, too, but you won't get the traction on slippery rocks that you'll find with felt soles. If you fish mostly in sand or mud, lugged soles will work fine. *Note:* On some streams, felt is illegal because of its tendency to transfer invasive species. To counter that, some manufacturers now offer soles made of things like crushed walnut shells. Look for these eco-friendly soles, or use cleats or lugs.

✔ **Stocking-foot waders:** Stocking-foot waders (which are also chest high) do not come with boots attached, so they require wading shoes. Many anglers prefer this style because they say sturdy wading shoes give them extra support while wading. To prevent abrasion of the stocking foot, you should always wear a pair of wading socks over the foot of the wader.

✔ **Hip waders:** Great for fishing streams in the summer. Hip boots reach your upper thigh, and can often be attached to your belt with garter-type straps (insert your own joke here). You can't go nearly as deep in hip waders as you can with chest-high waders, but if the river never gets that deep, why roast inside of chest waders? You'll also find it easier to go to the restroom while wearing hip boots.

Some wading shoes, like those made by Korker, feature interchangeable soles. You can also buy strap-on cleats that fit over your existing soles. These let you switch quickly from felt to cleats to match the conditions. Metal cleats are necessary when climbing on slippery jetty rocks.

Waders are often made of the following three materials, and vary in durability and comfort:

✔ **Neoprene:** The material used in wet suits, neoprene works well if you are fishing in cold waters. Walking around in neoprene waders on a hot day, you'll feel like a baked potato in a microwave oven. Neoprene punctures, like rubber ones, can be resealed. Neoprene waders keep you warm in water below 60 degrees F.

✔ **Rubber and nylon:** The least expensive of the bunch, rubber waders are basically rubber boots that "go all the way up." Most feature reinforced knee patches and factory-sealed seams. They can last a long time if cared for.

✔ **Breathables:** Made of Gore-Tex and other fancy materials, breathable waders are the most expensive, but they're ultra-comfortable. The breathable membranes of these waders allow you to stay cooler in warmer months.

When I (Peter) was a kid, we always had a laugh at the "old guys" who wore belts and suspenders. I still think it's kind of overkill for streetwear, but with most waders it's a must. You wear suspenders to hold up your waders, and the belt keeps water from rushing in if you get a dunking. This is a serious safety precaution. You can drown if your waders fill up.

Duct tape, the wader wonder

I (Peter) have one mounted fish on my wall. He's a 6¾-pound brook trout. I caught him on a stream in Labrador in early August. When I hooked him, I worked my way over to the side of the stream to continue the fight where I had a chance of winning. This required me to fanny walk across a number of midstream boulders. As luck would have it, one of those boulders had a sharp edge that tore a five-inch gash in my flyweight waders. When I had calmed down from the excitement of my gorgeous brookie, reality set in. When you're in the middle of Labrador and the nearest store is more than 100 miles away, you can't just hop in the truck and get a wader repair kit at the nearest tackle shop. I did have a roll of duct tape in my duffel bag. I ripped off a piece and ran it alongside the gash in my waders. I got another two full seasons out of them, and in the end, it was the seams and not my patch that gave out. Always carry a roll of duct tape.

Vests: Great for wading

Vests are such a common sight on streams that it's hard to imagine wading and fishing without them. Yet until Lee Wulff had the bright idea of sewing some blue jeans pockets onto a denim vest more than 70 years ago, there were no fishing vests. You can buy vests with a gazillion pockets and you can stuff every one of those pockets. And you can also make sure that you have every possible gizmo hanging off the little snaps and rings that many vests have. We know that some of you will because fishing, like every other pastime, has its share of gear freaks (like Greg). However, we recommend that you take as little as possible in your vest. When wading, it's advisable to travel light.

Here are the five features to look for in a vest:

- **Two large outer pockets suitable for holding a box of lures or flies:** The pockets should open and fasten from the top. If your vest has pockets that open on the side, you'll forget to zip up one day and eventually you will lose a box of expensive flies or lures.

- **Four inner pockets:** These are smaller, and it's okay if they only have Velcro and no zippers. You may put a box of split shot in one pocket, tippet or leader material in another, and bug repellent in another.

- **Four small outer pockets:** One should have a zipper for an extra car key. The rest are for a small box to carry flies, floatant, and this and that.

- **A metal ring:** You can tie your clippers onto this. They do make retractable pin-on gadgets that are designed as clipper holders, but we've had bad luck with those gadgets breaking. Save old fly line for these kinds of jobs instead. Tie your clippers on with them. Fly line is also a free alternative to Croakers for holding your sunglasses when you want to keep them handy.

✔ **Outside back pouch:** Put your rain jacket in here, or maybe your lunch, water bottle, extra reel, and so on.

Now that you have a vest, here are ten things you should always carry in it:

✔ **Sunscreen:** Use it for all daytime fishing.

✔ **Insect repellent:** For obvious reasons.

✔ **Clippers:** For cutting leader and trimming knots, clippers are preferable to teeth because clippers don't need to go to the dentist.

✔ **Thermometer:** Many tackle shops sell inexpensive thermometers designed to withstand being tossed about in vests and tackle boxes. With a thermometer, you can tell what species of fish may be most actively feeding.

✔ **A plastic garbage bag:** You may not keep fish as a rule, but every so often you will want to, and who needs a vest full of fish slime? You don't need a lawn-size Hefty bag; a wastebasket liner is more like it.

✔ **Forceps:** They help remove hooks more easily. This is good for the catch-and-release angler who wants to get the fish back in the water in a hurry. And it's always good for dealing with fish with sharp teeth.

✔ **Rain jacket:** It doesn't take up much room and it makes a big difference, especially when it rains!

✔ **Spare car key:** Everybody loses the car key sometimes. It's a bummer if this happens when it's dark and cold by the side of a trout stream 20 miles from home. If you have a key with electronics, keep it in an airtight plastic bag.

✔ **Flashlight:** They make small flashlights that you can clip on and aim so that you have two free hands for knot tying, removing hooks, and so forth. Then, on the way to the car, you can see where you are going.

✔ **First aid kit:** It's easy to find a compact first aid kit. Buy one and keep it in your vest at all times. If you're allergic to bee stings or other insects' bites, make sure you have something to treat severe allergic reactions.

Carrying Just What You Need to Fish

Okay, maybe it seems like we're loading you down with gear here. Admittedly, to be totally prepared for everything that can happen while fishing, you'd have to carry a truckload of stuff. You can't, and you shouldn't have to. Do this: Have what you need available, and bring the gear that a particular trip calls for, as well as you can predict. With experience, this process of choosing what to bring gets easier.

Bringing stuff also gets easier if you have the right tools to carry the stuff. A good fishing vest is one such tool (check out the previous section). A tackle carrier is another vital tool. Of course, an angler who shows up at the lake with his vest, foul-weather bag, and tackle carrier but no rod and reel looks like a ding-dong.

Start with your rod and reel

Everything you need to know about choosing a good rod and reel is covered in Chapter 7. You can choose a setup that best matches the kind of fishing you do, and most likely you'll end up someday owning more than one or two. Most beginners start with a medium-length rod, between five and six feet long, and either a spinning or spincast reel. That's a light outfit, with a relatively short rod, that transports well and carries easily.

As your fishing evolves to match your tastes, your rod and reel will likely change. With any rod and reel, remember that you have to get it to wherever you're fishing. The rod's most important job, of course, occurs on the water. But before it gets to the water, it has to survive inside of your car's trunk. Or a boat compartment. Or the mile-long trail down to the stream. Most rods "break down," meaning that they can be separated into sections. This makes packing easier. Some rods are one-piece, so think about your travel issues before you purchase a rod. Although you won't need them for basic fishing, rod carriers are available. Often made from tough plastic, rod carriers protect your gear while in transport. (Some require that you remove the reel from the rod first, which can be done fairly easily. Others are designed to hold the rod with the reel attached.)

Pick a tackle carrier and load up

In the old days, tackle boxes were metal and looked like miniature tool boxes. Today's anglers can choose from tackle carriers that are as varied as the selection of suitcases in a luggage store. Tackle carriers house your lures, flies, hooks and other terminal tackle, and maybe a spare spool of line. Most have varying compartments to keep gear organized, and the plastic is often designed to keep soft plastic lures from melting. As there are different kinds of fishing, there are different kinds of bags. (Some are built to hold many spinnerbaits, for example. Others, the giant plugs of the muskie fisherman.) You have a lot to choose from when it comes to the latest tackle carriers.

Anglers can still buy the traditional tackle box, although plastic has replaced metal. These are a good choice because they are waterproof when sealed, available in many different sizes and styles, and tough as nails. Some feature drawers with compartments to hold things like lures and hooks, others have removable utility boxes that can be filled with your stuff. Others offer trays that fold out when you open the box. A good tackle store will have a range of boxes available, and there are even more options online. Shop around and handle a few before you buy. They come in hundreds of different sizes and styles. Some are difficult to carry for long distances; others work better on the floor of a boat.

Soft-sided tackle bags are increasingly popular now. These come in different sizes, as well, and can be filled with plastic utility boxes that you can mix and match for different trips. You might have one box of largemouth bass plugs; another box might hold all your walleye jigs. Some of these bags have handles that double as shoulder straps, allowing you to wear the bag as a backpack. Bags come in colors ranging from green to pink, and can have nifty zippered compartments, d-rings, and built-in sunglass holders.

A word on size: You need a tackle box or bag big enough to hold your gear, but the bigger the carrier is, the clunkier and heavier it gets. My advice is to buy a bag or box that feels right for your current needs, then sell it or give it to a friend when and if you outgrow it. Lugging around a tackle box half full is like seeing a stadium half full of fans. There's a lot of wasted space.

Don't forget food and drink for yourself

We cover the importance of drinking a lot of fluids in Chapter 6 because staying hydrated is both a safety issue and a comfort issue. You need to pack a lot of drinking water or sports drinks (say, a bottle every couple of hours or so, because it's never a good idea to drink from the water you're fishing. Drinking plenty of fluids (that you brought from home) will keep you sharp and clear-headed. If you pack a cooler, freeze some water in plastic bottles. It will keep your food cold, and as it thaws, you'll have nice cold water to drink.

But you don't want to go hungry, do you? Bring a sandwich or two, and some apples, bananas, and nuts. A plastic container of peanuts can be tipped to your mouth without having to handle the goods.

On my boats, I (Greg) carry a plastic container of handi-wipes. Meant for things like road trips with little kids in the car, these containers fit in a cup-holder and offer an easy way to clean the bait and fish slime off your hands. I always feel better eating my PB&J after having cleaned the shad guts off my fingers.

Some sandwich thoughts from Peter: I'm taking it for granted that you already know how to make a sandwich. Over the years, I have found just a few common-sense things that have resulted in better sandwich eating or at least less sandwich disasters in the bottom of the cooler:

- **Wrap it small and tight.** A big hero sandwich looks great, but you will not normally eat it all at once. Then you are in the position of having to rewrap it, which hardly anyone ever does properly, and the result is a lot of salami, lettuce, and tomato bits rolling around the cooler or the back of your vest. Cut the sandwich into smaller pieces and wrap each piece individually. I use wax paper or cling wrap for wrapping and then I put everything inside a plastic bag.

- **Dry is good.** Although soggy bread may be good for bait, it's lousy on a sandwich. Remember that a sandwich to take along on a fishing trip is not the same as a sandwich that you make at halftime while watching the game on TV. Often, you are not going to eat your fishing sandwich for a few hours. That mayonnaise that tastes so good on a ham sandwich in the den is going to squoosh right through the bread when you unwrap your sandwich at the stream. Sliced tomatoes will soak through the crustiest, freshest roll. My solution is to cut down on the wet stuff, and if I absolutely need some, then I put it next to the meat and cover it with a piece of lettuce or a slice of cheese.

Tucking Your Fishing License in a Safe Spot

Fish are a natural resource, and as such, they belong to everyone and to no one. Actually, if you fish legally and catch a legal fish, then that fish belongs to you. But you still have to follow the rules. Fish populations are monitored and sometimes managed by your local Department of Natural Resources and Fish and Wildlife divisions, and their goal is to ensure healthy, well-balanced populations of fish. Those rules and laws governing wild game help maintain that balance, and Conservation Officers are the law enforcement branch of the DNR. When fishing, you may be visited by a Conservation Officer, and he or she might ask to see your license and inspect your gear.

Obviously, to prepare for this event, you need to have your license with you at all times. You also need to know the laws affecting the kind of fishing you are doing. Be courteous and let the officers do their job. They work to protect the same resources and places you love.

Carry your license in a waterproof container, or place your license in your wallet and your wallet in a sealed plastic bag.

Like anything governed by rules or laws, in fishing there are those who knowingly break the laws for their own gain. Most often this involves an angler taking more fish than he is legally allowed to keep, or by catching fish using illegal methods. Most states have a toll-free number that you can call to report this sort of activity to Conservation Officers, and we recommend you do just that if you see someone wantonly breaking the fishing laws in your area. After all, a poacher is taking fish illegally — fish that you and other law-abiding citizens will no longer be able to catch. It is your right to report poaching.

When you need a license

Check the laws for the state in which you are fishing before you wet a line. Some states, especially those that offer both salt- and freshwater fishing, have varying rules about when and where you need a license. But, as a rule, if you're fishing public property, you need a license. If you're fishing private property, you may not need a license, but you need permission from the landowner. If you're fishing in the state in which you reside, you qualify for a less-expensive, in-state license. If you're visiting the state you're fishing in, you must buy an out-of-state license, and these tend to be more expensive. For example, in Indiana, a resident annual fishing license is $17. An out-of state annual license is $35. Seniors often get a discount, and often children under age 16 don't need a license. Check your state's laws.

Where to buy fishing licenses

Most baitshops can still sell licenses, along with big-box stores like Walmart. It has become increasingly common to buy your fishing license online, though. Find the website of your local Department of Natural Resources, and you will most likely find a page where licenses can be purchased. Often you pay for your license with a credit card, then simply print a copy of your license to carry with you at all times. You can print more than one copy, in case one gets wet or lost. Try to buy your license before your fishing trip commences, so that's one less thing you have to worry about the morning of your trip.

Chapter 3

Finding and Evaluating Water for Fishing

Simply put, every decision I (Greg) make about how and what I'm fishing for follows the first, crucial decision: where I'm fishing. You don't fish streams the same way you fish ponds. Big rivers aren't lakes. Public piers jutting out from the beach aren't exactly like an untouched tidal inlet. So begin your fishing adventures by studying the body of water you intend to fish. When you know the water, you'll begin to know the fish in it. And then the fun — the catching — begins!

Wherever you fish, follow the same advice I give writing students: Pay attention to the world around you. Watch the water. Every swirl and splash tells you something. The fish's world is largely hidden from you, but if you pay attention, you'll find that every body of water provides hints about what's happening below the surface. Watch the prey (frogs, minnows, and the like) and fellow predators like birds, and they'll tell you where the gamefish are.

All fish, in any body of water, relate to two key things: *structure* and *cover*. Structure refers to what lies beneath the surface of the body of water; a sharp drop-off or a *point* (a finger of land jutting into the water) is structure, for example. Think of structure as permanent features. Cover could be things like a weedbed or a sunken log. Manmade cover, like docks or piers, hold fish just as natural cover does. Be aware of structure and cover and you'll find — and catch — more fish.

This chapter helps you figure out where to fish and then how and when to fish that location. There are a lot of variables at play when it comes to finding and evaluating fishing waters, but we do our best in this chapter to call out some typical conditions for both freshwater and saltwater locations.

Knowing Where to Go

As Chapters 4 and 5 make clear, there are hundreds of species of fish await-ing you. While they prefer a variety of habitats, some of those fish invariably live close to you. Although no two waters are exactly alike (and that's part of the fun of this whole adventure!), streams in the Midwest share some things in common with streams in the east or anywhere. Farm ponds are alike wher-ever you go. What you learn in one spot will add to your understanding of how to fish the next.

Fishable water is where you find it. Train yourself to look for water with the following two characteristics:

 ✓ **Access:** Fishable water is either open to the public or privately owned. Public water is governed by rules, and your first step is to investigate and learn those rules. Is fishing allowed only during certain hours? Are there rules in addition to state laws that regulate the fishing? If the body of water is open to the public, these rules should be posted or otherwise available. (See the section on fishing licenses in Chapter 2.)

 If the water is privately owned, then you must ask that owner's permis-sion. Never fish first, intending to ask later! It's not only rude, but illegal. However, many landowners will grant you permission if you ask politely. Common sense rules apply: Ask in a courteous manner; take rejection if it comes; be honest about your intentions (whether you intend to keep or release, for example); and don't bring all your friends. In other words, it's a lot like asking a father for permission to date his daughter. If you're fishing in a farm pond, remember to shut all gates behind you — you don't want to let any animals out!

 ✓ **Fish:** Sometimes giant bodies of water hold only stunted populations of scrawny fish. Occasionally the little pond on the golf course yields a ten-pound largemouth. The only real way to know is to study the water. Private landowners often know what fish have been stocked in that body of water. Some public places will post notices about the fish available, too. Better yet, check your state's Department of Natural Resources (DNR) Web site. It will most likely list popular fishing areas as well as the fish you can expect to find there. Ideally, you should seek water that carries a healthy supply of your favorite kind of fish in an aesthetically pleasing environment. How do you find such a paradise? This chapter helps you locate it.

Fish the one you're with: Finding fishing water close to home

Familiarity breeds success when it comes to fishing. Show me (Greg) a person with a shack on the river, or a bay house with a boat tied to the dock out back, and I'll show you someone who can catch fish when others cannot. The more time you spend on a body of water, the more you get to know it, and the better you understand its personality as seasons pass. Living along a stream will acquaint you with the length of time it takes to return to normal flow after a flood. Visit a lake every weekend for a year, and you begin to understand when baby shad congregate in the shallows, and when bluegills spawn. Guides know their home water because it's their job: They fish it five or six days a week.

But you can get to know a piece of water, too, even without quitting your day job. Just give the water time; even if you can only fish for an hour after work, every hour adds to your understanding. Now, I know some anglers only fish a particular place for a particular species, even if this place is far away: say, fishing for pike in remote fly-in camps in Canada. These anglers save up and go once a year, and that's the sum of their fishing. Fine, but that's not the way I do it, and I don't think it's the way to really understand and love fishing.

Locate a fishing spot close to your home or work, and fish it regularly. Keep your eyes and ears open every time you visit. Take note of the fish you catch: What did it bite on? Where was the fish when it hit? What was the water like? The weather? Every fish you catch helps you complete the puzzle. Fishing a place regularly — and throughout the seasons — helps you become a better angler.

Finding fish when you're on the road

A big part of the fun of angling is fishing in new places, for new and different fish. If you travel with a packable fishing rod, a handful of lures or flies, and a small collection of terminal tackle, you can be ready to fish anytime, any-place. (Just make sure you're fishing legally! See the section on licenses later in Chapter 2.) Perhaps you could steal away during the next family vacation for a visit to the beach. Maybe you could skip the evening cocktail hour at the next conference. If your travels bring you closer to new and exciting fish-ing, even a short foray could make a great angling memory!

You won't know this water well, and you won't have time to study it. But bodies of water share characteristics. Also, techniques that work in one stream will work in another. (See Chapter 17 for more on techniques.) And local baitshops can provide the best baits for that area or lures, as well as helpful advice.

Investigating fishing waters on Google Earth

By now, you've probably seen your house from space. That's certainly cool, but what about putting that technology to better use by using satellites to plan your next fishing trip? A program like Google Earth makes it possible to follow streams and rivers, seeking public access landings. You can also find hidden coves on big lakes, or small ponds hidden from the public eye. You'll still need permission or a license to fish these finds, of course, but finding the water is the first step. Visit `www.google.com/earth` to download the application.

Even without local help, though, you can catch fish. Certain lures, like small in-line spinners, tend to work everywhere. And you can always try giving the fish some version of whatever it is they're feeding on. Fishing far from home will challenge you. You're not likely to match your catch totals from your home waters, but there's always that chance. . . .

Getting the Scoop

Okay, so you find some fishable water. You fish it a few times, and try to pay attention to what the water (and the frog and minnow) tells you. But you still can't catch fish, or catch enough of them. There's no shame in asking for a little advice. Every angler has done this a few times.

But you might find that everyone has advice when it comes to fishing. Everyone! Some old guy at the gas station who hasn't fished since before color television will tell you to dangle a marshmallow under the bridge out on Tailbone Road to catch trout. Then he might tell you about transmissions or what the President is doing wrong. You need advice you can use, and you don't have all day. There's fish to be caught! This section takes you on a tour of reliable places to gather information.

From baitshops

Local baitshops are a tried-and-true source of fishing insight. Baitshops probably came into existence right after bait, and good ones carry an established reputation along with hooks and sinkers. Baitshop owners (and your fellow customers) often know the water nearby. They can refer to the handy map taped to the wall, or even mark the copy they sell you. They stock lures and livebait that works in local waters, as well as advice on how to use them.

The baitshop is a business, and that business isn't Free Advice. They need to sell items to keep the doors open, so I'll often buy something (even if it's just a candy bar for me) to get people talking. Another tip: Study the fish pictures tacked to the walls. Just knowing what fish are out there helps you plan your approach. Now, if all the fish pictures look as old as your grade school class photo, that's telling you something else.

From online forums

People say all fishermen are liars, and I (Greg) suppose there might be some truth to that. But I've found that anglers are surprisingly forthcoming in online forums. Often dedicated to a particular species or region, forums and Web sites can save you a lot of time on the water. And unlike baitshops, they're open all night long, allowing you to do your research at night and your fishing during the day. Use a search engine to find and bookmark the best ones for your area or your kind of fish. The free forum I'm a member of allows me to search every state, and then I can select "local talk," "streams/rivers," or "lakes/ponds." Within each section are countless threads about what's being caught and through what methods. Often members will offer to take strangers fishing. Like all things online, it's good to be cautious, but it's a pretty amazing resource when you think about it.

You should also check out your state's Department of Natural Resources Web site. They sometimes post fishing reports and even survey results from local bodies of water.

From guides

Guides are anglers who get paid to take you fishing, and the best guides are equal parts anglers and teachers. A good guide will know the water and a great deal about the fish within it. You can find guides online, in the yellow pages, or through word of mouth at the baitshop or boat ramp. Most can be hired for either half- or full-day trips, and in return, you can expect the guide to do most of the work for you.

What do you do as a client? Pack, sunscreen, rain gear, a camera, and a good attitude. (Ask if lunch and drinks are included; if they aren't, pack those too.) Pay attention and ask questions. Guides fish their home waters five or six days a week, and that kind of experience is invaluable. Most guides will offer advice on technique, lure selection, and habitat. Costs vary from location to location, but plan on tipping a bit over the initial charge if your guide works hard for you. (Don't punish a guide for the morning's cold front that shut the fish down. Even the best get skunked sometimes.)

When no one knows: Walk the bank

Suppose you find a fishing hole no one has seen before. Let's say it's on another planet. There's no local baitshop; no online forum mentions it. Can you still figure out this lake, and what lives within it? Of course you can. It comes back to paying attention: Walk the banks and watch the water. What's the water clarity like? Cloudy or stained water means fish probably aren't feeding visually — a loud, noisy lure like a spinnerbait might work. Are weeds prevalent? Moss? Baitfish will hide under moss and in weedbeds, which mean predator fish will patrol nearby. See schools of baitfish? Can you identify the species? If there are babies, there will be adults to catch, of course. Be on the lookout for dead fish or skeletons because these, too, will tell you what species live here. Without wetting a line you can learn a lot about a body of water and the fish that live there.

Evaluating Freshwater Sites

From a backwater slough to the Mississippi River to Lake Tahoe, how can an angler approach such varying freshwater? First, he or she realizes that only knowing one approach won't work. Different kinds of water call for different techniques (see Chapter 17), different gear, and different mindsets. Sure, all fishing has a lot in common, and your angling knowledge is transferable from one situation to another, but great anglers adapt to the situation and habitat they're facing.

Ponds

Natural and manmade ponds dot the landscape. They range from farmponds made as a source of drinking water for animals, to strip pits — stone-lined quarries left behind after mining companies move on. Ponds can support a lot of fish if carefully managed, and they provide a safe fishing environment for millions of anglers. Some ponds have fish populations that are carefully monitored by humans, others have wilder, more natural populations that self-regulate. Contrary to popular belief, birds don't spread fish eggs from pond to pond.

Who's home?

Largemouth bass, bluegills, and crappies are the classic choices for pond stocking, but channel cats are popular, too. If a pond has water that stays cool enough year round, trout can survive. (This is true of some quarry ponds, where the water is deep and clear.) A well-managed pond will feature all the habitat of larger natural bodies of water, with plenty of cover, good water quality, and a healthy balance of fish populations.

A poorly managed pond, though, is little better than a mudhole, with strangling weeds, silted water, and bare, eroded banks. Ponds like this often endure fish kills due to insufficient oxygen caused by things like excessive sediment or chemical run-off from yards and fields.

With the right stewardship, ponds offer healthy fish that are great for eating, and worth bragging about, too. Check your state's record list — I bet about half of the fish came from private ponds.

How to fish the water

Ponds suit themselves to the bank angler. If the banks are clear, and the pond is small enough, it's sometimes possible to fish your way around a pond, casting as you go. (And that's not a bad approach!) Most ponds have access points where you can get near the water and cast. Because there may not be a lot of structure to a pond (they are often bowl-shaped), one spot may be about as good as any other. Still, a visual inspection will usually call your attention to a few key spots — cover like fallen, partially submerged trees or floating docks draw fish. If the pond has a *dam* or *levy* (the earthen bank built across the lower end of the valley to hold back the water and form the pond), the water in front of it is often the deepest, and that might hold fish. Corners or coves often attract fish. Casting lures or flies allow you to cover a lot of water, and still-fishing with livebait is another good way to catch fish.

Streams, small rivers, and big rivers

Small rivers and streams often feature everything that makes for a great fishing trip: interesting fish, ever-changing environment, and beautiful scenery. Unlike small ponds, which usually start with an introduced population of fish, streams run wild and may carry wild populations of fish.

The majority of streams and rivers follow a pattern known as *riffle-hole-run*. A riffle is often visible — the water will churn as it flows over a harder bottom. Riffles are shallower than the surrounding water, and mark the beginning of a hole — the area where the current carves away the bottom after tumbling through the riffle. Holes are the deepest parts of the river. Runs occur where the river assumes a fairly stable depth until the next riffle. (Turn to the color section to see how these three elements come together.) Although the depths of a hole might range from a foot or two in a stream to a hundred feet in a large river, the basic pattern remains.

Who's home?

Trout favor cool streams, and some stream or river somewhere probably has about every species of freshwater fish, from trout to smallmouth bass to catfish to walleye to stripers to spawning American and Hickory shad. The largest rivers are deep enough to hide the biggest fish in freshwater. Streams and rivers allow for fish mobility, so fish can move up and down rivers seasonally.

Many fish move upstream in the spring (often seeking spawning sites) and downstream in the fall, seeking deeper holes for wintering. That varies from place to place and by species, but you should see the river as a highway with no roadblocks — it flows from place to place, and unless there's a dam to stop them, fish can move freely up- and downriver.

How to fish the water

What makes a stream different from a pond is its current. A stream's current influences a fish's life about as much as a paycheck affects yours. Fish in streams make most of their decisions based on the current, so you need to understand how current works. Start with this nugget: Fish face into the current, so they can see food being swept downstream toward them. Therefore, you should present your lure or bait so that it looks natural: In other words, cast upstream of your target and retrieve your offering downstream. Now, this doesn't mean always casting straight, or directly, upstream every time. You can still cast to different spots and at different angles. Just make sure that you are generally casting above your target — even if it's at an angle. Fish often want to be near the current (to take food from it), but they don't like expending more energy than necessary to maintain a position. For this reason, fish will often hide behind a large boulder or other obstruction, so they can be near the current but out of it. (You can find more on how to fish current in Chapter 17.)

Fishing large rivers is difficult without a boat, as fish are not spread out equally along the length of the river — most of the fish are usually in the riffles and holes. If you have shore access to one of these spots, you could be in luck. But on a large river, good holes might be miles apart.

Lakes and reservoirs

Lakes are natural and range widely in depth, age, and fish populations. Reservoirs are manmade lakes, formed when a river is dammed. Because reservoirs quite literally grow out of rivers, they feature a *channel,* which is the now-flooded river. Lakes and reservoirs range in size from a hundred acres to thousands, and can feature all kinds of structure and cover within that space, as shown in the color section.

Who's home?

Lakes and reservoirs offer the size needed to grow large fish. Almost any freshwater fish could be found in these large bodies of water, provided the water offers the temperature, food base, and so on that a particular species of fish requires. Because reservoirs are still connected to a river, and because many lakes have creeks draining into them, fish populations vary as fish move in and out of the waterway. Check with baitshops and the local Department of Natural Resources to see what fish species are present in a particular lake or reservoir. (Simply type your state and "Department of Natural Resources" into your favorite search engine to locate the right one.)

Underexplored hotspots

Sometimes success is about fishing where others aren't. Constantly seek underfished water. Often, this means making more effort than other anglers are willing to expend. Walk farther than other stream anglers. Ask permission to fish the tiny golf course pond. Cast around the docks in the bay behind the packed tourist hotels. You never know where a big fish will appear. (And if your local water is packed with anglers on the weekend, fish when others aren't.)

How to fish the water

The size of any large body of water is intimidating. Don't let it be. Whereas boats offer anglers the advantage of covering more water, most lakes and reservoirs offer shorebound anglers some bank access. Some even feature fishing piers, often with sunken brushpiles nearby to attract fish. Fishing any lake or reservoir calls for ruling out the fishless water. The fish population won't be distributed equally over the acres, so whether you're fishing from boat or bank, seek out cover or interesting structure. A point will attract fish, especially if it provides cover, too. A bank with a rocky ledge will usually lure fish. A bridge over a lake will often appear in a narrower area where the banks are closer together and may feature banks of *riprap* (large stones or chunks of rock) to control erosion. Pay attention — the land above the water line provides clues about the bottom. A sharp rising bank usually means the water is deep below the surface, because the bottom will fall away just as steeply. Fish will be drawn to edges, or differences — where one bottom type meets another (say where a sandy bottom becomes rocky, or where a weed-bed stops).

Generally, fish will be in shallower water in the spring, seeking warmer water (the sun warms shallower water faster) and potential spawning sites. As the summer passes, fish move into areas offering the right structure and cover all over the lake, and as fall approaches, fish tend to move to deeper sections of the lake or reservoir. Usually, the closer you are to the dam, the deeper the water will be. Plan your location around the season and you're on the right path.

If mobility is possible, don't fish too long in one spot. Move and learn more about the water.

Evaluating Saltwater Sites

Saltwater fishing can be intimidating due to the vastness of the oceans. Chances are, though, if you're reading this book, you're going to do most of your saltwater fishing within three miles of shore, in water less than 100 feet deep. To fish the deep blue of the sea, you need a serious boat, gear, and experience. You may not have those things yet, but you can always hire a guide to get a taste of fishing the biggest water. A guide will have the proper gear and knowledge, which takes the pressure off you. You can relax and enjoy the trip! But fear not — even if you fish on your own, closer to shore, plenty of adventure awaits the coastal angler.

Approach saltwater fishing as you would freshwater — seek access and fish (refer to the earlier section "Knowing Where to Go" for the full scoop). Pay attention to your surroundings, and watch for clues about what's happening beneath the surface. Saltwater species often come closer to shore to pursue prey because the shoreline offers the habitat that creatures like crabs, shrimp, and baitfish need. In a freeding frenzy, larger gamefish chase huge schools of bait to the shore and, once its corraled, feed voraciously and fearlessly. You can catch feeding fish if you understand the saltwater fishing basics of tides, structure, and cover.

Tidal inlets, marshes, streams, and bays

To fish saltwater, you need to understand tides. Tides affect all oceans, of course, but the *tidal range* varies from place to place. Sometimes the tidal range, which is the difference between high tide and low tide, can be less than a foot. But with irregular coastlines with inlets, bays and streams, the tidal range can be as high as 40 feet! Tides affect fishing just as current does in any stream: The fish understand that tides move baitfish and other prey, and they respond accordingly.

Tides are basically predictable, and you can find charts informing you of the *high,* or rising, tide, as well as the *low,* or falling, tide. But even predictable ones can be very affected by storms and other natural events thousands of miles away. When the tide is neither rising or falling, it's known as a *slack* tide. As in a river, where too little current often makes for difficult fishing, a slack tide tends to slow or stop the bite (there are few rules that don't have exceptions).

Who's home?

Gamefish can't survive with food, and tidal inlets, marshes, streams, and bays offer a smorgasbord of baitfish, crabs, shrimp, eels, and the like. In warm climates, places like mangrove coves and flats provide plenty of food, so many species of gamefish will come close to shore in pursuit of it. Tarpon smash through baitfish near the pilings of a causeway. Snook chase bait in the shadows under docks. Stripers run off the jetty. Bonefish often cruise the flats. Sharks dash through the crashing surf. In late spring and early summer, stripers on the East Coast do the same, and redfish along the Gulf Coast fit this pattern. It's all here.

How to fish the water

In places like marshes or brackish streams, a high tide offers gamefish a chance to chase baitfish and other prey in prime habitat. But a low tide will force fish back into deeper water, so time your trips to coincide with moving tides. Falling tides are often as good or better than rising ones. Gamefish will often be either rushing out or rushing in with the tide, chasing the displaced bait. Fish inside harbor, bay, and creek mouths during high tides, as fish will be moving into shallow water, and outside bay mouths as the tide recedes (see Figure 3-1).

All tides can consolidate and move fish. Look for ambush points like rock out-croppings that gamefish use (just as freshwater fish do) to jump prey being carried by the tide. Look for variances in structure — reefs, sandbars, and drop-offs — and watch for signs of fleeing baitfish. Birds won't help you as much in most freshwater fishing situations, but in saltwater, they're a valuable aid. Watch birds like terns and seagulls — they'll respond to schools of baitfish, and if the birds are following the bait, you can be sure the gamefish are, as well. Sightfishing works better in saltwater, too, as you can sometimes spot fish like bonefish, tarpon, stripers, bluefin, bluefish, seatrout (specks), and redfish when they come into shallow water to feed. Polarized sunglasses, which are recommended in Chapter 6, will help you see the fish.

Surf fishing

Waves shake things up and attract everything along the food chain. Stirred up sand displaces everything from zooplankton to crabs, which attract small fish, which of course attract big fish. Surf fishing allows you to fish from the beach or shore, capitalizing on the feeding frenzy triggered by breaking waves.

Who's home?

Striped bass are popular quarry, but anglers catch everything from bluefish to snook to red drum while surfcasting. Small sharks are often spotted cavorting in the waves, much to the dismay of beach-goers! Understanding the seasonal movements of particular species of fish will help you understand when and where to cast from the surf. Some species make what is called a *run*, or migration, up and down the coastline, sometimes traveling hundreds of miles. Ask the locals or in baitshops for information about the local runs of various species. DNR Web sites should help with this, as well.

How to fish the water

Although most coastal fishing can be done with quality freshwater tackle, surfcasting requires a longer rod. A long spinning or baitcasting rod, say about 10 to 12 feet, allows you to cast heavy weights out beyond the breakers. You can use livebait or lures, depending on the species being targeted.

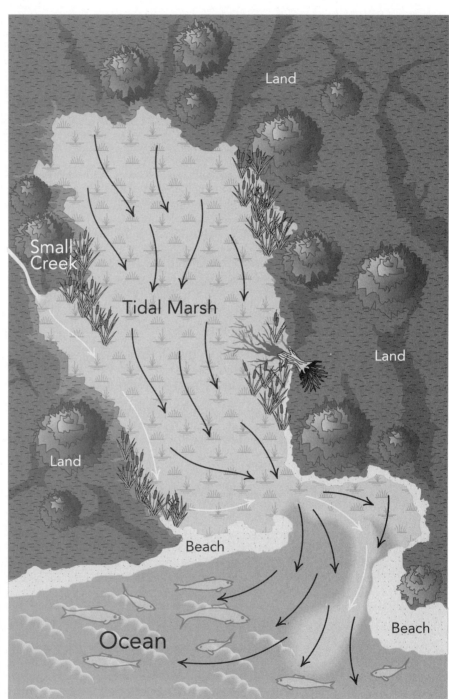

Figure 3-1:
Fish staging
outside a
marsh
during a
falling tide.

Watch the water to see the subtle differences in a long stretch of breaking waves. Running roughly parallel to the beach is what's called the *outer bar,* essentially a sandbar that's higher than the bottom on either side of it. Fishing cuts and dips in the outer bar can be effective, and fish may hold in the drop-offs in front of or behind it.

As with all fishing, the more you observe, the more you learn. Experience trumps anything we can say about surf fishing here. Many anglers wade and fish at night while surf fishing, so know your limits before you imitate more experienced anglers.

If you use your freshwater tackle to fish in saltwater, be sure to rinse it thoroughly after you're done. If you don't, the saltwater will corrode the inner workings of your reel. If you plan to fish saltwater regularly, buy gear rated for saltwater use, which will feature higher-quality bearings and better seals. Rinse saltwater off all equipment, regardless of the grade.

Fishing piers

Pier fishing lacks the beauty and serenity, perhaps, of stalking bonefish on the flats. But it makes up for any shortcomings with convenience. Piers provide a high, stable vantage point for shorebound anglers (including those who are physically disabled), and offer a safe, inexpensive opportunity to pull fish from the ocean. Most anglers bottom-fish, but it's possible to cast and retrieve from piers, and some enterprising anglers have developed special techniques to present baits far from the pilings.

Who's home?

Although it's hard to imagine a cleaner, easier way to fish, pier fishing isn't just for lazy anglers catching baby fish. Major fish are caught from piers every year, including big striped bass in New Jersey, sharks in South Carolina, and salmon in the Pacific Northwest. Depending on the season and location of the pier, it's possible to catch a major tarpon or a mess of great-tasting weakfish.

How to fish it

Many fish move in and out of the protection offered by the pilings of the pier itself, meaning that good fishing is literally underfoot. You may want to use bottom rigs to present livebait straight down (see Figure 3-2), although you can also cast away from the pier, or let the tide or current carry your offering out.

One way to present a livebait far from the pier is to use a three-way rig or try this trick: Cast only a sinker far from the pier, then attach a short leader loaded with a hook and live baitfish to the main line with a snap swivel. The baited leader then slides down the line and into the water. After hooking a big fish, either walk down the pier to the beach, or use the landing net on a rope that many piers leave available. Other anglers will likely assist you with the landing.

Figure 3-2:
Anglers
bottom-
fishing
from a pier.

Finding the Right Time to Fish

This one is simple: Fish whenever you can. I (Greg) often fish at night because flathead catfish pursue baitfish then, and the waters are never crowded with other anglers. Flatheads almost stop eating when the water cools to 50 degrees in the fall, but other species of fish feed all winter long and can be caught from open water or through the ice. At any moment, year-round, some fish are biting somewhere. Go experiment until you catch them.

Of course, some times are better than others. Low-light periods of dawn and dusk encourage most fish to feed. Spring and fall, often marked by heavy rainfall and wild temperature swings, can make for unpredictable fishing. (Although it can be as good as it is bad!) The *spawning season* (time for breeding, eggs, and nesting) of each species of fish will definitely affect the angling for that species. While spawning, some fish become almost impossible to catch, whereas others become emboldened. There are ethical issues to consider when fishing for spawning fish, as well.

All fish are affected by lunar cycles, too. Traditionally, the three days on either side of a new or full moon make for better fishing. (Although it will alter night fishing and daytime fishing differently. Some anglers swear by fishing a full moon — others feel like it's impossible to catch fish at night then.) Lunar cycles also change the tides — a full moon marks an especially high and low tide.

In rivers, a steady rise of the water level can excite fish. A sharp fall can shut them down. A big rain can raise a lake or pond level, and this activates fish.

There's a lot of opinion out there about the right time to fish. The bottom line: Fish when you can. Let's face it — your work and family schedule will dictate your fishing time, anyway. But if you begin to notice a pattern, like a new moon triggers a hot dawn bite on your favorite smallmouth stream, you may need to schedule some mental health days.

Watching the Weather

Everyone knows that the weather affects fishing. Beyond that, there are no agreements regarding the two subjects. Much of what you hear about fishing weather patterns will be discounted or contradicted elsewhere. Most anglers agree that a cold front makes fishing tough, as fish go deep and grow sluggish. (Although fishing before the cold front arrives can be super.) High pressure, bluebird-sky days look like the perfect fishing days, but they've often marked tough bites for me (Greg).

Planning a trip around the weather

It won't take you long to notice how weather patterns affect your kind of fishing. This summer, I caught some of my biggest blue catfish from the Ohio River while fishing on hot, cloudless days — exactly when I would not have expected a bite! But when I noticed this pattern, I fished more of those dog days. As a rule, though, cloudy, overcast days make for better fishing than sunny, bright days. Some anglers are uncomfortable fishing in the rain, but a steady rain can trigger ferocious feeding.

If you're planning a trip a week or two in advance, how can you predict the weather? You can't. Just go and make the most of it. You might find, though, that shifting a day trip by a couple of hours in either direction could make a big difference on that day.

Reacting to changing weather while fishing

The joke about "If you don't like the weather in _____, wait five minutes and it will change!" seems to be told in every state in the Union. You know the weather will change, and sooner or later, a fishing trip will be affected by a sudden development overhead. Will this turn the fish on or off? It's impossible to say, but you need to be prepared. Your safety should come first. Some anglers have found that an approaching storm triggers the best bite of the day, but don't get struck by lightning because you're unwilling to leave a hot bite. Be prepared for weather changes because although you can't predict what it will do to the fishing, you know it will affect you. (For advice on how to prepare a foul-weather bag, turn to Chapter 2.)

Chapter 4

Putting a Face on the Fins: Common Freshwater Fish

*W*herever you are, chances are you're close to some fishable water: mountain streams, Great Lakes, little lakes, farm ponds, deep reservoirs, or mighty rivers. Freshwater fishing is so popular in large part because of this incredible wealth of habitat, which is home to some pretty amazing fish.

You probably have — or will soon have — a favorite species of freshwater fish. And you might already have a favorite place to pursue that fish. Although traveling long distances to fish is one of the greatest joys and challenges in angling, most people usually fish in water close to home. Either way, getting to know various species of fish (and their habitats) is the first step toward discovering your favorite quarry, or your next piscatorial challenge. Anglers find themselves drawn to particular fish for various reasons — they like the way a smallmouth bass leaps when hooked; they love the quiet streams where brook trout live; they enjoy catching perch because they taste great; or they simply like the action of casting large plugs for northern pike. The more fish you know, the more fish you begin to understand and appreciate, the longer your list of options for fishing on any given day.

Sunfish

Odds are, more "first fish" are caught from the sunfish family than from any other family of freshwater fish. Consisting of 30 species, the sunfish family includes the widespread and feisty bluegill, the sporty crappie, and the ever-popular largemouth and smallmouth bass. These are the most popular species from this family, and they appear throughout North America. They likely wait near your house to offer you great sport and table fare.

Bluegills: America's spunky little sweetheart

Sometimes known as *bream,* bluegills range in color from dark blue to yellow to almost white. (The habitat they reside in can influence their color — in clear water, such as that found in a quarry; they tend to be lighter, for example.) These hand-sized fish love ponds and lakes, and appear in running water, as well. They eat a variety of insects and crustaceans, and bite willingly on a variety of baits. Bluegills rarely exceed 15 inches in length, and are often much smaller. They seek quiet, weedy water where they can feed and hide. They like shade during the hottest parts of the day and usually remain near some kind of cover because they are common prey for fish such as largemouth bass. Bluegills adapt well to a variety of habitats, and are often stocked in retention ponds and community lakes. Bluegills fit easily in the hand, but take care with the dorsal fin, which consists of spines that can deliver a painful stab. Bluegills fight with every ounce when hooked, similar to a lightweight boxer bouncing around the ring. You can see a bluegill in the color section.

Crappies: A little bigger, a bit sportier, still tasty

Crappies fight well on light tackle and can taste great. They tend to school, so catching one is a good sign of things to come. Crappies might grow to nearly 20 inches and 5 pounds, but that would truly be a monster specimen. There are white crappies and black crappies, and although both are common, the white crappie is more widespread. Both species are popular with anglers all over North America because they bite eagerly on all kinds of bait and small lures (see Chapters 11 and 12 for more on bait and lures). Minnows work well for crappies because adults usually feed on small fish, although they won't pass up insects and crustaceans. Crappies do well in a variety of waters and prefer the silted, slow-moving water found in ponds and reservoirs throughout the country.

If you catch a crappie, you can quickly tell which kind you have by looking at its dorsal fin. Check out Figure 4-1 and consider the following:

- **Black crappies** have seven or eight dorsal spines. Black crappies prefer cooler, clearer water, and this is why the white crappie is more widespread. As the name suggests, they're a little darker, and the speckles on their sides are spread throughout, not in noticeable bars.

- **White crappies** have a maximum of six dorsal spines. White crappies also are more barred on their sides.

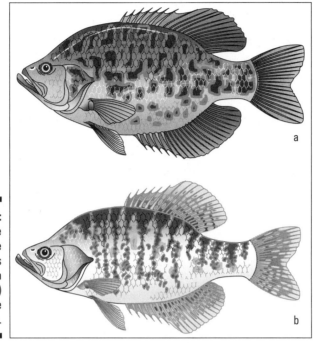

Figure 4-1:
Notice the subtle differences between the black (a) and white (b) crappies.

Largemouth bass: The most important gamefish in America

Largemouth bass appear all over the country, and are pursued with feverish intensity. Bass tournaments have become high-dollar affairs, with professional anglers chasing down fish from gleaming boats with arsenals of gear. Many lakes, rivers, streams, and brackish coastal waters have populations of largemouth, and anglers don't need fancy equipment to get in on the excitement of catching this hard-fighting sportfish. Largemouth bass take lures, plugs, flies, plastic worms, real worms, crayfish, and crickets. In short, they are opportunistic feeders that often strike aggressively. As shown in the color section, the jaw of the largemouth extends farther back than the eye (which is not true of the smallmouth). The largemouth is usually dark gray to dark green in color with a dark band along the lateral line. The dorsal fin is divided into two distinct portions: hard spines in front and softer ones in the rear. The largemouth is also known as the bucketmouth because of its large mouth, which appears even larger when it attacks your lure, fly, or bait. Bass grow larger in warmer climates like those found in Florida or California, where 20-pound largemouths appear; in the Midwest, an 8-pound bass is a trophy.

A true fish tale

It was rainy and windy on June 2, 1932, and 19-year-old George Perry was out before dawn with his fishing buddy Jack Page. "My father died the year before," Perry later recalled. "I had my mother, two sisters, and two brothers. We lived three creeks further back than anybody else, and in those days it was a good deal of a problem just to make a living. I took money we should have eaten with and bought myself a cheap rod and reel and one plug."

Perry remembers that he wasn't feeling very lucky that morning on Montgomery Lake near Helena, Georgia. He tied on an imitation of the local bait fish, the creek-chub. A bass took the lure. Perry struck but couldn't budge it. Then the fish moved, and Perry knew he was into a major bass. When it finally surrendered, even though it was enormous, Perry later said, "The first thing I thought of was what a nice chunk of meat to take home to the family."

Thankfully, Perry had the presence of mind to make a detour at the general store in Helena, Georgia, where the bass that he had pulled out of Montgomery Lake tipped the scales at 22 pounds and 3 ounces, duly notarized and witnessed. It is a world record that stands to this day. With his place firmly enshrined in the history books, young Perry went home and prepared a very large largemouth meal for the family.

Smallmouth: The gamest fish

In what's perhaps the most-quoted phrase in angling literature, retired Civil War surgeon James Alexander Henshall called black bass (meaning largemouth, smallmouth and spotted bass), "Inch for inch and pound for pound, the gamest fish that swims." Many people now mistakenly believe he was referring to only the smallmouth bass, because the description is so apt.

Similar to its largemouth cousin, the smallmouth is a native of the Mississippi drainage, which makes it a true heartland (or maybe "heartwater") fish. Where the largemouth likes slow or still water with lots of food-holding weeds, the smallmouth prefers clean, rocky bottoms and swifter water. Lake-dwelling smallmouth often school up, which means that if you catch one, you can catch a bunch. In rivers and streams, they are more solitary. Similar to the largemouth, the smallmouth is an opportunistic feeder; but if you give smallmouth a choice, both crayfish and hellgrammites score well. But unlike its largemouth cousin, the smallmouth has a series of dark vertical bands along its flanks, shown in Figure 4-2. The dorsal fin of the smallmouth is marked with a shallow notch between the spiny part and the softer part, while the largemouth's dorsal fin reveals a deeper notch (one that almost separates the two parts). Another difference is that the smallmouth's upper jaw does not extend backward beyond the eye. Smallmouth bass, on average, are smaller than largemouth bass, but under ideal conditions can grow upward of 12 pounds.

How to pick up a bass

If you try to pick up a bass by grabbing its body, you'll find it's about as easy as trying to diaper an angry baby. The little suckers can *really* squirm. Even worse than babies, bass have spiny fins that can deliver nasty pricks. With a bass (and with many other soft-mouthed fish), however, you can nearly immobilize it if you grab it by the lower lip, depressing its tongue and lip between thumb and forefinger as shown in the adjacent figure. Be very careful of hooks, especially of lures that have multiple treble hooks. Picking up your catch by grasping the lower lip between thumb and forefinger works very well with bass.

Figure 4-2: The mouth of the smallmouth isn't *that* small, but its upper jaw is shorter than the large-mouth's.

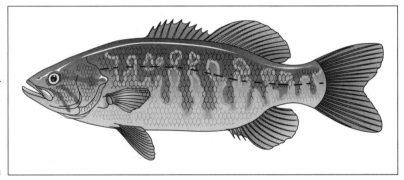

Catfish

Many species of fish look like other fish at first glance, but a catfish looks only like a catfish. Covered in skin, not scales, catfish are smooth, muscled bruisers. Members of the catfish family have *barbels* around their mouths — whiskers they use to taste their environment. In fact, they taste with some of the skin covering their bodies and, for that reason, they've been called "swimming tongues." They are growing in popularity as sportfish due to their large size, good taste, and tackle-busting fight. In this section, you discover the four most popular species of catfish.

When you handle a catfish, especially a small one, be wary of its pectoral and dorsal fins. The projecting spines are very sharp, especially on younger specimens. Though not fatal, a wound from these spines can be nasty and painful. If you are pricked while handling a catfish, treat the wound immediately with a disinfectant because swift action often nullifies the bacteria.

Blue catfish: King of the big water

Blue catfish (see Figure 4-3) are the kings of big rivers. Although they also appear in some large reservoirs, blue cats thrive in the rolling, rollicking waters of wide rivers such as the Ohio, Mississippi, and Missouri, and also in tidal rivers such as the James. They feed primarily on fish like skipjack herring and gizzard shad. A ferocious fighter when hooked, blues attain sizes in the triple digits. Because blues are big fish found in big waters, anglers often fish from boats using heavy rods and reels to cast or drift big chunks of cutbait (cut fish). Despite the myth that catfish feed only at night, blues are active day and night and can be caught during the winter months, as well. They can be found near the bottom, but they also suspend throughout the water column.

Figure 4-3:
Notice the broad, muscled body of the blue catfish, which is built for big water.

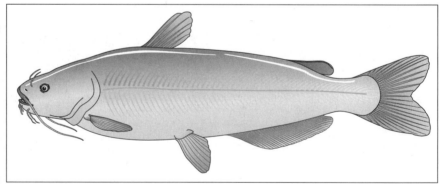

Flathead catfish: Denizens of the deep lair

Similar to the blue catfish, flathead cats can weigh more than 100 pounds, and they also thrive in America's big rivers, reservoirs, and lakes. However, flatheads tolerate muddier, slower water better than blues, and can be found in some surprising small streams. Flathead catfish feed on crustaceans and small minnows while young, but adults subsist on a diet of primarily fish (some of them quite large!). Although anglers occasionally catch flatheads on night-crawlers or cutbait, most foraging flatheads are more attracted to a struggling, live-hooked baitfish. Flatheads are most likely to be caught at night, when they leave the logjams and rockpiles they take shelter around during the day. Flatheads live in nasty environs and have an attitude to match. Anglers target-ing them use heavy tackle (think 80-pound braided line) and expect to horse them out of gnarly cover. Figure 4-4 shows a flathead catfish.

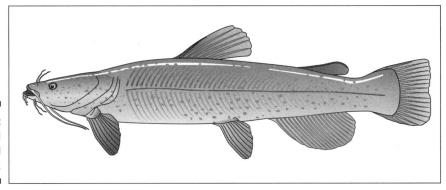

Figure 4-4:
The flathead catfish is all mouth.

Channel catfish: Prince of the pond

Channel catfish taste great, which is why they're raised on fish farms throughout the South. When you order "farm-raised catfish," you're getting channel catfish on your plate. But channel cats make great quarry for all anglers. They hit hard and fight long, and will outpull almost all fish of simi-lar size. An extremely adaptive fish, channel cats can be found in everything from the largest rivers to the smallest ponds. They feed on everything from fish to insects, and grow quickly as a result. They can be caught on prepared stinkbaits, grocery store baits such as cheese and hot dogs, and natural baits like nightcrawlers and minnows. (Sometimes, anglers catch them on lures meant for bass or walleye.) They will hit night or day, and when in rivers or streams, can be found feeding in surprisingly swift current. Channel catfish (see Figure 4-5) are not as big as their blue and flathead cousins, but a chan-nel of more than 20 pounds is possible, and it will fight like nothing else.

Figure 4-5:
The adaptive channel cat is one of the most popular gamefish.

Bullhead catfish: Tough as they come

Rounding out the catfish lineup are the bullheads — small catfish commonly found in small ponds, streams, and lakes. Although there are different species of bullheads — including brown, black, and yellow bullheads — all bullheads feed on crustaceans, fish, and insects, and so are easily caught by anglers fishing with bait such as worms. Highly tolerant of low oxygen levels and pollution, bullheads live in waters that would fail to support other fish life. In the event of a nuclear holocaust, providing you survive, go fishing for bullheads (shown in Figure 4-6). They should still be there.

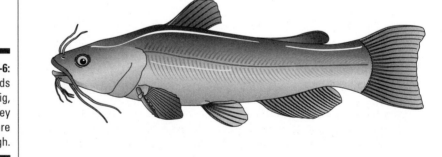

Figure 4-6:
Bullheads aren't big, but they sure are tough.

Perch

Like the sunfish family, the perches include several species popular with anglers. Two of the most popular are covered here, and they well represent the challenge and the great taste of this family. Yellow perch congregate in schools, can be readily caught, and are fine table fare. Walleyes taste great, too, but they also inspire anglers with their challenging habits. Like many species of fish, members of this family have been introduced beyond their native range, but it's fair to say that the perch family tends to favor cooler, cleaner water, traditionally found in the northern part of the country.

Walleye: Popular like a largemouth, toothy like a pike

Walleyes are the largest members of the perch family, and like largemouth bass, they command a loyal following. Their excellent flavor may explain why walleyes are often the preferred fish where they are available. In addition to being delicious, they are found in schools, hang out around underwater structures, and usually locate themselves near drop-offs. Walleyes require a great deal of water and are rarely found in smaller lakes or ponds. Clear water and a rocky bottom are also high on its list of environmental preferences with water temperatures in the mid 60s (and never higher than the mid 70s) being optimum. It eats any baitfish available, and for that reason walleyes are often caught on minnows, although leeches and nightcrawlers work as well.

The walleye is a very light-sensitive fish, so although you may take one in shallow water, chances are that you will do this only in low-light conditions. Their eyes allow them to see well at night, and their prominent white eyes might be why some people insist on calling them "walleyed pike." They're not pike, though, so this is a misnomer.

As shown in the color section, the walleye is a torpedo-shaped fish with big eyes (hence wall-eye), a brownish-greenish color, and a white tip on the lower lobe of the tail. Walleyes could reach 25 pounds, but anything bigger than 6 to 8 pounds is a winner.

Yellow perch: Food for everyone

If walleyes share similarities with largemouth bass, yellow perch (as shown in the color section) have a lot in common with bluegills. Yellow perch are primarily lake fish, and they favor cool water with sand and rocky bottoms. They're especially important and popular in the Great Lakes and Lake Erie in particular. Yellow perch have been stocked in lakes throughout the United States simply because they serve as great forage for predator fish and humans alike. Yellow perch grow slowly, so many of them end up as prey for fish such as walleyes and pike. But humans like the taste of perch just as much and target this fish with worms and minnows. Perch eat crustaceans and insects until they are large enough to consume minnows, and find protection from predators by forming schools. Any fish that schools could mean fast action for anglers; yellow perch can be caught year-round and are delicious to eat anytime. A torpedo-shaped fish like the walleye, yellow perch feature bands of yellow and green, and seldom get larger than 3 or 4 pounds, with the average well under that.

Pike

For flat-out mean looks, nothing in freshwater rivals the looks of a pike, pickerel, or muskellunge — all part of the pike family. A long fish with big eyes, a pointed snout, and rows of stiletto teeth, the average pike looks like what you might get if you crossed a snake, a bird, and a shark.

When landing a pike, be extremely careful of its sharp teeth. They are about the nastiest thing in freshwater fishing. (This advice goes for the pike's cousins, the muskie and pickerel.) As shown in Figure 4-7, the safest way to land a pike is with a landing net, and then grab the fish gently but firmly behind the gills.

Figure 4-7: The finger-preserving way to land a pike, muskie, or pickerel.

Northern pike: Water wolf

The most popular member of the pike family is usually known simply as the *pike,* but it's really a northern pike, and it's a native of the Great Lakes and its cooler tributaries. It prefers cooler water and can be found in any habitat that provides a steady source of it.

Pike are clearly designed to attack and devour (see the color section). All forms of baitfish and gamefish, birds, muskrats, frogs, snakes, snails, leeches, and anything else it finds within striking distance can (at one time or another) find its way into a northern pike's belly.

You are liable to find pike in weedy shallows (especially if the water's cool) where they wait to ambush their prey. As stealthy as a lion in wait, or as swift as a springing panther, pike stalk and pursue their prey. For this reason, anglers pursue pike by using livebait (usually a good-sized sucker) or by casting a variety of lures designed to entice an angry strike. They'll also take flies and popping bugs. Anglers desire pike more for sport than for food — they are too bony for many cooks to mess with. Northern pike reach weights into the lower 40-pound range, but anything larger than 20 pounds is an ornery trophy.

Chain pickerel: Pike junior

Though smaller than the pike and the muskie, the pickerel is (in every other way) as pugnacious and predatory as its larger cousins. When fishing a shallow bass pond on a day when nothing is happening, look for the arrow-head-shaped wake of a feeding pickerel. Whether the pickerel is cruising or sprinting from its lair in a weedbed, I think you will agree that it is exciting to watch a well-equipped predator going about its deadly work. More common in the eastern and southern states, pickerel thrive where their larger pike cousins are absent. They seldom weigh 10 pounds but grow quickly and offer great sport. Figure 4-8 illustrates a chain pickerel, whose dark green side markings appear to line up like the links in a chain.

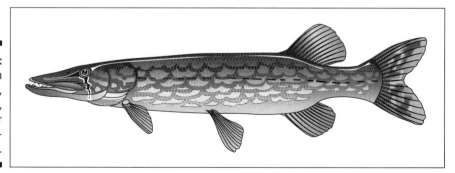

Figure 4-8: The chain pickerel, shown here, looks similar to a miniature pike.

Temperate Bass

Members of this family of fish, including striped bass, white bass, and their cross, the wiper, or hybrid striped bass, are taking the country by storm. Extremely popular with anglers wherever they are found, these bass strike hard, fight well, and taste great.

Things get a bit confusing here. Largemouth and smallmouth bass are in the sunfish family, not the bass family. And one member of the temperate bass family — the striped bass — exists in both salt- and freshwater (meaning it's *anadromous*). And two members of the bass family — the striped bass and the white bass — can be crossed to form a hybrid called a hybrid striped bass or wiper. What anglers really need to know is that all the species in this family make wonderful sportfish.

Striped bass: Strong enough for saltwater, happy in freshwater

Striped bass, or stripers as they are commonly called, exist along both coasts and delight saltwater anglers casting from shore. But stripers enter rivers to spawn, and they have been successfully introduced into landlocked reservoirs throughout the country. These landlocked stripers are the true freshwater striped bass, and they challenge anglers everywhere with their size and fighting ability. Stripers can weigh more than 100 pounds, and can test even the strongest tackle. They feed primarily on fish, and anglers target them using livebaits or lures, either cast or trolled, often with planer boards presenting baits off to the side of the boat. Not often found near shore, stripers are often caught by anglers fishing open water from boats. Stripers are silver with unbroken black stripes running from head to tail, as shown in the color section.

White bass: Little fighters

White bass look like miniature stripers (as you can see in Figure 4-9), and a 3 to 4 pounder is considered a trophy. Similar to their larger cousins, white bass consume fish, along with crustaceans and insects. White bass may be small, but they're ferocious, especially when pursuing a school of baitfish. It's not uncommon to see baitfish exploding from the surface when a school of white bass move in to feed. They can be found in rivers and large streams, but they prefer large lakes with relatively clear water.

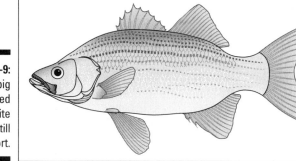

Figure 4-9: Not as big as striped bass, white bass are still great sport.

Wipers: A bit of both

This popular hybrid shown in Figure 4-10 favors big water reservoirs and the tailraces found below their dams. Often stocked by state DNR agencies, wipers school and chase shad and other baitfish along rocky points and through open expanses of water. Anglers target them by casting lures that imitate popular forage fish, and wipers tend to be more aggressive than stripers. Because they school, catching one may lead to quickly catching another. Like striped bass, they tend to remain on the move, however.

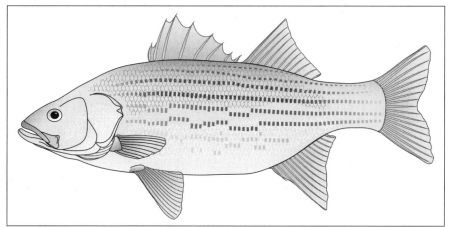

Figure 4-10: Hybrid or wiper bass, a cross between a white bass and a striped bass, are often stocked in reservoirs.

Carp

There are approximately 200 species in the minnow family, and most of them are what you'd expect — they're, well, minnows. One exception deserves mention in this book, because it offers anglers great sport: the common carp. Carp were abundant in Europe (Aristotle mentioned them in 350 B.C.) but their American story began in 1876, when we imported them from Germany. Carp spread rapidly, and now exist almost everywhere. They prefer warm water streams, rivers, and lakes, where they feed on everything from insects and crustaceans to mollusks. Anglers take them with natural baits like corn, grasshoppers, and worms, and fly fishermen can take them on flies. They grow large — more than 70 pounds — and fight like crazy when hooked. Figure 4-11 shows a carp, which really looks like an overgrown goldfish.

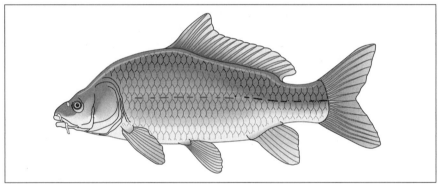

Figure 4-11: The common carp is a big, deep-bodied fish, capable of testing even stout gear.

Trout

Known widely as the quarry of fly fishermen everywhere, trout are fish of moving, cool water. Popular as both sportfish and table fare, members of this family are held in high esteem by anglers. Similar to the temperate bass family, the trout family has some odd twists in its family tree, as species can cross-breed and might be *anadromous* — that is, live part of their lives in both salt- and freshwater. The salmonid family is divided into five groups: trouts, including the Atlantic salmon; Pacific salmon; char; grayling; and whitefish. Fish from the first three groups are represented here, as they're the most pursued by anglers. Don't worry — you don't need to understand that to catch or eat a trout.

Who was Izaak Walton anyway?

Without question, the most famous book ever written about angling is *The Compleat Angler* published by Izaak Walton in 1653. Since that time, it has been through more than 300 editions and is probably the most widely read (or at least widely owned) book after the Bible and the Koran. Because *The Compleat Angler* is an all-around handbook for fishing in England, people who are not familiar with Walton have an idea that it is only for purist fly fishing snobs. It isn't.

Izaak Walton was primarily a bait fisherman who came late to the fly. He was a self-made businessman who retired in his 50s and wrote the book that would earn him immortality at age 60. His prose is so simple and clear that most people today could read his book with much less difficulty than they could read the plays of, for example, Shakespeare.

Much of the best advice in the book was actually written by Charles Cotton, a young man of leisure who was an amazing fly rodder. It was Cotton, not Walton, who wrote "to fish fine and far off, is the first and principle rule for Trout angling." In other words use a light leader, and keep your distance from the fish so you don't spook it. This advice is as valuable today as it was three-and-a-half centuries ago when Walton and Cotton filled their days fishing and talking. What a life!

Many states, including those far from the original range of certain species of trout, often raise trout in hatcheries and release them in select locations. There may be an additional license or charge to fish for these trout, but they provide anglers a shot at wonderful-tasting fish. Check with your local DNR to see if trout are either native or stocked within your area.

Rainbow trout: High jumpers

The colorful rainbow trout is one of the most sought-after gamefishes in the world. Rainbows coexist nicely with brown trout in many streams (see the following section for details on the brown trout). Whereas the brown prefers slower water and calmer pools, you can depend on finding the rainbow in the more oxygen-rich and swift-running riffles. This scenario is what you would expect from a fish that predominates in the mountain streams of the Rocky Mountains.

As seen in the color section, the rainbow may have spots over the whole body (although in many rivers and lakes, the larger rainbows are more often an overall silver). A much more reliable sign of "rainbowness" is the pink band or line that runs along the flank of the fish from shoulder to tail. But even this indicator is not always 100 percent foolproof because some stream-borne rainbows have a faded, almost invisible band and many spots, as do the brown and brook trout.

Brown trout: The champ of the stream

The brown trout is a fish designed for the angler. It often feeds on the surface. It rises to a properly presented fly. It fights like the dickens. The brown didn't acquire a reputation as a "gentleman's fish" because it had particularly good manners and went to the right school. The brown trout is a cold-water fish that lives in lakes and streams and is most active when the water temperature is in the 60s. A temperature much higher than 80 degrees F is liable to kill brown trout. As shown in Figure 4-12, the brown trout is covered with spots everywhere but its tail. The majority of the spots are deep brown, like coffee beans, with a light yellow halo. Sprinkled around its skin, you also find a few red and yellow spots. Brown trout are long-lived animals and can reach weights up to 40 pounds, but most stream-bred fish average less than a pound each. They say that a few wise browns in every stream usually reach weights of 10 pounds or more.

Figure 4-12:
The brown trout is a wily and rewarding fish when taken on rod and reel.

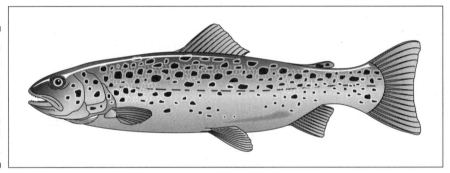

Brook trout: Sentimental favorites

The brook trout, or *brookie,* fills the trout niche in the cooler streams of the northeastern United States, east of the Allegheny Mountains. The brook trout is actually a char, which makes it a relative of the lake trout, the Dolly Varden, and the Arctic char.

We think that the fact that the brookie is found only in wilderness areas explains part of the fondness that anglers have for him. He's a sign of pure water and a healthy ecology. Brook trout like cooler water and cannot stand the higher temperatures that the brown and the rainbow can tolerate. Before Europeans cleared the great hardwood forests of the northeastern United States, most streams had the shade and pure water that brook trout need.

Steelhead: A salty rainbow

Almost all species of trout, if given the chance, drop downstream to the ocean where they usually grow to much greater size than trout confined to streams and lakes. Sea-run brookies and browns (those that forage in the ocean and return to spawn in freshwater) also appear in North America, but the main target for anglers of sea-run trout is the steelhead, which is nothing more than a rainbow that has gone to sea. Steelheads have usually lost the distinctive coloration of the freshwater rainbow (although they still have the pink lateral line). As their name suggests, steelheads have a bright, metallic coloration. Steelheads have been introduced inland, most notably in the Great Lakes, where they're managed by several state fish and wildlife agencies. These fish leave the Great Lakes, where they're a common quarry, and travel up tributary rivers, where more anglers await them. Like landlocked freshwater striped bass, these fish never see saltwater but are extremely popular with anglers fishing far from the sea.

The brook trout has many red spots that are surrounded by a blue halo. The fins have a telltale black and white tip. The belly and fins have an orange cast that can be quite brilliant and almost crimson in spawning season. The tail of the brook trout is more squared off than that of the brown and rainbow (see Figure 4-13), hence the nickname *squaretail*.

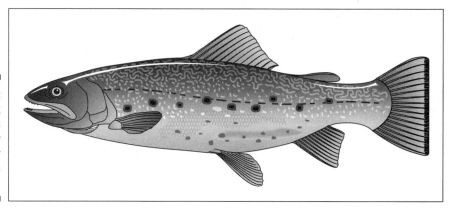

Figure 4-13: The brook trout is universally admired for its gorgeous coloring.

The cutthroat: Yellowstone beauty

You may think of the cutthroat — which is really a cousin to the rainbow — as the Rocky Mountain version of the brook trout because in many undisturbed waters, just like the brookie, the cutthroat is the native fish. After ranching, logging, and the introduction of other gamefish takes place, the cutthroat often retreats to unpressured headwaters. The cutthroat is the native trout in the drainage of the Yellowstone River, where it is protected by a complete no-kill policy in all of the flowing water in Yellowstone Park. To fish them at the outlet of Yellowstone Lake is one of the great angling experiences in North America. (See Figure 4-14 for an illustration of the cutthroat.)

Figure 4-14:
The cut-
throat trout
is most eas-
ily identified
by red and
orange
slashes
around the
lower jaw
and gills.

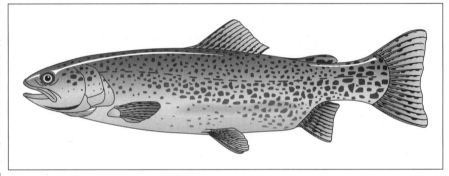

Lake trout: Big macks

Widely known as Mackinaws or gray trout, the lake trout (or *laker*) is the largest char. Unlike all the other trout, the laker spawns in lakes, not streams. As shown in Figure 4-15, the laker, similar to the brook trout, is heavily spotted. It has a forked tail (in contrast to the square tail of the brook trout). The Mackinaw requires colder water than any other freshwater gamefish, optimally about 50 degrees F, and it will die at 65 degrees F.

Right after ice-out in the spring and right before spawning in the autumn, you may be able to take lakers in shallow water. But during the rest of the season, you have to fish deeper, often trolling using downriggers.

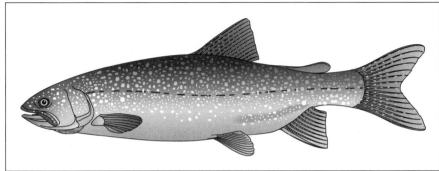

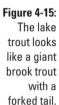

Figure 4-15:
The lake trout looks like a giant brook trout with a forked tail.

Pacific salmon: Now appearing in the Great Lakes!

Pacific salmon come upstream to spawn just as Atlantic salmon do (see the next section for more info on the Atlantic salmon). The Pacific salmon's flesh is pink, just like the flesh of an Atlantic. They even taste the same. But the six species of Pacific salmon are completely different animals than the Atlantic salmon, which is the only *true* salmon. The Pacifics are the much larger, mostly ocean-going cousins of the rainbow trout.

Some years ago, Pacific salmon were introduced into the Great Lakes to help control the spread of the alewife herring. The alewives were so plentiful and the salmon fed so well on them that the Great Lakes now hold the greatest fishery for both the coho and chinook sportfisherman. In the Great Lakes, Pacific salmon are a favorite among trollers. This method of taking fish, of course, requires a hefty boat and expensive gear. Shallow-water and stream anglers have the most luck when the fish gather at stream mouths and within the streams themselves during their spawning migrations. Fishing when the salmon are still *bright,* or fresh from the ocean or lake, can be great sport with these brawny, athletic fish. As with many saltwater fish or as with fish that spend a good amount of time in saltwater, the chinook and coho like flashy, bright-colored lures that imitate the smelt and alewives they feed on.

Figure 4-16 shows the coho and chinook salmon. The usually smaller coho has black spots only on the upper part of its tail, although the chinook's tail is spotted on both top and bottom. The chinook's dorsal fin is spotted; the coho's isn't. The gum in the lower jaw of the coho is grayish, but the same gum in the chinook is black.

Few fish are as delicious as the Pacific salmon (which is one of the reasons they are so heavily harvested by commercial fishermen). In many areas, particularly in the Great Lakes, fish can pick up toxic pollutants. The presence of pollutants doesn't make Pacific salmon less fun to catch, but eating fish from these waters is not a good idea. Always check the local health advisories before you take a fish for a meal.

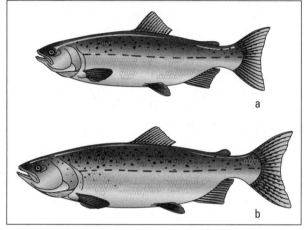

Figure 4-16:
The coho (a) and chinook (b) salmon present fun big-water challenges.

Atlantic salmon: The leaper

The Atlantic salmon is regarded by many as the aristocrat of fishes. Perhaps it has this reputation because you have to be an aristocrat to be able to afford a few days on one of the choice salmon rivers. Not surprisingly, with something that has become the sporting property of upper-class gentlemen, one is usually required to fish for Atlantic salmon with a fly rod; and on many rivers, one also has to rent a guide. Don't hold any of this against the salmon. He had very little to do with all the tradition surrounding him.

Known for its acrobatic jumps, the Atlantic salmon is a cousin to the brown trout but spends most of its time at sea (although a salmon's infancy is passed in a river, and it is to that river that it returns to spawn). The Atlantic salmon (shown in Figure 4-17) does not die after spawning once, so you may return a salmon to the stream after catching it and be confident that it may well return to spawn and fight again. If plenty of action is what you crave, salmon fishing is not for you: Just one fish a day is a very good average on most streams.

Like the Pacific salmon, Atlantic salmon exist in inland bodies of water, too. Known as *landlocked* salmon, these fish are just like their more-traveled siblings but are a bit smaller. Although many landlocked salmon spend their lives in rivers, some stay in lakes year-round, usually staying in the deepest, coolest water. These landlocked salmon are more accessible to anglers. Wherever they're found, anglers love to pursue Atlantic salmon for a chance to see their great leaps.

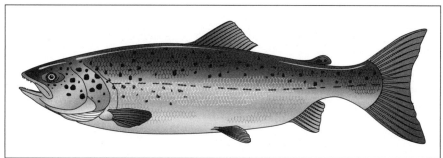

Figure 4-17:
The Atlantic salmon is prized for both food and sport.

Chapter 5

Familiarizing Yourself with Common Saltwater Fish

*T*hey say there are many fish in the sea, and this time, they're right! Anglers face a tremendous array of options when it comes to pursuing saltwater fish; the variety of fish is mind-boggling. And habitat? Saltwater fishing offers anglers the opportunity to fish everything from mangrove coves to public piers to the deep blue sea. Saltwater fish tend to be bigger, faster, and stronger than their freshwater cousins, simply because their environment demands it. Add to this the fact that saltwater fish often taste great, and you can see why saltwater fishing is a terrific experience anywhere you find it. To walk along the shore with the surf crashing, flights of ducks cruising overhead on their way to winter quarters, pods of gulls wheeling and diving over acres of baitfish, and with big schools of gamefish showing in the breakers — that's a great place to be!

Bluefish

The bluefish is hyper-aggressive and eats whatever it can find, including at times its own young. The bluefish is fishdom's version of that guy in the bar who asks every newcomer, "Hey, buddy, are you looking at me?" and then, without waiting for an answer, throws a punch. The guy can be big or little, can win or lose a fight, but he keeps coming back for more. Fighting is in his nature.

When blues are around, they hit anything — livebait or cutbait, plug, jig, or fly (see Part III for more about each of these ways to entice fish). Bluefish are excellent fish for newcomers because they're strong fighters that hit much of what you offer them, and they travel in schools, so the action can be fast. They also taste great, as long as you eat the fillets while they're fresh. (They don't taste nearly as good if frozen for a long time.) They can weigh close to 30 pounds.

Bluefish spend a good half of the year in deep ocean water. In the warmer months, when surf temperatures are 55 to 75 degrees Fahrenheit, the blues follow baitfish into shallow coastal waters. When they do, they can be taken on all kinds of tackle with all sorts of bait, lures, and flies.

Bluefish have very sharp teeth, so whatever method of angling you use, you often find that you lose fewer fish if you use a wire leader. To avoid the chance of a bite, pick up a blue as you would a pike, by squeezing it behind the gills (see Chapter 4 for detailed instructions for pike pickup). Use pliers to unhook a bluefish.

Figure 5-1 shows a typical bluefish that, sure enough, looks kind of bluish on top when out of the water; when you see them in the surf, however, they appear more coppery green.

Figure 5-1:
The blue-fish has extremely sharp teeth, a white belly, and usually a black blotch at the base of the pectoral fin.

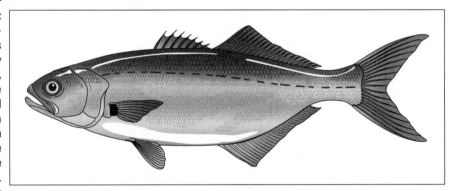

Flatfish

The scientific grouping and naming of fish can be a confusing business, but in this case, it isn't — fish in this family are flat. Flatfish share common features, such as a thin body that is white on one side and brownish green on the other. This allows flatfish to lie on the ocean floor and blend into their surroundings. Both eyes of the flatfish species are on one side of the body — either the left or right side, depending upon the species. These fish make for delicious food.

Winter flounder: Another snowbird

In addition to being highly catchable and delicious, the winter flounder (shown in Figure 5-2) is one of the great early-season fish. When the first warm days of spring make it harder and harder to think about work, nothing is more pleasant than giving winter the kiss-off by catching a bucketful of flounder. A small boat and a simple rig with a piece of clam on the hook are all you need to explore the protected bays and sandy coves where early-season flounder rest on sandy, muddy bottoms. They will strike your bait with a persistent tap-tap, which is your signal to rear back and strike. These small fish (less than ten pounds) range along shallow coastal Atlantic waters, and they go to colder, deeper water in the summer. In the winter, they're found near shore.

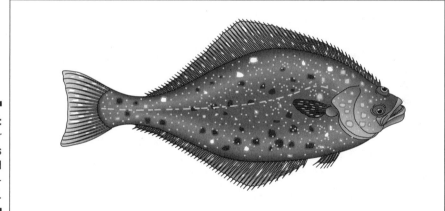

Figure 5-2:
The winter flounder is right-eyed and right-mouthed.

Fluke: Mr. Dependable

Fluke is the common name for the summer flounder (shown in Figure 5-3). The fluke is a little spunkier than its cold-weather cousins; and although fluke are found mainly on the bottom, they sometimes surprise you by chasing your bait when you're after blues or weakfish. Fluke range into bays, canals, and estuaries in the summer months, making them a common catch of shore-fishing anglers. They frequently weigh less than ten pounds.

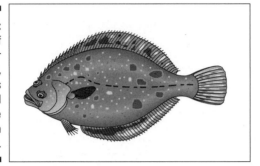

Figure 5-3:
Opposite of
the winter
flounder,
the fluke's
mouth and
eyes are
located on
its left side.

Halibut: Like catching a doormat that fights back

The halibut (shown in the color section) is a member of the flatfish family; and in contrast to the flounder, it will often use its broad, flat body to put up a terrific fight that may have you thinking that you're into a nice striped bass. There are Pacific and Atlantic halibut, and both make for great eating. Atlantic halibut hang out in deeper water, and all halibut are susceptible to anglers who drift bait rigs or jigs, primarily from boats over deep water. Halibut can weigh hundreds of pounds.

Drum

This interesting family of fish includes species like croakers and drums, which are named after the sound they produce by thumping muscles against their swim bladders. This distinctive sound is audible underwater, and anglers above the surface can hear it, too. Anglers seek these fish because they fight well and taste even better.

Spotted seatrout: Pretty like a trout, even if it isn't

The seatrout (see Figure 5-4) looks a bit like a trout found in freshwater, but this species exists in saltwater from New England through the Gulf of Mexico.

Seatrout flesh is tasty, but it will spoil quickly if it isn't iced. Seatrout love shrimp, and anglers do well to present this common food. But they also take jigs, and are often pursued in shallow water grassflats. An inshore species, seatrout can be found in shallow bays, bayous, and Gulf Coast beaches.

Figure 5-4: The seatrout has a torpedo shape and spotted skin.

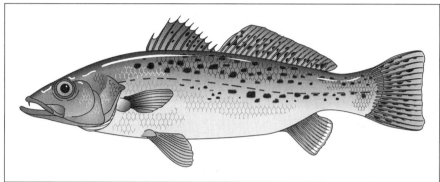

Weakfish: Not a weakling

The weakfish, shown in Figure 5-5, is exclusively an Atlantic Seaboard fish, but weakfish and seatrout live side by side in the Mid-Atlantic states. These fish aren't super big and can be taken on a variety of tackle.

Bait fishermen do well with sandworms in the early season, switching to crabs and shrimp as the warm weather progresses. In the grass beds of Florida and the Gulf of Mexico, shrimp are far and away the preferred food of the weakfish; and the trick for the angler is to get a shrimp (or an imitation shrimp) to ride just above the top of the grass beds to avoid getting hung up if a fish strikes. Weakfish cruise these beds like white-tailed deer grazing in a pasture.

In the absence of any grass beds to hold shrimp, you need to fish tidal structures (rocks, inlets, drop-offs) just as you would with any other fish, looking for areas that are likely to carry baitfish in the moving tide. Surfcasters do well with spoons. Fly rodding with shrimp imitations or poppers can be productive. No matter how you angle for weakfish, remember its name and how it got it: The mouth is soft; so even though it requires steady pressure to keep the fish out of the weeds, you also need a light touch so that you don't pull the hook out.

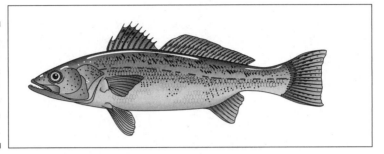

Figure 5-5:
The weak-fish has telltale coffee-bean-like spots.

Redfish (red drum): For cooks and anglers alike

This crustacean-loving gamefish is caught from New Jersey to Houston, Texas; but it is on the grass beds of Florida and the Gulf of Mexico that the redfish (shown in the color section) becomes a super-challenging opponent. And the shallower the water, the more thrilling the fight. As revered on the plate as it is on the line, redfish rank high with anglers everywhere.

When fishing in less than a foot of water for ten-pound fish, this is hold-your-breath, one-cast fishing. It's also very demanding. You need to put the fly right in front of the fish's nose (within two inches). And you have to avoid spooking him with your line at the same time. The best fly for a red in Louisiana is a crab imitation. Shrimp also score consistently. Red drum can reach lengths of nearly five feet, but this is not common. Fortunately, most signs indicate that the population of redfish was not too severely affected by the oil spill of 2010.

Puffing for reds

With redfish and seatrout, I (Peter) have found that if you don't *see* them on the grassy flats, it doesn't mean that they aren't there. They could be following in the wake of a ray and picking up shellfish that the ray has stirred up as it cruises. Look for tight puffs of turbid water that indicate a recently made cloud of mud. Cast into the trailing edge of the cloud and begin to retrieve line. I have caught many fish by this kind of blind casting. (Actually, it's not so much a blind cast as it is blind hope!)

Temperate Bass

Striped bass are sometimes classed in the sea bass family, but they really belong here, in the same temperate bass category found in the freshwater fish chapter. (For more on freshwater fish, check out Chapter 4.) Because these fish are *anadromous,* meaning they live in both fresh- and saltwater, anglers can pursue them using different techniques in very different environments.

For the surf fisherman or fisherwoman, the striped bass (shown in the color section) is the peak of the game, the serious fish that makes your day. It offers a special challenge and a special satisfaction. The striped bass, as its name suggests, is easily identified by the thin black stripes that run the length of its body. They can weigh more than 100 pounds.

Found from the Carolinas to Maine, and transplanted to the west coast and a number of reservoirs all over America, stripers are a favorite gamefish. *Schoolie* (small) stripers can be caught on any form of light tackle, but the little guys aren't the only ones that run in schools. During the great migrations of spring and fall, stripers tend to travel in packs in which all the fish are of uniform size. (Peter has had days in early December off Montauk when they were all 30 inches long and gorging on herring.)

Stripers take a variety of baits. Baitfish such as the bunker (also known as menhaden) produce well, as do herrings and bloodworms. Live eels can yield enormous fish. Plugs and spoons (the latter often fished with the hook buried in wiggly surgical tubes) both work well for stripers, as do surface lures.

Fly rodding for stripers has revolutionized fly fishing in the northeastern United States. Now, instead of making the long drive to crowded trout streams in the mountains, fly rodders are finding great sport close to home with stripers, often with major league fish in the 20- to 30-pound range.

Similar to the trout, the striper hangs on the edge of the current and looks for feeding opportunities. For that reason, stripers like tidal rips (strong flows) and are found around sheltering structures, picking off similarly minded bait. In this case, jetties and rocky shorelines can produce good striper action. This affinity for a rocky habitat no doubt accounts in part for the name *rockfish,* by which the striper is known in the waters south of New Jersey.

Striped bass often chase schools of baitfish to the surface, where their noisy splashes attract birds and anglers alike. Watch for gulls and terns attacking a particular spot offshore — chances are, stripers, blues, or false albacore are there, too. This is fast action, calling for anglers to move quickly from spot to spot as the panicked schools of baitfish appear.

Cod

Codfish seek cold water, and for this reason, they are found in the Northern Hemisphere, in both the Pacific and Atlantic oceans. Commercially fished to the point of decline in spots, cod are extremely valuable as a food fish.

The cod, a delicious fish, is probably the most important commercial fish in history. Ever since Europeans arrived in the Western hemisphere, commercial fishermen have made the long voyage from Europe to the once fertile but now seriously endangered fishing ground of the St. Georges Banks. Their catch could be sold fresh or salted and dried. And cod, which prefer water temperatures in the mid 40s, can be taken through the winter when other fish desert the continental shelf for mid-ocean depths or southern waters.

Because you can catch cod in the cold months, they're a lifesaver for anglers on the Atlantic Seaboard. Party boat captains know where to find the wrecks that concentrate forage (bait) fish, and the cod that feed upon them.

Cod angling is pretty much of the meat-and-potatoes variety: simple bait fishing or jigging just off the bottom. A sturdy boat rod with a bait-casting reel or a surf stick with heavy spinning tackle are the preferred instruments of most cod anglers. Because cod can often tip the scale at greater than 30 pounds (and can weigh up to 200), you want heavy line (at least 30-pound test). Figure 5-6 shows an Atlantic cod with the telltale single *barbel* (whisker) hanging from its lower jaw.

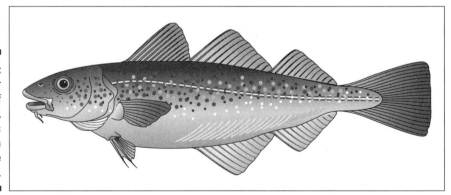

Figure 5-6: Like other members of its family, the Atlantic cod has a goatee-like whisker.

Grouper

This family of fish make for common catches in any warm sea. They don't really school, but individuals might congregate in the same habitat. Some species of groupers have the ability to reverse their sex later in life, which is interesting, although not exactly knowledge that might help you catch him or her.

Groupers tend to be caught near the bottom, and whereas they can be found in water 100 feet deep, they also can be caught inshore, in areas like mangrove coves or bridge pilings. (This is especially true of juvenile fish, which are still big!) Groupers lie in wait and then pounce, feeding on animals such as other fish, squid, crab, and mollusks, and can be taken with heavy tackle and wire leaders using the same for bait. Because groupers live near snags or even in caves, anglers must quickly turn fish, or they risk losing them to the crags where they reside. Figure 5-7 shows a goliath grouper.

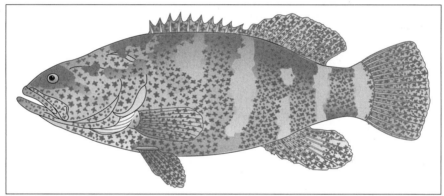

Figure 5-7: The goliath grouper can weigh up to 1,000 pounds.

Snapper

The snapper family contains more than 100 species, but all snappers live in schools in the tropical waters of the Indian, Pacific, and Atlantic oceans. Care must be exercised with these fish because they do have canine teeth that appear, on some species, downright freaky. The red snapper is one of the most sought-after food fish around.

The distinctive yellowtail snapper, shown in Figure 5-8, doesn't grow large (less than ten pounds), but it's a beautiful fish that can be caught on a variety of fishing gear, including fly rods. Most anglers fish for them after attracting them with *chum,* a concoction of ground fish parts placed in the water to lure fish in with its scent. Yellowtail snappers can be found among bridge and pier pilings, and over grass beds and reefs.

Bonefish

Scientists now put five species of fish into this family, but the bonefish is seen as the desired sportfish. Although they have little value as a food fish, they're extremely popular as fly fishing quarry. They might reach 20 pounds, but a specimen well under that would be a prized trophy, especially when taken on a fly.

If one fish is responsible for kicking off the saltwater fly-fishing craze, it's this silver-gray denizen of sandy and coral flats in the world's warm-water oceans. From the west coast of Africa to the Caribbean to the paradise of the South Pacific, the bonefish is among the wariest shallow-water fish and, like the trout, responds well to the right fly, properly presented.

The conventional angler can do well with live shrimp or an imitation shrimp jig. An effective fly is a little shrimp imitation. The first trick to learn in fishing for bones is to see them. Initially, if you go with a guide (which is the *only* way for a newcomer to start bonefishing), you may have a hard time seeing the fish that your guide points out. You simply have to train your eyes to spot what the more experienced guide will see. Eventually, you'll be able to pick out the telltale black tip of their tails (and then their silver-yellow-green outlines) as they cruise. When you do, the trick is to cast four or five feet in front on the same line on which the fish is moving.

With its big eye and downturned mouth, as shown in Figure 5-9, the bonefish is well designed to find food on the flats. When bonefish feed in shallow water, their tails will often stick up in the air. This activity is known as *tailing,* and it is to the bonefish angler what a rising trout is to the freshwater fisherman.

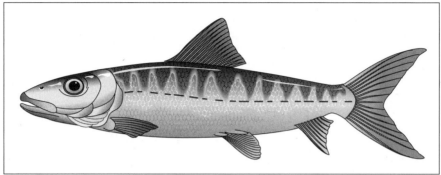

Figure 5-9:
The bone-fish has a large eye and downturned mouth.

Snook

There might be 12 species of snook, but the common snook, shown in Figure 5-10, is the most abundant and the most sought-after by anglers. Like the largemouth bass of freshwater, snook ambush prey and fight hard when hooked. In fact, because snook will enter freshwater rivers, snook and bass might overlap.

Snook seek warm water and are usually found in water less than 65 feet deep. This habitat puts them in close proximity to anglers, particularly in Florida. They feed ravenously on fish, shrimp, and crabs, and jump them in mangrove coves and along docks and bridges. They can be caught on a variety of lures that imitate their prey, and are a popular fly rod quarry, as well. They can reach weights up to 50 pounds, and an angler tangling with one that size would have a whale of a fight on his or her hands because snook will leap, tug, and dive for heavy cover when hooked.

Dehooking a snook by holding it by the lower lip — just like you would dehook a bass — is best. You should not put your fingers in gill covers because they are super-sharp.

Snook are like savage bass when they hit a plug, and we've also had great luck catching them with a fly rod and bass bugs. At night, when they congregate under the lights of bayside docks, the fishing can be unbelievable. When the tide is running, the snook hang around the lights, picking off bait fish. By casting a streamer, first at the outside of the group and then further into it, you can take a half-dozen nice fish before you have exhausted the possibilities in any one *pod* (small group of fish).

Although snook make great eating, they're susceptible to cold winters (when winter-kill occurs in snook populations) and are under so much angling pressure that we would advise you to keep them rarely, and only as a special treat. Follow the local laws, which may include strict bag limits or slot limits.

By returning them to the water alive, you can do your part to help maintain a classic sport fishery.

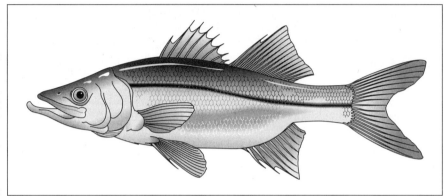

Tarpon

This is another small fish family with a large, feisty, and dominant member. The tarpon can grow to 250 pounds and provides some of the most memorable fights in any kind of fishing. As shown in the color section, the tarpon is easily recognizable because of its protruding lower jaw and huge eye.

The tarpon is a big fish — a very big fish — that can be taken on light tackle in shallow water. It can run forever and leap ten writhing feet in the air. They take squid, shrimp, or baitfish as well as plugs. Anglers catch them while casting, using both bait and fly fishing gear, and while drifting or stillfishing livebaits from boats. These hardy fish live in a variety of inshore habitats, and some tarpon (particularly juveniles) travel upriver in freshwater rivers. They like the shade of long causeways and bridge pilings, and can be found in bays and lagoons, and along mangrove-lined banks. Many times, a tarpon is hooked but not landed because these fish will often throw the hook during one of their spectacular leaps.

Sharks

Sharks are popular in large part because they're, well, sharks. The fascination with sharks runs deep and is well earned. They're often called "killing and eating machines," and are among the most impressive of any predators on land or sea. The range of shark species runs the gamut from deep-water whale sharks to the haunting great white to the bull shark, which can enter freshwater rivers and has been sighted far inland.

Although great whites get most of the attention from the general public, for people who pursue sharks with rod and reel, the mako is top dog. A streamlined shark capable of great speed and gravity-defying leaps, the mako (shown in Figure 5-11) feeds on fish, including other sharks, and the largest of its kind can kill and consume whales and dolphins. They're found throughout the oceans, and are typically pursued from boats. They readily take cutbait but also take flys. They can weigh close to 1,000 pounds, and yes, they have attacked humans. Like many sharks, makos suffer from commercial over-fishing and should probably be released.

Figure 5-11:
Like all
members
of the shark
family, the
mako shark
is highly
streamlined,
with rough
skin and
super-sharp
teeth.

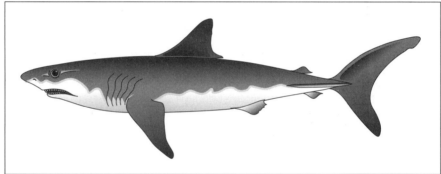

Tuna

Tuna are so common and prized as food, only anglers know about their immense fighting power. Species of this family can be huge — think 1,500 pounds — and fast. Schools of tuna can cruise at 30 miles per hour. Tuna travel almost constantly, and some make grand migrations. Because they swim without pause, they eat large amounts of baitfish, and oddly, can maintain a body temperature warmer than the surrounding water. Tuna are found throughout the world's oceans — often in deep water. Some species of tuna, like the albacore, can be taken on a fly rod, whereas others are big-water, big-boat game.

Billfish Family

It might be fitting to end this chapter with the billfish family, which includes the marlin; the high dorsal fins and swords of these fish probably make them the most recognizable image of saltwater fishing. Famous from Hemingway's *The Old Man and the Sea*, marlin are prized catches. The white marlin, the smallest of the group, is primarily an Atlantic fish. Blue, black, and striped marlin can be found in parts of the Atlantic, Indian, and Pacific oceans.

The blue marlin leaps like a tarpon, runs line like a bonefish, and dives like the most stubborn grouper. The only difference is that a *small* striped, black, or blue marlin is the size of a defensive tackle on the Cincinnati Bengals, and a big one is the size of a pickup truck. (Blue marlin can be up to 16 feet long and weigh 1,800 pounds!) If you want to take your measure against a fish, the marlin can test all of your angling skills (and your strength and endurance, too).

Baitfishing is the most effective angling method with bonito and wahoo common choices for bait. Trolled lures can be very effective, and marlin have even been caught on flies.

If and when you do catch a blue marlin, bear in mind that they evolved that big sword (shown in Figure 5-12) for something, so our advice is this: Don't touch it if the marlin is alive, and assume that the marlin is alive until somebody tells you otherwise. Because marlin are such prized fish, almost all should be released.

Figure 5-12:
The distinguishing feature of all marlin is their sword, a dangerous weapon to other fish and anglers.

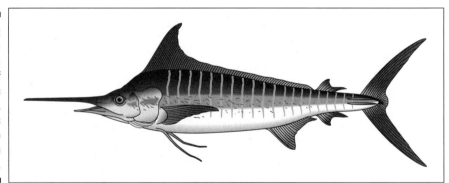

Chapter 6

Staying Safe On (Or Near) the Water

*F*ishing is one of the safest, most enjoyable outdoor pastimes available to you — especially when compared to hobbies like mountain biking, skiing, or rock climbing. But like any passion that brings you into the natural world, fishing has its own inherent dangers. You need to be close to the water to fish, of course, and it's possible to take a dunking or worse. And good, sharp hooks practically wait with keen anticipation for a chance to hook their owners. Fishing from a boat increases the risk of something going wrong because you could fall into deep water, and it may be harder to get help should something happen. Like any outdoor sport, fishing also puts you at the mercy of the weather and all its challenges.

You'll also find that fishing, like a bag of potato chips, perhaps, is something that you'll stick with a little longer than you should. You want to catch one more fish, explore one more bend in the river. Stay out just a little longer before the storm hits. These traits — which all good anglers share — sometimes get us into trouble.

Still, you can make your fishing experience safer. Safety begins with you being prepared for the bad stuff. A prepared angler is not only a successful one, but one who comes home just as healthy as he or she left.

Planning Ahead for Your Trip

An angler on foot is like an infantryman. You have to carry equipment for fast-changing weather, food and water, and (after you get to the scene of the battle) fishing gear. To carry all of this, you have to balance two variables:

> ✔ **Pack light:** There's a law of physics (or at least a law of the physics of anglers) that every pound that you pack to go fishing feels like two pounds coming back. Take only what you need.
>
> Regardless of your feelings about the solitude of nature, bring a cellphone. Turn it off if you choose, ignore it all you want, but carry it for emergencies. Don't forget to put it in a plastic bag first! Cellphones have a nasty habit of jumping into the water.
>
> ✔ **Pack completely:** If you aren't comfortable, you'll be miserable. The cold feels colder, the wet feels wetter, and hunger and thirst seem more insistent. Think of what you'll need and make sure that you take it with you.

Leave a note or a message with a friend about where you're going and when you expect to return. Be specific — you might say, "I'll be on the west side of Shipley Lake," or "I'll wade downstream from the landing at Heron's Point." If you don't have anyone to tell, leave a note at your home. If a search party is involved later, directions like this will make the searching easier.

You look at the map and it shows two miles to the stream you plan to fish. So you figure "Two miles in; two miles out: No big deal." But it is a big deal if those two returning miles are on an uphill grade, in the dark, on an unmarked path, in a snakey area, with landowners who like to sight in their deer rifles before going to bed. Also, after you get to the fishing spot in the first place, you have to fish. Often, this means a good deal of wading, stream-crossing, and rock-hopping, all of which can be very tiring. Bottom line: Think about how far you can reasonably walk — then cut that distance in half. Then see how it all works out. The worst thing that can happen if you follow this advice is you will have more time to fish.

If you are in a new place and the path is so-so, don't wait until dark to start the walk back. One of these times, you may lose your way, and being lost in the woods at night will remind you of what it was like to be a scared four-year-old in a strange, dark house. Make a mental note of how much time it took to get to the stream, and leave that same amount of time to get back while it is still light.

Water, Water Everywhere: Bringing Food and Drink

Regardless of where you fish, don't let the water you're fishing in touch your lips. Sure, you might drink from a pristine wilderness river and be fine. Or you might contract something like giardiasis, an illness commonly referred to as "beaver fever." It occurs when bacteria from tainted water enters your body, and the results are severe. (As in severe diarrhea and vomiting. But are those things ever not severe?) Even accidental contact, such as eating a sandwich after rinsing your hands in the river, should be avoided. You don't need to be paranoid about it, but you should be smart.

Bringing plenty to drink is a necessity, but don't overlook your body's need for food, too. You may get too involved in the fishing to remember to eat much of the food you've packed, but it's better to have it and not need it, than to need it and not have it. Hunger makes you ditzy and irrational, and prone to making mistakes. Come to think of it, my (Greg's) brothers must be hungry all the time.

Both food and drink may call for ice. A small cooler, well packed, can carry all you need for a trip. Keep your food sealed in a bag to prevent ice water from ruining it.

Dehydration hurts

Ironically, sports involving the water often tend to dehydrate people faster than other activities. The sun's rays reflect off water, increasing the effects of light and heat. Wading in current or walking with gear burns energy. For these reasons, anglers need to drink plenty of fluids, and drinking water is best. Just remember to drink it throughout the day! Bring about twice what you think you'll need, and drink it all. Once, on a fishing trip in South Carolina, my (Greg's) cousin grew more loopy and foggy-headed than normal. He couldn't string together a sentence and could hardly stand. We'd been fishing hard for days, and he had simply gotten dehydrated. With plenty of water and rest, he returned to his normal levels of foggy-headedness. Dehydration is nothing to play around with.

Alcohol kills

People often connect angling with drinking alcohol, and it's true that nothing goes better with fried fish than a cold beer. But beer and the hard stuff pairs better with the end of the trip than the beginning. Drinking alcohol exacerbates the effects of dehydration, and the alcohol tends to take hold sooner. Drinking while operating a boat is illegal and especially stupid. Drink, if you choose, to celebrate a good trip, but don't use it to kick one off.

Don't forget the bait for yourself

I (Greg) find that I fish smarter when I'm comfortable. Most of us fish to get away from work, so make your time on the water as hassle-free as possible. In addition to plenty of water, I also bring a candy bar or two and a couple of sandwiches. The food not only makes the day more comfortable, but if something were to happen and I was forced to spend the night on the water, I'd have plenty of energy to survive.

A big hero sandwich looks great, but you will not normally eat it all at once. Then you're in the position of having to rewrap it, which hardly anyone ever does properly, and the result is a lot of salami, lettuce, and tomato bits rolling around the cooler or the back of your vest. Cut the sandwich into smaller pieces and wrap each piece individually. Use wax paper for wrapping, and then put everything inside a plastic zip-top bag.

Although soggy bread may be good for bait, it's lousy on a sandwich. Remember that a sandwich to take along on a fishing trip is not the same as a sandwich that you make at half-time while watching the game on TV. Often, you are not going to eat your fishing sandwich for a few hours. That mayonnaise that tastes so good on a ham sandwich in the den is going to squish right through the bread when you unwrap your sandwich at the stream. Sliced tomatoes will soak through the crustiest, freshest roll. My solution is to cut down on the wet stuff, and if I absolutely need some, then I spread it right on the meat and cover it with a piece of lettuce or a slice of cheese.

Serious Safety: First Aid Kits and Sun Protection

You can always make and pack your own first aid kit, but I (Greg) prefer to buy pre-packaged kits and store them in both my boat and tackle bag. That way I have the basic supplies I need, whether I'm afoot or afloat. Available at most sporting goods stores, first aid kits list their contents on the packaging, and you can pick the one that matches your needs.

I like kits in waterproof packaging, and I don't even open it when I buy one: I simply stow it away, sealed. A good first aid kit will have what you need to address the most common scrapes, cuts, and stings a trip might bring. Likewise, my tackle bag has a bottle and a stick of sunblock, as well as a bottle of insect repellent.

Making your own kit

You know your medical needs better than anyone, so you may be more comfortable just making your own kit to bring what you need. If you're highly allergic to bee stings, bring your EpiPen. Chronic sinusitis sufferers should bring sinus relief medicine. You're prone to heartburn? Pack the antacids! Bringing these common medicines sounds obvious, but many anglers forget them in the morning's rush. Don't let a minor affliction ruin your trip. A small plastic container, such as a small tackle box or a plastic kitchen container, makes a good miniature medicine chest that can be tucked into your vest or tackle box. One more thing to include: Bring a tube of superglue. Use it to mend both torn plastic lures and minor lacerations.

The sun is a fair-weather friend (sort of)

When you're on the water, sunlight gets you two times — when it comes down, and again when it reflects back up off the water. Sunscreen is a must. Spread it on before you begin fishing and reapply once or twice. A serious sunburn is no joke. Covering exposed skin with clothing and a good hat really helps, too.

Why polarized sunglasses make a difference

I (Greg) started wearing contacts simply so I could wear nice sunglasses. I wasn't worried about their appearance, though — I just wanted a great pair of polarized sunglasses to cut the glare from the water's surface. On bright days, you'll be grateful for any pair of shades. Polarized lenses, though, cut through the shiny glare on the water's surface, allowing you to see deeper into the water. This will help you spot cruising fish — like carp or bonefish on the flats — or spot underwater cover you might have missed. When boating, seeing more might make the difference between a missed obstacle and a busted prop.

Safe Wading

Even though wading is just walking, it requires much more skill and care than walking down the street does. First, you are often dealing with the force of moving water. Second, you can't always see the ground in front of you very well (or at all). And third, underwater rocks and plants can be slippery. For all of these reasons, there is one cardinal rule of wading: Take it slow!

Come to think of it, there is a second cardinal rule: Test the footing in front of you before you take the weight off your back foot. Drop-offs, unseen rocks, and current surges are often invisible, so you need to wade slowly and cautiously, one foot at a time.

In addition to these cardinal rules of wading in any body of water, this section gives you some additional advice for staying on your feet as well as what to do if you take a tumble.

Thy rod and thy staff, and thy friend, too

I (Peter) do most of my wading without a staff, but there are times when one really helps, either as a probing device or as a third leg.

Although a stick lying around on the ground may make a serviceable wading staff, what do you do with it after you're in the middle of the stream? For greater convenience, many people like commercial wading staffs that can be tied to a belt. If you can't find such a staff, a cheap and easy alternative is a ski pole with the little rubber circle cut off of the bottom. I say cheap because in the summertime, ski poles are not a hot ticket, and you can often pick up a bunch at bargain-basement prices.

You would think that if one person can easily slip and fall in a stream, then linking two people is a sure recipe for a dunking. But the opposite is true. By linking arms together, two anglers can actually gain strength and stability. If one of you is a stronger wader, that person should take the upstream position because that is the more difficult one. (This is also a good way to get a new angler a little more used to handling moving water.)

Handling the current and the occasional mishap

When a fish is hooked and it wants to use the force of the current to fight you, it turns broadside to the current. This may work fine for a fish trying to escape. For an angler trying to wade, it's precisely the wrong thing to do.

You want to present the thinnest silhouette possible. In other words, stand sideways. I realize that some of us older anglers may have a shape that looks more like a soup spoon than a steak knife, but sideways is still the most efficient way to deal with the physics of moving water.

Suppose you see a nice fish rising behind a midstream rock. Inch by inch you begin to wade across the treacherous stream. It's slow going, but you're slowly getting in position for that perfect cast. And then the bottom drops sharply and you realize there's no way you're going to make it. Whatever you do, don't turn around and wade out! This action simply presents the broadest part of your body to the flow, and it's a great way to get knocked off your feet. Just take your time and back out slowly, inch by inch.

Still, one of these days, you are going to take a tumble into the water. If you are careful, you will tumble much less often than you think. In 25 years of angling, I (Peter) have fallen into the stream exactly twice. I've come close to falling more often than that, but in terms of bona fide butt-soakings, that's it. That makes me lucky. If you fall in, you should be able to right yourself pretty quickly. It helps if you keep your waders tightly cinched with a belt. If the current does take you, don't fight it: The river always wins. If possible, keep your feet in front of you so that if some part of you strikes a rock, it probably won't be your head. Although taking an involuntary ride is a little scary, try and remember that most dunkings will leave you in calm water in less than half a minute. And if you just can't manage to stay safe and hold on to your rod, let the rod go. After all, you can buy a new rod easier than the rod can buy a new you. For this reason, you might also wear a life jacket.

Danger Amplified: Boating Safety

You can get into trouble while wading or walking the bank, but as soon as you climb into a floating vessel, you assume more risk. Boats (even self-powered vessels like canoes and float tubes) allow you to move faster and over deeper water. And while there's nothing more peaceful than floating in a little jonboat on a shallow pond, a high-powered bass boat can cross a reservoir at 70 miles per hour! Ocean-going fishing boats are even bigger and faster. Whether you own a boat or fish from a friend's, you need to be smart about your own safety.

It starts with life jackets

State and federal agencies come up with different slogans to encourage you to wear a life jacket, including "It Only Works If You Wear It!" and "A Life Jacket is an Expensive Seat . . . It Could Cost You Your Life." A phrase that worked for me (Greg) came from a conservation officer after a body was recovered from a local river. He said, "We never find a corpse wearing a life jacket."

When we talk about life jackets, you probably picture the classic orange, upside-down U yoke that fits over your head. Well, life jackets have come a long way in terms of comfort. Figure 6-1 shows different styles of life jackets, including belts and vests that inflate only when they hit the water. Modern life jackets are comfortable to wear, cool in the summer, and unobtrusive, so you can wear one all the time while boating. The fanciest life jackets are quite pricey, but others are equally effective and inexpensive. Besides, isn't your life worth it?

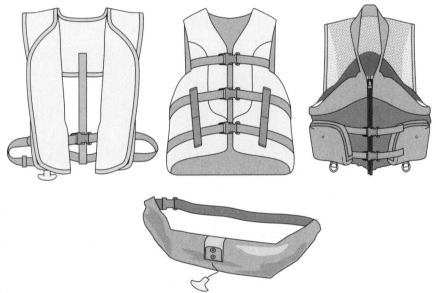

Figure 6-1:
A range of modern life jackets.

Your call, Captain

If you own the boat, you're in charge. That's a lot of pressure: You need to ensure that your boat is seaworthy, legal, and equipped. Any guests will have varying amounts of on-the-water experience, and before you worry about getting everyone fishing, you need to make sure they know the rules of the boat. After all, if an accident occurs, you might be held responsible.

The first thing the owner of a boat has to do is make sure everything is legal. The bigger a boat is, the more regulations it has to follow. Rules vary from state to state, but make sure you have a proper license. This will probably require stickers placed on the hull to mark your boat, as a license plate identifies a car. Your boat will also bear a metal tag that limits the number of persons it should carry. Obey that limit.

A safe boat is properly equipped. You need a good accessible life jacket for everyone on board. Some states require boats to also carry a "throwable" type of float, like a boat cushion. Make sure the boat has the proper lighting, bow and stern, and that it works. You might also be required to carry a horn or additional safety devices. Weather or marine radios are a good idea. Fire extinguishers rated for marine use are a must. Figure 6-2 shows a safely equipped boat. Check with your local state department of natural resources for specific rules.

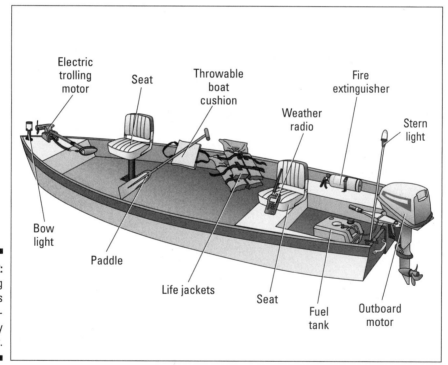

Figure 6-2:
This fishing boat carries the necessary safety gear.

In any boating situation, you want to ensure two things: that the boat maintains its power, and that the boaters stay aboard. To ensure the first, I (Greg) follow the three-kinds-of-power rule: Every boat needs to have three methods of movement, should one or two fail. In most cases, this will include a gas engine, an electric trolling motor, and a paddle or two. Check before each trip to make sure your boat has three kinds of power, and that each is in good working order. Boaters need to stay aboard for obvious reasons — when in the water, anyone could fall victim to drowning or hypothermia, or risk being hit by another boat. Even on mild days, someone treading water could succumb to hypothermia quickly because the water sucks the heat from a body. Make sure life jackets are worn and people remain seated when the boat is moving. As a captain, avoid making sharp turns and excessive speeds. If someone does go overboard, keep an eye on them while you turn around and position your boat between the man overboard and any nearby vessels. Pull them to safety as soon as possible.

Of course, you also need to know the rules of the water. Unlike drivers, in most states boaters aren't usually required to pass a test to operate a boat, and this can be a scary thing when you're on a big body of water. You may feel like you're surrounded by nincompoops! And you might well be. States offer courses, often online, that you can take to learn boating safety. Take the course. Boat with experienced captains first. And stick to smaller waters (and avoid popular boating times, like the weekends) until you learn the ropes. Or, in this case, the buoy markers.

Owning a fishing boat is a source of tremendous pride for me and millions of other anglers. But, like a car, a boat brings with it some additional responsibility. Know your guests before you take them out in your boat. If the trip isn't going well, make an excuse and cut it off early. If you're on someone else's boat, and you feel unsafe, cut it off early. It's just not worth it.

Part II
Gearing Up Without Going Overboard

"What kind of line do I use when I go fishing? Usually, 'I'm only doing this to save money on our food budget, Honey.'"

In this part . . .

You uncover all you need to know about the gear of fishing: everything from the different styles of reels, to all kinds of terminal tackle, to the latest in sonar units. While fishing doesn't have to be complicated, the latest technology offers a lot to the contemporary angler, helping him or her catch more and bigger fish. Fishing line has evolved. Rods are lighter and more sensitive than ever. Even the classic fish hook has a new twist. This part helps you decide what kind of gear you need, and what you can live without.

Chapter 7

Hot Rods and Cool Reels

· ·

· ·

*Y*ou can still catch fish with a cane pole. Find a long bamboo shoot or willow branch, tie a string to the end in lieu of a reel, and add a hook and a bobber. Flip over a dried cow patty for some worms, get your grandfather, and head down the dusty path of Mayberry. Catch a few fish and have fun. The iconic cane pole of yesteryear has been replaced many times over, though. Today's rods are constructed of everything from graphite to carrot fibers (no kidding). Modern reels now feature everything from one-piece aluminum or magnesium frames, up to a dozen bearings, and titanium parts.

As advanced as rods and reels are today, there remain four kinds of equipment that anglers use to store line, cast a lure or baited hook, and fight fish. Casting equipment breaks down into four categories: spincasting, spinning, baitcasting, and fly.

This chapter tells you how to distinguish among the four kinds of casting gear, as well as the advantages and disadvantages of each. You gain a good idea of what you need in your first rod and reel and how your gear selection might change as you evolve as an angler.

Getting a Handle on Fishing Rod Basics

A rod is used for catching fish. To do this, it must be stiff but supple, strong but delicate. If fishing were just a matter of cranking them in, you could use a broom handle. But angling for a fish is a three-part job that requires three different tasks of your rod:

- **Getting the bait, lure, or fly to where the fish is:** That is, your rod needs to deliver the goods.

- **Setting the hook:** Because not every take is a visual one, a rod has to be sensitive enough to let you feel the fish as it takes your worm (or lunges at your jig) and strong enough to set the hook.

- **Fighting the fish:** The rod is a big lever that transmits a great deal of force; and because of its ability to bend, it transmits variable force as required, acting as a shock absorber when the fish suddenly turns or bolts off again.

The way in which a rod accomplishes these three tasks varies. Sometimes the delivery has to be as light as goose down. In other situations, you need to heave your bait into heavy current and hold it there. To accommodate the key tasks as well as the differences in anglers, all kinds of rods are available. In time, if you fish enough, you will discover how to feel the differences in rods. You may like some but not care for others. Your personal fondness for a particular rod doesn't mean that one rod is necessarily better than another (although there are both winners and stinkers out there). It just means that one is better for you and the kind of fishing you want to do at any given time.

Unlike reels, all rods (spincasting, spinning, baitcasting, and fly) share many of the following common features, as shown in Figure 7-1. For more on reels, see the section "Catching Up with Reels" later in this chapter:

- **Butt:** The bottom half or third of the shaft, or *blank,* of the rod. As with the tip, on some rods, the butt really bends, while on others it doesn't.

- **Ferrule:** The joint where the rod blank can be separated. In the old days, this was a metal connector that decreased the rod's sensitivity. Now, the smaller section of the blank is made to fit inside a larger section, with little effect on performance.

- **Grip:** The handle part you hold onto. It can be made of cork or synthetic materials. Grips come in many shapes and sizes. The main point is that it should be comfortable for the way you fish.

- **Guides:** Small eyes that direct the line on its journey from the reel to the tip top. On a spinning rig and fly rod, in particular, the guides get progressively smaller as you go from reel to tip top, channeling the large coils that come off the reel into a straight line to your target. Guides, often formed of stainless steel or other metals, might be lined with ceramic or some other material to allow the line to slide smoothly through the guide. Check your guides frequently to ensure that they are nick-free, as a chink in the lining of the guide will damage your line.

✔ **Reel seat:** Usually a set of screw-tightened washers or rings that fit over the base of the reel and attach it to the rod.

✔ **Tip:** The last foot or so of rod. It can bend a little or a great deal and is critical in determining the action and sensitivity of the rod. See the later section "How slow can you go?" for more on how rods bend.

✔ **Tip top:** The uppermost guide, the point where the line leaves the rod on its way to the fish.

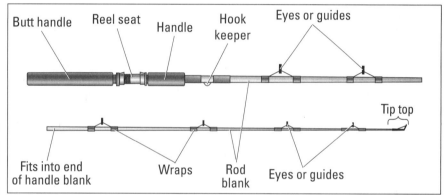

Figure 7-1:
Rod anatomy.

The writing on the rod

Fishing rods usually have the following information printed right above the handle:

✔ **Action:** When you apply force to rods, they bend quickly or slowly. Some flex only at the tip, although others bend all the way down to the butt. How fast and where a rod bends determines its *action*.

For the record, tackle manufacturers classify their rods as *ultrafast* (or *extra-fast*), *fast*, *moderate*, and *slow*. Which one is right for you? It depends on what fish you pursue and the kind of lures you use. Moderate or slow rods probably are the best bets for beginners, as they're more forgivable and more flexible.

✔ **Length:** The length of the rod is usually expressed in feet and inches. Printing the length right on the rod prevents the social awkwardness of having to hold the rod against your forehead in the store to determine how long, or tall, it is.

Shorter rods work better in tight spaces, like when you're fishing under overhanging branches, but in general longer rods allow for longer casts. And a longer rod acts like a shock absorber, making it easier to maintain a tight line while fighting a surging fish. Stay in the midrange — say, around 6 feet for your first rod.

✔ **Optimum lure/line weight:** Manufacturers also classify rods by how much weight they can optimally cast, listing the preferred range in ounces. So you may see "1–4 oz." on the rod, indicating that this rod works well when casting lures or rigs weighing between one and four ounces. In addition, the rod should print the preferred line test, usually labeled as such and in pounds, as in "Line 12–20 lb."

✔ **Power:** In addition to a rod's action, most manufacturers will print the rod's *power,* the amount of weight required to bend the rod, on the blank. They generally use the terms *ultralight, light, medium,* and *heavy,* or some combination of these terms, such as *medium-heavy.* An ultralight rod bends easily under light weight. A heavy rod might flex only slightly when lifting a bowling pin.

How slow can you go?

As shown in Figure 7-2, a rod can bend a little or a great deal. Fast rods bend in the tip, whereas slower rods bend through the whole length of the rod (from the tip to the butt in a gentle arc). In general, a fast rod casts well when distance is a priority. It is punchier than a slow rod. It is also sensitive in the tip, so that you can feel a strike or even a nibble right away. A slower rod generally allows for a more delicate presentation. Whereas a fast, or *tippy,* rod may have a tendency to tear bait off the hook, a slower action will give a nice even heave.

If you're doing a great deal of jig fishing, for example, the stiffness of a fast rod is desirable. On the other hand, if you're working crankbaits, many anglers prefer a slower rod so that they don't yank the lure out of the fish's mouth the second it shows any interest. Although a fast rod can be more sensitive than a slow rod (with a fast rod, you can feel the tiniest tap-tap of a fish), a slow rod acts as a better shock absorber when you're battling big fish. Slow rods also work best with circle hooks. See Chapter 9 for more on hooks, circle and otherwise.

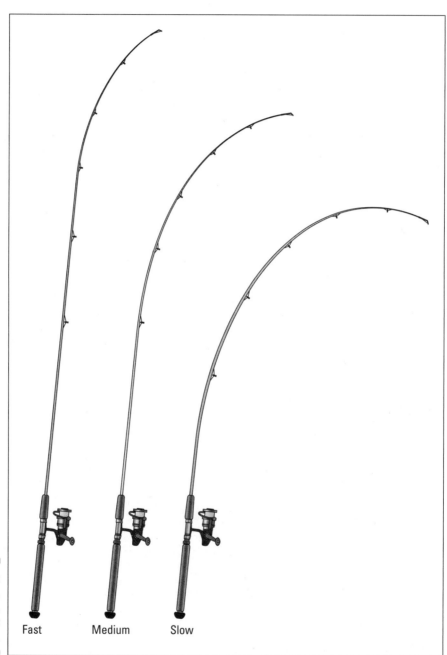

Figure 7-2:
Fast,
medium,
and slow
rod action.

Fast   Medium   Slow

Catching Up with Reels

Saying every reel works the same is akin to saying every automobile works the same: It may be true on a basic level, but everyone knows the difference between a Hummer and a SmartCar. The four kinds of reels range widely in performance and function. But all reels, like all rods, share a few commonalities. Figure 7-3 points out the basic parts that reels share:

- ✓ **Anti-reverse:** This lever can be found on most reels, and when switched on, this device prevents the crank from turning in reverse. Some anglers leave the anti-reverse off so they can crank line in, or crank line out (by turning the crank counter-clockwise). But most find life easier when the anti-reverse is on because, while fighting a fish, you can take your hand off the crank and not worry about the fish taking line off the reel. Put simply, with your drag properly adjusted, you're better off with the anti-reverse on.

- ✓ **Bail/line release:** Every reel except the fly reel features a button, lever, or device that allows the release of line. Because every reel completes two basic jobs — sending line out or bringing it back — a reel is either *disengaged* (allowing line out) or *engaged* (bringing line in).

- ✓ **Crank:** This is the handle of the reel. You see single-grip cranks, double-grip cranks, cranks with grips so soft your fingers rejoice when they touch them. But they all turn to bring line into the reel.

- ✓ **Drag:** A knob, usually on the crank, or in front of the spool on a spinning reel, that tightens the spool to control the fight of a fish.

- ✓ **Reel base:** This part connects into the *reel seat* of the rod.

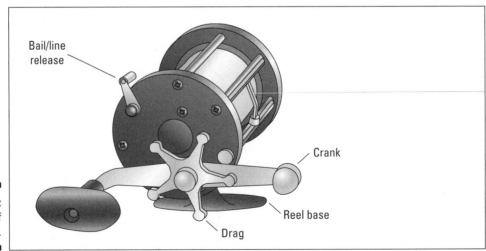

Figure 7-3: Anatomy of a reel.

It's a drag, but it works

The *drag* on a reel works with you to control a fighting fish. On a spincast or baitcast reel, you might find a star-shaped knob inside the crank (or a roller-type knob built into the body of a spincast reel). A spinning reel usually features a knob in front of the spool, although some have a rear-mounted drag on the back of the reel's body for easier access. A fly reel's drag is often a knob right on the axis of the main spool.

All drags work to control surging fish by controlling the speed of line leaving the spool once *engaged*. You might wonder, but if a reel is engaged, line can only come in, right? Not quite. A strong fish could pull a reel out of your hands if there were no give. (More likely, it would break the line first.) Drag lets a fish take line out, while leaving the reel engaged. A big fish, in its strongest moments, might take out some line against even a tight drag. (One of the sweetest things to happen in all of angling!)

You "set" the drag using the knob on your reel. With the drag set too loose, you can't even pull in your lure. You turn the crank and nothing happens. A hooked fish could simply swim away, towing your line. But make the drag too tight, and a big fish might take your rod and reel to Davey Jones's locker. So do the following before you cast the first time: Engage the reel, then pull the line off the reel with your hand. (Grab it right in front of the reel.) If it comes off easily, tighten the drag a bit. If it appears to be locked down, loosen it up a bit. Adjust again once you begin fishing, and after you catch (hopefully!) a few fish. All we can say is, you get a feel for your drag.

Know where your drag is *before* a big fish catches you off guard. You should be able to reach down and adjust the drag (just a little now!) while fighting a whopper.

The writing on the reel

Reel manufacturers make your life a little easier by telling you a reel's *capacities* right on the reel itself. Most reels are stamped with a series of numbers, and, like the numbers on the side of a car's tire, knowing what they mean can help you understand more about what you need.

The first number refers to the size of line a reel can hold. This is usually given in pounds, referring to the *pound test* of the line. The second number refers to the amount of line the reel's spool can hold. This number is usually given in yards. The bigger the reel, the more line it can hold.

As reels get bigger, they also get heavier, bulkier, and often costlier. It's easy to overestimate the amount and size of line you need. Start smaller, and if you discover you need more or heavier line, you can upsize later.

Suppose a reel is stamped "12/245." This means the reel likes 12-pound test line, and it holds 245 yards of it. I say "likes" because reels are built to utilize a particular range of line tests, and you can fudge that range a bit, but don't be surprised if your reel no longer works as well. A reel that likes 12-pound test can hold 20-pound test, but it may not cast as far or as smoothly. (And it won't hold as much of it.) Sometimes, reel manufacturers give you several sets of numbers, allowing you to choose the line that fits your fishing: 10/245, 12/200, 17/150. See how it works? The heavier the line, the less you can put on the reel. Carp fishing close to the bank? Sure, go 17-pound test. Casting across the pond for bluegills? Stick with 10. (Chapter 8 covers line in detail.)

Classic Beginnings: Spincast Gear

The odd label of *spincast* — a combination of spinning and casting — might confuse you, but you know exactly what I (Greg) mean when I say that these are the "push-button" reels that so many anglers cast first (see Figure 7-4). Long associated with beginning anglers, people love spincast reels because they work, cost less than other types of reels, and require low maintenance. Indeed, some anglers begin their fishing adventures with spincast gear — likely a Zebco 33 — and never experiment with other kinds.

Figure 7-4:
The spin-casting reel is good for kids and beginners because there's little opportunity to mess up the cast.

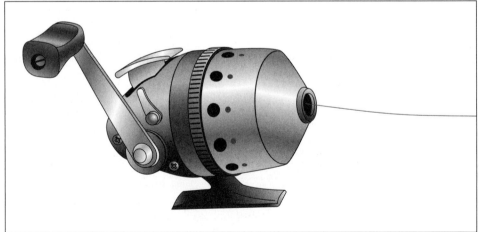

Many refer to spincast reels as *closed-face* reels because they have a cover that hides the spool. The spool is fixed (meaning it doesn't spin as line is retrieved) and mounted parallel to the rod, so when you turn the crank, the *spinnerhead* turns and picks up the line, laying it around the spool. Casting is simple: You push in the button with your thumb (and hold it down) while you bring the rod overhead. As you swing the rod forward, you release the button, allowing the line to peel off the spool. (You can stop a cast suddenly by pressing the button down again.) After a cast, you engage the reel when you turn the crank a little and begin the retrieve. (More on casting in Chapter 16.)

The *spinnerhead* is the device that rotates in front of the fixed spool and lays the line onto the spool. Spinnerheads use either rounded edges (like smooth teeth) to pick up line, or pins (often ceramic) that pop out of the spinnerhead to snare the line. I suggest a reel with pop-up pins because they treat the line better, causing less wear and tear.

Advantages and disadvantages of spincast gear

Spincast reels couldn't be easier to operate. They're durable enough for years of hard use, able to withstand accidental dunkings and drops from bike handlebars. They're less likely to tangle, so kids are less likely to get frustrated. All in all, this is great, entry-level equipment and the best choice for beginners. You cannot go wrong starting out with a push-button reel.

But the mechanics of a spincast gear inherently increase friction. The spinnerhead that picks up the line and lays it on the spool will knick and fray the line over time. (Even if it utilizes pins instead of teeth.) The spool itself is often small, limiting the size and amount of line that can be used, limiting fishing applications. The gear ratios don't allow for fast retrieves (useful when fishing a lure like a buzzbait). The drag range is limited. Improvements have been made in the design of spincast gear, to be sure, and the newest reels are much, much improved over the models our grandparents started with. For example, now you can buy spincast reels that mount underneath the rod like a spinning reel, and these tend to work well, especially with light line. These hybrids are called *underspin* reels and use a trigger instead of a button, but they're equally user-friendly. Not ideal for big fish or heavy lures, they work well when pursuing fish like panfish.

So although this is the perfect choice for a beginner, a spincast reel, with its fixed-spool design, will never operate as butter-smoothly as a good baitcasting reel, and will never cast as far as a good spinning reel.

Considering a rod and reel combo, or striking out on your own

You have two options when purchasing spincast gear from a store: You can buy a combo, or you can buy your rod and reel separately. Tackle companies know that spincast gear works perfectly for beginners, so they package ready-to-fish kits that pair a spincast reel with a rod. Buying them together like this often saves the angler money, and it's a good way to know the reel is paired with a rod that matches it in terms of size. (Basically, the size of the line and the weight of the lures intended for them. In other words, the writing on the rod and the reel match up.) It's not unusual to find kits targeting specific species — we see combos designed for bass and catfish, for example. Some even include lures or hook and sinker assortments.

Most big-box stores carry these combos in their sporting goods sections. These are great starter kits. Most anglers find that it takes longer to get the rod and reel free of the plastic packaging then it does to figure out how to cast with them pretty efficiently! You could buy a combo in the morning and fish with it that afternoon. Most reels sold in a combo come pre-spooled with line, but check to make sure.

We trust these kits and believe that most big tackle companies work hard to lure younger anglers into the sport by offering affordable kits with quality gear. You can find a good combo at a fair price for sale close to your home. But, as you fish more and perhaps begin to focus on a particular species or kind of fishing (say, smallmouth fishing in a tiny stream outside your town), you may want to pair a particular reel with a longer rod, for example.

Spincast reels mount on top of the rod, as do baitcasting reels (covered in the later section "Baitcasting Gear: Complicated, but Worth It"). This means that they require a rod that accepts a top-mounted reel. These rods are simply known as *casting* rods. As long as the size of the rod is pretty close to the size of the reel, any casting rod should work with any spincast reel. But you cannot pair a spincast reel with a spinning or fly rod. Those rods (covered elsewhere in this chapter) are designed for reels that mount under the rod.

The same big box stores that sell combos will sell individual reels and carry racks of rods overhead. Remember to examine the writing on the rod near the handle (refer to the earlier section "The writing on the reel") — is it for spinning or casting, and what are the recommended weights? Look at the line rating for the various rods and reels, and pair them up yourself. Have fun with it! No one says you can't match a rod and reel based on accent color alone. (Although if I [Greg] admitted to my brothers I had done that, I might get heckled out of the boat.)

If you're limited to just one

Start with something middle of the road, size-wise. You can find ultralight spincast reels that aren't much bigger than an egg for panfish and trout. Likewise, they make spincast reels for catfish and stripers that are as big as coffee cups. Go for something in the middle, about the size of a peach. Look for line rated between 8- and 12-pound test. That size casts well and handles most fish.

You want an all-purpose rig — something you can take after bluegill or pinfish off the pier. (Although check the manufacturer's specs before you take it too far afield — most spincast gear cannot handle saltwater.) Maybe you're targeting a streaking largemouth bass or the pike that lives under the dock at the lake house in Wisconsin. You want a rod between five and six feet long, medium action, rated for 8–12 pound test line. A rod of this length will allow you to cast well without snagging every tree branch overhead. Several companies make good reels, and you can always go with the classic — the Zebco 33. It's what your grandparents used, after all.

You see a lot of pre-packaged combo kits featuring cartoon characters. Cute, aren't they? Kids love them, and maybe you should buy one for that reason alone. But don't be surprised if little Johnny fails to catch a fish with one. With their stubby poles and tiny cranks, these combos are cute, but impractical for fishing. Kids may have a hard time hooking any fish that bite, simply because the rod is too short to set the hook. (When using these kits, even experienced adults have a hard time hooking up!) Blasphemy, I know, but I recommend buying a small spincast reel and a longer rod (like a five footer). Give Little Johnny a fighting chance, and catching fish will make him happier than seeing a cartoon on his reel. (You can find more on fishing with kids in Chapter 23.)

So Smooth: Spinning Gear

Spinning gear takes a step up from spincast gear, both in terms of function and utility. While a little trickier to use, spinning reels tend to be smoother operators that can cast farther than most spincast gear.

Spinning reels, like spincast reels, feature a fixed spool. That means a device must lay the line around the spool as you crank, and with a spinning reel the *bail,* a curved piece of wire that rotates around the spool, accomplishes this task (instead of the spinnerhead of a spincast reel). To cast a spinning reel, you pick up the line with your forefinger of your casting hand, hold it tight against the rod, and open the bail with your other hand. You then bring the rod overhead and swing it forward as your forefinger releases the line. (Find more on casting in Chapter 16.) Already you see how things have gotten more complicated over spincast gear: no button. Instead your finger controls the line's release. Gone, too, is the cover that hides the spool and the moving parts. Now everything is exposed — no "closed-face" here!

Figure 7-5 shows a typical spinning reel. Usually, you can move the crank to the right or the left side. Sometimes, righties want the crank on the left, leaving their strong arm to assist the rod in fighting the fish. Other righties cast with their right, and then pass the rod to their left hand to reel with their right. (This assumes their left arm is strong enough to handle the fish they hook, which is usually the case.)

Figure 7-5:
A standard spinning reel with the reel mounted under the rod.

Advantages and disadvantages of spinning gear

When spinning reels cast, line peels quickly off the front lip of the spool in tight loops, which reduces friction and translates into longer, smoother casts. (Especially when compared to spincast gear.) Only a few key parts move on a spinning reel, so less can break. Any tangles are accessible. These reels tend to be lighter and sleeker. The best spinning reels feature silky-smooth retrieves and cast effortlessly, so they are perfect for everything from wading small streams for trout to surfcasting for stripers. When it comes to casting lighter baits, only a fly rod will outperform a spinning rod and reel.

Surfcasting with a spinning rod

Surfcasting rods can be very long, but I (Peter) find that the real sharpies go for the medium to short rods. Being able to lick a big fish with a light rod has a macho element, but macho only gets you so far. I think that the real reason most fishermen prefer surf rods in the eight- to ten-foot range is that such rods are more effective (and that means more fun) in the long run. If you're just baitfishing, a long rod doesn't have much of a downside (except for fitting it in your car or truck). But if you work a lure, fish a very long rod and you're reminded of the laws of physics as they apply to levers: Even a little weight feels like a big weight when you apply force over a long distance. In other words, using a long rod can be tiring.

In surfcasting, the basic fact you must confront is that there is only a little surf but a great deal of ocean, so the more water you can cover, the more chance you have of catching fish. I have spent days on end watching schools of feeding fish slashing through bait that was just out of reach of my gear. If I could only get another 20 or 30 feet out of my spinning rig, I would no doubt have been into fish like the guys with the baitcasting surf sticks, which just flat out cast farther. Mastering the technique of using baitcasting surf sticks does take longer, but for delivering the goods, the baitcasting rod is the champ.

But line twist can be a problem with spinning reels because the line winds onto a spool mounted parallel to the rod (and thus, counter to the direction of the line as it approaches the reel). Controlling the cast with your forefinger takes a while to get used to. (Although I (Greg) should note that some spinning reels, like my Shimano, feature a trigger that sort of picks up the line for you, so your finger finds the line every time.) Some anglers claim, and I'm one of them, that for truly large fish, spinning reels take a backseat to baitcasting reels. You get more cranking power out of baitcasting reels.

Spinning rods: What makes them different

Spinning reels mount underneath the rod, so they require a special kind of rod. Again, all rods are labeled either casting or spinning, and only spinning rods work with spinning reels. Spinning rods feature an upside-down reel seat, but the rod *guides* (the eyes the line goes through) are the real give-away — on a spinning reel, the guide closest to the reel is much larger (like an inch or more in diameter). This allows for less friction as the line comes "spinning" off the reel. The guides then get progressively smaller as they get closer to the tip of the rod. If you ever see a TV commercial where some hunk fishes with a spinning reel held above the rod, you can assume no one on the set has ever fished before!

As with baitcasting rods, spinning rods come in a range of actions and weights. I (Peter) own three rods: one ultralight rod for panfish, stream trout, and smallmouth bass; a medium rod for bigger bass, walleye, and pike; and a nine-foot, stiff-action surf stick for the ocean. The rules here are to match the rod to the fish and to use enough rod to catch fish but not so much rod that there is no fight. You could use a heavyweight rod to catch a bluegill, but that wouldn't be much fun. Likewise, a good angler could land a large trout on an ultralight, but do you want to fight one fish all afternoon?

If you're limited to just one

Our choice for an all-in-one spinning rod would be a six- or seven-foot, medium-action graphite rod. Such a rod can throw lures in the ¼-ounce to ⅝-ounce range. It's sporty enough to give some pleasure with small fish, but it can also fight bigger freshwater fish (and even the odd bluefish or striped bass).

Breaking down any rod

If I (Peter) lived out at the beach and had a pickup truck, I would probably have a one-piece fiberglass rod. All the sharpies out my way have this type of rod. And if you know how to handle one, the action that it provides is deliciously slow, and casting is more like relaxing and less like practicing for the Olympic hammer throw.

This leads to the larger question of *ferrules* (the joints where two pieces of a rod fit together). The old wisdom has it that the more ferrules you have, the more strength and action you give up in your rod. I'm not so sure that this wisdom applies to most modern rod designs. Instinctively, I like the look of fewer ferrules; but as a traveling fisherman, I can tell you that you can't fit a nine-foot rod in the overhead luggage bin on an airplane. Traveling rods that come in four or five pieces are probably less smooth than one- or two-piece rods, but I don't think that you really notice that much difference. For most fishing, most of the time, a multipiece rod works perfectly fine, and it has the advantage of being handy anyplace you go.

Although one-piece rods are neat, 99 percent of the readers of this book have (or will have) rods that break down into two or more pieces. Going

on the time-honored principle of "If something bad can happen, it will," you can count on a pair of ferrules getting stuck together someday. When this happens, remember the following do's and don'ts.

Don't use pliers. A blank is usually a hollow tube, and pliers are *guaranteed* to break your rod. It may not break right then and there — although it usually does — but take my word for it: You will injure the fibers in the rod, and it will break one day.

The same goes for twisting the stuck ferrule apart like a screw-top soda bottle. First, this technique probably won't work; and second, you could easily snap one of the guides. Use a gentle twisting motion when you disassemble a rod; but if that technique doesn't work, try applying ice to the joint. If you don't have any ice handy, try running cool water (such as from that stream behind you) over the joint. Wait a moment and then try again to separate the ferrules.

Before you assemble the rod the next time, apply ferrule wax (ask for it at your store) to the joint. Wax will prevent the rod blanks from sticking in the first place.

Baitcasting Gear: Complicated, but Worth It

The first truly modern reels were developed by the precision German watchmakers of Kentucky. By combining their love of angling for the native black bass with their skill with gears and machinery, they transformed the reel from a thing that conveniently held line to a machine that aided fishing. One turn of the baitcasting reel's crank or handle, assisted by the gear mechanism of the new reels, produced four turns of the reel.

Unlike spincast or spinning gear, *baitcast* reels feature a spool that rotates as the crank turns, and the axis of the spool is mounted perpendicular to the rod. This allows line coming off the rod to go directly onto the spool, without requiring a mechanical device to lay the line onto the spool. Examine the gear of any bass pro, and you're likely to find an arsenal of baitcasting reels. With hundreds of thousands of dollars on the line in bass fishing tournaments, this is the kind of casting gear most pros use. That tells you something.

The principle behind casting with a baitcasting reel is simple: the weight of the lure pulls on the line, causing the spool to spin as it feeds more line. (Gone is the "fixed" spool of spincast and spinning reels.)

A low-profile baitcasting reel (shown with a classic round reel in Figure 7-6) fits the palm of the hand well and lessens fatigue. The classic round reel can hold more line and works well for anglers fishing big water for big fish. (Note that the reel is mounted on top of the rod.)

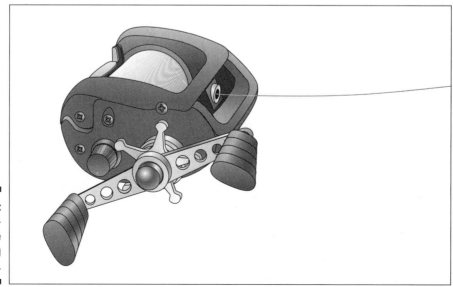

Figure 7-6:
A low-profile baitcasting reel.

Advantages and disadvantages of baitcasting gear

Let's be clear on this: Even with technological improvements, baitcasting gear is still tricky to master. And even when you "master" it, you still find yourself occasionally picking out a bird's nest fit for bald eagles. (Chapter 16 covers casting in more depth.) These reels, on average, carry more moving parts, more tiny gears, and more bearings than other kinds of reels. That complication brings reward, though — a good baitcasting reel is slick and both retrieves and casts line like a finely engineered machine. Which, in fact, some of them are. The best ones bear a cost that reflects that engineering, too.

A *backlash* is the bane of the baitcaster, and it occurs when the spool gets up a head of steam and moves faster than the line can peel off. When this happens, the extra line (that is no longer traveling down the rod) piles up around the spool in snarls. Bingo! The "bird's nest" of the baitcaster! Various design advances — like the *level-wind mechanism* that moves back and forth across the spool as it spins, stacking the line evenly, and adjustable *tension* (resistance) or *brake* — have somewhat lessened the frequency of backlash; but still, this is the most demanding reel to learn how to use properly.

Because the biggest negative with baitcasting gear is the dreaded backlash, you need to understand how to prevent one. To use a baitcasting reel properly, follow these steps:

1. **You adjust the tension (resistance) or brake to accommodate and compensate for the weight of the lure or bait.**

   Not to be confused with the drag, the tension knob is located on the side of the reel, and it adjusts the speed of the spool when the reel is disengaged. (The drag affects the rotation of the spool when the reel is engaged.)

2. **To make your initial setting for casting, hold the rod at a 45-degree angle to the ground. Release the lure or bait by putting the reel into** *free-spool mode* **— baitcasting reels have a button that lets the spool spin freely without the crank turning — and let out line.**

3. **With the tension properly adjusted, the lure/bait descends slowly. The spool should stop spinning when the lure hits the ground.**

   If it descends too fast, backlash occurs. Too slow, and you won't cast very far.

Adjust the tension as needed as you switch lures or baits. (You can find more on casting in Chapter 16.) The tension helps you control your cast, but your thumb really has to do the rest. Your thumb helps control the spool during a cast.

As is the case with all equipment, learning how your new baitcasting reel works helps you learn how to use it. The rotation of the spool controls the line, and thus your cast. Teaching yourself the basic mechanics of a baitcasting reel takes some time, and you're going to have to practice in order to improve your casting. But the practice will pay off and you'll make one of the most reliable and durable reels available your own. These reels come in a giant array of sizes and styles, and the best of them are built to sustain decades of use. I (Greg) don't own an heirloom watch to pass down, but I expect to leave behind a dozen nice baitcasting reels.

Baitcasting rods: Time to specialize

Any rod labeled "casting" will work with a baitcasting reel, assuming the reel and the rod generally match in size. But if you're using a baitcasting reel, it's a sign that you're ready to specialize your rod — that is to say, it's time to pick out a specific rod that works for the way you fish. For example, bass pros have "flippin sticks" they use for flipping lures (a particular kind of casting) under things like docks. Catfish anglers might pair a heavy duty baitcasting reel filled with 80-pound braided line with a heavy action eight-foot rod rated for up to seven ounces of bait. You may very well eventually own several reels, each paired with a different rod. You might have a bass casting rod, a heavy rod and reel for striped bass, and a third for panfish. Or you might have ten different reels, all for different kinds of largemouth bass fishing. You may have to explain the subtleties of this arrangement to your spouse, but it's true — you really do need different rods and reels for different kinds of fishing. (And many anglers own and use both spinning gear and baitcasting gear, using the spinning gear to cast lighter lures on lighter line.)

Some stores are chock-full of rods and reels. Thousands more await your attention (and your credit card) online. You might start with a pre-packaged combo for your first baitcasting rod and reel, but you really should look around and find the right rod and reel for the ways and waters you fish. This can be expert-grade equipment, and by the time you're ready, the experience you need to understand what to buy will be under your belt.

If you're limited to just one

Our choice for an all-around baitcasting rod would be a medium action rod, six feet long, with a pistol grip. It's light enough to respond to a bass, yet strong enough for northerns (and even muskies). If you're fishing in brushy cover and overhanging boughs, you may want a somewhat shorter rod, but stick with the medium outfit for an all-rounder.

Fly Fishing Gear: Artful and Effective

The three kinds of gear discussed so far all work in similar ways, and they all have one thing in common — they require the weight of the lure or bait to pull the line off the reel. (This is why heavier lures cast farther.) Flycasting is different. Because flies used for fishing weigh next to nothing, fly fishing gear is designed to cast using a different system. With flycasting, the reel has less work to do, so the rod picks up the lion's share of the work.

Of all the reels discussed in this chapter, the fly reel often has the simplest mechanism. Its first function is for storage of line. Action, gear ratio, drag, and the like are secondary considerations in fly fishing. The basic fly reel is a *single-action reel,* which means that one turn of the crank handle equals one revolution of the spool. You can buy *multiplier reels* that employ the same kind of gear-driven principle that you find in baitcasting: One turn of the crank produces a number of revolutions of the spool. I (Peter) have never found a need for this kind of reel. Figure 7-7 illustrates a basic reel. It has a spool, a housing for the spool, a crank, and sometimes, a drag adjustment. Like a spinning reel, a fly reel is mounted below the rod. With most reels, you have a choice of configuring your reel for winding with the left hand or right hand. Because I (Peter) cast with my right arm, I like to hold the rod in my right hand and reel with my left. This way, I don't have to complicate my life and change hands to fight a fish using the strength of my more powerful arm to assist the rod during the struggle. Others switch hands after a cast, and this becomes second nature to them. If you're unsure of how to configure the crank, ask the people in the tackle shop to set it up for you when you buy it.

 Don't forget to oil your reels. Because reels are made with moving metal parts, they need to be lubricated. Manufacturers often include oil with their reels, and many stores sell reel oil and grease. Check with the manufacturer's reel instructions to see where to apply oil or grease. Oil works well for gears. I (Peter) like to lubricate spools and spool posts with silicone lubricant, which holds up under a wide temperature range. I use silicone lubricant on everything from my ice fishing gear to the gear stored in the trunk of my car in a Florida parking lot.

Advantages and disadvantages of flycasting gear

So the flycasting reel is a simple machine — certainly when compared to a baitcasting reel. What makes casting a fly rod such an art, then? Part of the challenge lies in the fact that the reel, while it doesn't hurt you with complicated mechanics, doesn't help you much, either. The reel is basically just a device to store line. This keeps the cost of flycasting reels relatively inexpensive (although, like anything, it's certainly possible to spend a pretty penny if one is so inclined!) and relatively easy to maintain. The reels are light and unobtrusive. Landing a fish on a fly rod is not like landing a fish on other tackle, though. Gone is the anti-reverse and the cranking power of a strong baitcasting reel.

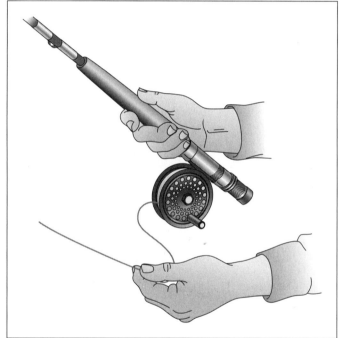

Figure 7-7:
The fly reel is a very simple machine.

Fly rods: Choosing the right one

Although fly rodding is steeped in tradition, fly rods aren't. In Izaak Walton's day, there were no fancy split-cane bamboo rods — only solid pieces of pliable local woods like willow and ash. Bamboo technology came along only in the last century and only dominated for about a hundred years. Bamboo is fun to cast, and there's something pleasurable in using material that was once living. No question about it, when fiberglass came along, many more people could afford to get into fly fishing. And now, the successor to fiberglass — graphite-based — is the most high-performance material so far.

Casting is the name of the game in fly fishing. Much of the pleasure of the sport comes from laying out a good cast.

Casting a fly is kind of like throwing a baseball: Almost everybody has a different style. I (Peter) have a kind of three-quarter, sidearm kind of cast that is miles away from the classic English style of straight-up-and-down cast with the elbow held tight against the chest. Some rods that more-traditional casters love give me a problem. Some rods work for me at short distances; but when I really want to lay the line out there, a "dead spot" appears that probably has more to do with my casting motion than it has to do with the rod. So when people ask "What rod is best for me?" I can make recommendations, but in the end, you are going to have to feel your way into this and get the rod that feels best for you. If no one had said it before, then I am sure that some fly rodder, somewhere, would have come up with the saying "different strokes for different folks."

The following sections cover my preferences for different situations.

Small streams, small rods

In general, fishing in small streams with overhanging boughs often leads to a tangle of rod and line. Watching anglers fish in such a setting is almost like watching people in an old slapstick movie: the angler looks in front for obstacles, and then, with equal care, looks in back. Then he or she very carefully casts and — boing! — the line is hung up in a tree in back of Mr. or Ms. Fly Rodder. Apart from your being very conscious of where your line is going to go when you cast, using a short rod with a fast tip enables you to cast with very little line out of the guides.

Fast rods for most trout

There is an old saw about dry-fly rods having fast action and wet-fly rods having slow action. I don't agree. A fast tip makes for a tighter casting loop, which is good, especially with small flies. But you need to be careful when setting the hook with a fast rod, especially when using light tippet. If the rod doesn't have much give, you will break right off. To avoid this situation, you need to learn to strike with firm, but not explosive, pressure. As far as wet flies go, when you are fishing a nymph upstream (which is an increasingly popular and effective method of fishing them), you need the same sensitivity that a fast tip affords the dry-fly angler. What my recommendation gets down to is this: I (Peter) like a fast rod for most trout situations. For starters, a nine-foot, five-weight is my pick.

Slowing down for bass and saltwater

Flycasting has a great deal to do with *line* speed (which many anglers, unfortunately, confuse with *arm* speed). When you're fishing with big, air-resistant flies (and when you add to them the amount of line you need to carry in the air for distance-casting in saltwater), you don't want to do a great deal of hurry-up casting with a bunch of false casts. Fast trout rods tend to reinforce this tendency to speeding up, and the one thing I (Peter) tell trout fishermen when they begin saltwater fly fishing is to slow down. A slower, somewhat softer rod encourages an angler to let the fly line have that extra second or two in the air to load up (flex) the rod fully. The result in your cast is less false casting and longer distances. Ideally, I like a fast tip with slower action through the body of the rod. A nine-foot, nine-weight is a good saltwater all-rounder. (Make that an eight-weight if you want to catch some freshwater bass and pike while you are at it.)

Chapter 8

The Bottom Line on Line

*Y*our fishing line forms a crucial link between you and the fish. It should be matched to the kind of gear you use and the fishing you do. Some anglers routinely cast line that won't break under 80 pounds of pressure. Others use line that you could easily snap with a light tug. While some situations, like deep-water trolling, call for weighted lines made of wire, the lines we discuss in this chapter are made from things like nylon, Dacron, and microfilaments. Fishing line, regardless of what kind it is or what it's made of, has two jobs to perform:

✔ It must deliver your lure, fly, or bait to the fish and present it in a natural manner.

✔ When a fish bites, the line should help you land the fish without breaking.

The concepts are pretty simple, and although you have choices to make, our guess is that you're going to wind up using good-old-fashioned monofilament line. But just in case, this chapter also introduces you to the other basic types of fishing line and what to consider when buying your line, as well as how to care for it and attach it to your reel.

Fly line is a whole different kettle of fish, but even with fly line, the leader at the end of the line is usually made of nylon monofilament, so much of what we say in this chapter about the lines you use for spincasting, spinning, and baitcasting also holds true for the last few feet of your fly fishing rig as well.

Getting to Know the Three Kinds of Line

Fishing line companies work tirelessly to improve their product. Many of the improvements take place on a microscopic level — what looks like just another line to you may feature a revolutionary new way of blending things like copolymers, alloys, fluorocarbon crystals, and other fancy fibers. That's all well and good, but what you really need to know is that three basic types of fishing line exist: monofilament, braid, and fluorocarbon. We fill you in on all three in the next sections.

Monofilament: Best for beginners

Monofilament line (often called just *mono*) is really just a single strand of nylon line, and it's the line you should start with if you're a beginning angler. Mono has been around for a long time and for good reason. Mono possesses the following characteristics:

- Knots well
- Comes in a wide range of pound tests, colors, and varieties
- Matches almost every fishing style
- Is relatively inexpensive and quite durable
- Stretches (which can help you hook and fight a fish smoothly)
- Casts well off any kind of reel, provided it's properly matched

Braid: For those who don't like to stretch

Braided line consists of strands of fibers intertwined or braided. It's extremely strong for its diameter, a characteristic that allows you to put more line on a spool. This is important if you're fishing deep water for big fish. Braid also

- Has very little stretch (meaning you feel every bite)
- Is super strong
- Works great on baitcasting reels

Fluorocarbon: For serious anglers

Fluorocarbon line, a monofilament nylon alloy, is a more expensive line that essentially disappears from sight in the water and is used by serious anglers fishing in situations where precision and extreme sensitivity count. Fluorocarbon line is

✔ Super sensitive

✔ Easy to cast

✔ Dense enough to sink

✔ More resistant than mono to ultraviolet rays

✔ Better suited to baitcasting reels than spinning reels

Buying Line 101

Finding the right type of line for your rod, reel, and needs is pretty simple, provided you take the time to gather some basic information before heading to the store. Of course, you also need to consider a few important character-istics of line when you're standing there in front of your options. If you don't, you may come home with the wrong line and have to waste time returning the undesirable line when you could've been fishing.

Like anything else, as you gain experience, line shopping becomes second nature. After you cast a lure a thousand times or catch a hundred fish, you know what you like. Then buying line is just like buying socks: You know what size and style fits you best.

Information to get before you leave home

Any sporting goods store that carries rods and reels most likely boasts an aisle filled to the rafters with colorful boxes of fishing line. Usually, the boxes are marked with jumping fish, flashy graphics, and a handful of numbers. It's a lot to process. But just as you shouldn't go grocery shopping on an empty stomach, you really shouldn't shop for line until you do just a little home-work. Here's a breakdown of the important information you should find out before you ever set foot in the store:

✔ **Your reel's size limitations:** The manufacturer built your reel (and labeled it) for a particular size of line, and if you don't know what your reel is made to handle, you won't know what line to buy. (If you buy your reel in a combo pack, it may well come prespooled with line — meaning that you won't need to buy line for some time.) So check your reel first and see what size of line it recommends.

✔ **Your rod's size limitations:** Also check your rod — it, too, is marked, right above the handle, for a particular size of line.

✔ **Where you fish and what you pursue:** Line comes in a wide range of styles and sizes, but it's not complicated if you know your quarry. Is it a lake mostly open and free of snags like sunken trees? Are you fishing a stream lined with sharp-edged rocks? Are most of the fish in the pond under ten pounds? Often, line of the same size can be bought in either extra tough (more abrasion resistant) or extra limp (better castability).

Be realistic about what you need for your conditions and buy the line that best fits your equipment and fishing situation.

Factors to consider when you're at the shop

Even if you have a rough idea of what you need in a fishing line, you can get confused at the store. Some line is expensive but lasts forever. Some line is cheap and fishes like it: It kinks readily and breaks easily. Other spools may promise great strength but cast like a length of garden hose. Some line sacrifices strength for sensitivity. It's easy to get confused, but understanding the numbers on the spool will help you make the right choice.

Although you can buy line at almost every place you buy tackle, some clerks are more knowledgeable and willing to help than others. Don't be afraid to ask for advice, especially in a serious tackle shop. But even if you're alone in a big box store, you can choose a good line by following the advice in this section.

Most spools of line carry about 300 yards of line — that's plenty. (Your reel may only hold 100 yards.) You can save money by buying a bigger spool (allowing you to respool your reel many times over from one spool), but you may not want to commit to a giant spool of line until you're sure it delivers the performance you're seeking. And some shops carry bulk supplies of popular lines and will fill your reel for you. This eliminates the wasted line left on a filler spool, as well as the slight hassle of having to do the job yourself.

Test

The word *test* as it applies to fishing line means that somebody tested the line and guaranteed it won't break if you apply a specific amount of force to it. In other words, if you apply anything less than 12 pounds of pull to a 12-pound test line, you *should* be fine. Apply more than 12 pounds of pull, and the line may part. A line made for ultra-light gear can be 2-pound test, and a line made for heavy duty work can be 100-pound test (or more!).

Line test isn't an absolute measurement. The give or stretch in the line, the kind of knot you use, how many fish you've caught with that line, and other factors all figure into the equation, often to the advantage of the fish, not the angler. On the other hand, most manufacturers play it on the safe side when they list the line test, the same way that the weather people on TV do: They leave a little wiggle room.

After you learn how to play a fish, you might be surprised at how much fish you can subdue with a relatively light line. Notice we said "subdue." Line isn't designed to *lift* fish. You use special tools such as nets, gaffs, and special leaders for that task (see Chapter 18). Just because the fish weighs 6 pounds doesn't mean you need 6-pound test line.

Look at it this way: Suppose you weigh 140 pounds. If we stuck a hook in your lip, we bet you it would take a lot less than 140 pounds of force to lead you around. In fact, human beings are so wimpy that a pound or two of pressure should have you following along quite nicely. Fish are a little tougher, but still, Peter has caught 100-pound tarpon on 20-pound test. He's also lost 3-pound trout on 6-pound test. And remember: Sometimes you need to break your line by choice. If you snag on the bottom, you must break or cut your line. The heavier that line is, the harder this task becomes. Trust us — when you get snagged, it's better to have 6-pound line over 20-pound line.

Thickness

In fishing line, thin is usually better. Thin line cuts through the air with less resistance and likewise cuts more easily through the water. You can fit more of a thinner line on your spool. It throws less of a shadow in shallow water (a big consideration with spooky fish like trout or bonefish). It also usually knots more easily. For any given line material, the thinner product has a lighter line test rating: 6-pound test mono is thinner then 12-pound test mono of the same brand and style. But 12-pound braid is thinner than 12-pound mono. Again, it's all about balancing out your needs for a particular fishing situation.

A little quarter-ounce lure has a hard time pulling 20-pound test line off your reel. On the other hand, a two-ounce lure might snap off or give you a royal backlash if you try to cast it with 6-pound test line. Many lure manufacturers recommend a line weight and you can always ask the person at the tackle shop for a recommendation. But understand that it may be impossible to match your line to one exact lure, as you're sure to fish more than one kind of lure. Still, if you know you fish most of the time with lures or baits weighing less than an ounce, you can spool up line accordingly. You'll learn quickly what lures fish well on what kinds of line.

Flexibility

Flexibility, or limpness, is a good thing when you're fishing lures with a delicate action. Heavy or stiff line can interfere with the action of the lure or trolled bait. (Sometimes anglers say that heavy line "clotheslines," meaning that it drags the bait or lure through the water with a very unlifelike action.) Generally, lighter, thinner line is limper than heavier line. Nylon monofilament is not as flexible as braided line.

When the action of a lure is all-important, go light and limp. On the other hand, when jigging or using a popping bug, you want your rod motion transmitted directly to the jig or bug. A stiffer or heavier line works to your advantage here. (For more on fishing particular lures, see Chapter 13.)

Stretch

If you have a tendency to set the hook really hard, you should probably stick with monofilament line. Many newcomers, as well as a lot of longtime anglers, rear back the minute they feel a bite, sometimes yanking the hook right out of the fish's mouth. Thankfully, most mono lines stretches in these situations. In fighting the fish, mono absorbs more of the shock of any sudden twists or turns. And mono really shines when fishing circle hooks, covered in Chapter 9. For all these reasons, monofilament is a good line for beginners.

On the other hand, stretchy line isn't ideal if you're the kind of person who has really sensitive fingertips and who can feel that tiny bump when a bass picks up a plastic worm. If you're in this group, you probably want a line with less stretch in it so you can set the hook with a single, firm stroke. Braided line has almost no stretch, and fluorocarbon has just a little, so both types offer more sensitivity and control. Just know that they're less forgiving than monofilament, so you may need to adjust your techniques, such as trying softer hooksets. You may also need to adjust your gear to fish with braided or fluorocarbon line, such as using a longer rod and less drag on the reel.

Visibility

Almost all kinds of line can be found in different colors, including bright fluorescent ones. Some lines are made to literally glow when seen under a blacklight, which is helpful for anglers fishing at night for fish like walleyes or catfish. But what do these colors mean to the fish?

How line appears in dry air varies from how it appears underwater. Fluorocarbon line practically disappears underwater, although it can be seen above it. Some fluorescent line shows up nicely in the air but becomes pretty invisible in the water (especially at night). If you need a little extra help in seeing the above-surface part of your line, then fluorescent or brightly-colored line can be worthwhile in detecting those subtle bumps that mean a fish has picked up your bait.

Many anglers fish in ways that require the line to be watched closely, as this is primarily how they detect bites. But as a general rule, you don't want the fish to see the line. Opaque or gaudy lines, as well as thick lines, put you at a disadvantage in clear water. The cloudier or dingier the water, or the less sunlight overhead, the less this factor comes into play. Bottom line: If you need to see your line, get line that you can see. But if your style of fishing isn't dependent on seeing the line, you're better off with fluorocarbon or neutral-colored mono or braided line.

Working out the kinks

Line, especially the monofilament kind, has a habit of coming off the reel in pesky coils. This is doubly true when you pick up your rod and reel for the first time after a winter layoff. Look at it this way: You have a hard time straightening out right away after an hour or two nap in your recliner, so it's not surprising that fishing line acts the same way after three months in the closet. Spinning reels are major offenders in the line-curling department.

One way to straighten your line is to let all the line trail behind you as you slowly motor or paddle along in your boat or canoe. Don't tie on any weight or lures. The resistance provided by the water's surface tension will lay the line out straight and remove the coils and twists within it. Without a boat you can knot one end of your line around a tree and then walk backward. When you've fed out all the line, pull firmly. ("Firmly" doesn't mean a violent yank: Use steady, medium pressure.) Repeat a few times, pulling and maintaining pressure for ten seconds, to straighten out your line.

In both cases, when you reel up, keep uniform tension on the line with the thumb and forefinger of your noncranking hand. (You also can hold the line with a towel, between the reel and the first guide, which will prevent friction burns on your hand.) Applying steady pressure assures that the line goes evenly onto the spool, which makes for smoother casts.

Spooling Up: Attaching Line to a Reel

A reel must be spooled correctly, or your new line won't function as smoothly as it should, and it might twist. Follow the instructions included with the line, but the basics are as follows:

- ✔ **For spinning and spincast reels:** Attach the line to the reel's spool (see Chapter 15 for the correct knot) and lay the filler spool on the floor. Remember to run the line through the reel's cover (spincast) or around the bail (spinning) first. (Don't worry if you forget; you'll officially be the one-millionth person to do so! *Tip:* Rather than retying your knot, remove the spool, run it around the bail, and reattach it.) Holding the line in your free hand to apply some pressure, turn the crank with the other hand and begin to fill the reel's spool. Stop when it is halfway full, disengage the reel, and pull some line back off the reel. Does it twist and spin wildly? If so, flip the filler spool over on the ground. Remove the twist and resume filling the reel's spool. (Note: Leave a bit, like a ¼ inch, of the reel's spool showing.)

- ✔ **For baitcasting reels:** Attach the line to the reel's spool (refer to Chapter 15 to find out which knot to use). Now ask someone to hold the filler spool by threading a pencil through the center of the spool. Your helper should hold the filler spool so that it is parallel to the reel's spool. This will allow the line to come off of one spool and smoothly go onto the other. Applying pressure to the line by pinching it a bit with your free hand, crank the reel slowly and proceed to fill the reel's spool. (Note: Leave ¼ inch of the reel's spool showing.)

Caring for Your New Line and Knowing When to Let It Go

You need to take care of your line. Great line that's worn out is still worn out line. After all, you only get so many chances at a dream fish, like the 54-pound blue catfish I (Greg) caught one August while driftfishing the Ohio River in Indiana. As soon as I set the hook into what felt like Secretariat with fins, my mind went directly to the thin little fiber connecting me to this thrashing fish 40 feet below the boat, and I began wondering when I last put fresh line on the reel. (In this type of situation, you desire confidence in your line, which makes respooling often worth the added expense.)

Of course, a huge part of keeping your fishing line in good condition is knowing when line is past its prime. The sections that follow help you care for line and get rid of it when the time comes.

Protecting your line from wear and tear

The most common type of wear and tear is *abrasion,* weak spots in the line that can appear when a fish drags your line over rocks or against an overhanging bank. (Think of an abrasion on your line like the nick you get on your knee when you take a spill on the sidewalk.) The newest lines are extremely resistant to nicks and scuffs, but all lines eventually abrade to some degree. Braided line abrades fairly easily; monofilament lines less so. Damaged line will fail, sooner or later — usually, later, as in, later when a big fish is on your line.

After catching a fish (and sometimes after losing one), run your fingers along your line, especially that last 20 feet or so. If you feel a nick or rough spot, cut your line above the nick and re-tie your lure or re-rig your terminal tackle. (Check out Chapter 15 for more on tying rigs.) In fact, after you've caught five or six fish with the same setup, it's a good idea to re-rig anyway. Many times, your line will develop invisible fatigue or stress points.

Note: Most of the time, when you lose a fish, your line breaks because of a poor knot or structural failure of the line. Although it's true that the fish has to win sometimes, it's also true that many anglers (ourselves included) lose fish because they just don't take the time to re-rig.

You also need to watch out for damage caused by the following:

- **Sunlight:** Sunlight can affect your fishing line, especially if it's mono. So can heat. Like wine, fishing line should be stored in a cool, dark place. For most folks, storing means stacking a bunch of rods together in a corner of the basement or closet.

✔ **Saltwater:** If there is one chief enemy in the war against fishing tackle, it is salt, as in saltwater. It rusts and corrodes metal, dissolves synthetics, and in general, does the same number on your tackle as it does on all those pitted out cars you see when you're on the coast or driving salted roads in a Midwest winter. Rinse all your tackle after fishing in saltwater, and that includes your line. You shouldn't let it sit for even a day.

Saying goodbye to old line

How often should you replace your line? Well, it depends on how you use it. If you fish once a week in an open lake, your line may well last you all summer. If cared for, line retains its strength for a long time. But certain factors speed up the wear and tear process: Fishing around snags hurts line, as does saltwater or sunlight. Catching a lot of fish will wear out a line. So inspect your line visually and with your fingers before every trip.

If your line has been on the spool for more than a year (or even if you're not quite sure that it has), replace it. To remove line from a reel, just disengage the reel, pull the line off the spool, and cut the line-to-reel knot (see Chapter 15 for the scoop on this knot).

After you take line off your reel, you're left with a handful of line that is really of no use to anyone. Some stores keep a box for old line — it can and should be recycled. (Greg stores his old line in a grocery bag until it gets full and then takes the whole bag in to be recycled.) At the very least, throw used line away in a proper waste receptacle. Line litter is an eyesore and a serious hazard to birds and other wildlife.

Setting Your Sights on Fly Lines

A fly line is a totally different animal from all other fishing line. In spincasting, spinning, and baitcasting, the weight of your terminal tackle pulls the line off the reel and carries it to the fish. Fly fishing is just the opposite. The weight of the line carries the relatively weightless fly to the fish.

Way back when, fly line was made from braided horsehair. If you wanted a heavy line, you braided more hairs. The modern fly line is a smooth plastic coating around a core of braided nylon or Dacron. Most lines are 70 to 90 feet long and are spliced to another hundred yards or so of thinner backing line (usually braided Dacron). When you buy line or a reel, have the store put the backing on and splice it to your line. You can also do this yourself.

The sections that follow fill you in on some of the basics about fly lines, as well as their ever-present companions and leaders. If you want to read more in-depth about fly lines and fly fishing in general, pick up a copy *Fly Fishing For Dummies,* written by Peter Kaminsky and published by Wiley.

Looking at the types of fly lines

Originally, the only type of fly line available was braided horsehair. But now that fly fishing no longer exclusively means dry-fly fishing for trout in a stream, fly rodders use different kinds of lines for different fishing situations. Often, this means using some kind of weight to get down to fish that aren't surface feeders, such as stream-borne trout hanging on the bottom, bass 3 feet down in a pond, or stripers 15 feet down in a bay.

These days, you have the choice of using *sink tip lines* where the front of the line is weighted and the rest floats for easy casting. There are a couple types of sink tip lines:

- **Intermediate line** sinks very slowly so that it can be fished as a floater or a sinker. This is the preferred line for saltwater fly fishing in the northeastern United States. It gets the line below the surface chop and keeps you in contact with your fly.
- **Full sinking (FS) line** gets down fast and deep. The best are the really thin lines that have come on the market in recent years. They are slim, so they cut through the wind, and they aren't so hellish to pick up and cast as the old lead core.

Considering the weight and taper of fly line before you buy

Buying fly line is a little different than buying line for other types of fishing. Instead of looking at characteristics such as test and stretch (see the earlier related sections), you're more concerned with the weight of the line and the type of taper, as explained in the following sections.

The weight of the line

The weight of the line is what bends the rod, allowing the rod to spring forward and shoot the line toward the fish. Fly lines come with different ratings according to their weight, and rods are rated according to the weight of the line they throw. A One Weight is a very light line that is used with an extremely delicate rod. As the numbers go up, so does the weight. Most trout fishermen prefer something in the Four to Six range. Peter's first fly rod was a

Six Weight, and he caught trout, bass, an 18-pound pike, many bonefish, and two barracuda on it. (The second barracuda finally broke that rod.)

Although there are no hard and fast rules, Table 8-1 lists some recommendations for line (and rod) weights for common game fish.

Table 8-1	Fly Line Weights and Common Game Fish
Line Weight	*Type of Fish*
One, Two, and Three Weight	Panfish, trout
Four Weight, Five Weight	Trout, freshwater bass
Six Weight, Seven Weight	Trout, bass, small blues, stripers, bonefish, pike
Eight Weight, Nine Weight	Salmon, stripers, bonefish, permit, bluefish, redfish
Ten, Eleven, Twelve, Thirteen, and Fourteen Weight	Tarpon, tuna, marlin, and other big game

With graphite rods, you can usually go up or down one line weight from the recommended number and still be well within the optimum performance range for your rod.

The type of taper

Most fly lines have a *taper;* that is, they are fatter in one part than another. The most common taper is *weight forward*. It is heavier in the head, which is the first 30 feet or so of line to come through the guides of your rod. The principle behind this is that you want to get a lot of leverage on the rod to develop momentum quickly, and then, when you have rapid line speed, the weight of the head will carry the rest of the line. In other words the weight-forward line is ideal for *delivery* of the fly.

You will see some fly lines marked with a saltwater taper or bassbug taper. These, too, are weight-forward lines with a more exaggerated taper.

Less common these days than it used to be is the *double taper.* This design is thin in the head, gradually fattens out, and then slims again. The idea is you have a good amount of line in the air to develop momentum, yet the line that lands nearest to the trout does so more delicately than the weight-forward variety. You have to be a pretty sensitive angler to be able to appreciate double taper; when you want more delicacy of presentation, it may be easier to just go to a lighter rod and line.

Threading your fly line

Usually, when you thread line through your spinning or baitcasting rod, you pick up the end of the line and thread it through the guides. When you try to do this with heavy fly line, it will find a way to slip back down and make you start all over again. The easy way is to pull off about six feet of line, double it over, and pull the doubled line through the guides. That way, when you accidentally drop the line, the loop catches on the guides and doesn't slip all the way through to the reel.

Throwing leaders into the mix

After the *fly* (your offering, often a tiny hook covered with feathers or yarn and made to look like an insect or other prey), the most critical element of the fly fishing setup is the *leader,* meaning the nylon monofilament line that connects the fly line to the fly. A fly line is big and thick, and a fly is delicate and small. The leader must also be light; otherwise, it will overpower the fly, giving it a lifeless action. A big, fat fly line landing next to a spooky fish is guaranteed to send it straight for cover. A leader that makes as little disturbance as possible increases your chances of connecting with a fish.

As you can see in Figure 8-1, the thick section of the leader that joins to the fly line is called the *butt.* What happens between the butt and the fly is a gradual *taper* as the leader gets progressively thinner and lighter. The result is a smooth and even transfer of force from the rod to the line and down through the leader. The last section of the taper is also known as the *tippet.*

Figure 8-1:
The sections of the leader are the butt, taper, and tippet.

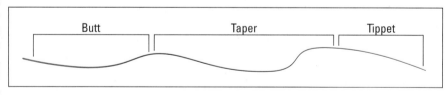

Leaders are usually between 7 and 12 feet in length. You can buy them knotted or knotless. The taper of a knotted leader is made up of progressively lighter lengths of monofilament line knotted together. The knotless type is just a single strand that smoothly tapers.

X marks the tippet spot

If you ever catch a nice trout — make that *when* you catch a nice trout — you will be asked, "What did you take it on?" This is actually two questions. The first is "What fly?" and the second is "What tippet?" Tippets are rated according to their thickness, which is directly related to their strength. Where the spin fisherman might say "I caught it on 12-pound test," the fly rodder's answer would be "1X."

Why X? In the old days, leader tippets used to be made out of silk worm gut. They were sized by being passed through a die that shaved down the thickness of the gut. If you ran it through the die once, it was 1X; twice gave you 2X; and so on. The more shavings it got, the thinner the leader. So the higher numbers represent thinner, lighter leaders.

When you change flies a lot, you end up cutting off and replacing tippet. Using a knotted leader is a handy way to remember what thickness you are fishing. On the other hand, if you are just starting out, knotless is pretty simple, so keep it simple. Tippet material is sold in tiny spools, which makes it convenient to replace.

For more information on leaders, including how to match your fly to your leader, check out Peter's book *Fly Fishing For Dummies*.

Chapter 9

It's Terminal (Tackle): Hooks, Sinkers, Snaps, Swivels, and Floats

In This Chapter

▶ Understanding how a hook works

▶ Picking the right range of hooks

▶ Choosing between J hooks and circle hooks

▶ Getting a handle on sinkers

▶ Knowing when to use swivels and snaps

▶ Exploring the world of floats

At first glance, this may appear to be one of the most boring chapters in *Fishing For Dummies*. It lacks the illustrations of the fish ID chapters, the excitement of the fishing techniques chapter, and the gratification of the cooking chapter. But wait, there's more here that you need to know; in fact, what we cover in this chapter is both interesting and crucial to your fishing success! *Terminal tackle* refers to the equipment that accompanies your line on its way to the fish. Although rods and reels matter, and it's hard to overstate the importance of line, your understanding of terminal tackle will greatly influence the number of fish you catch.

Hooks: What They Do and Why They Matter

Put simply, the invention of the fish hook changed history. More effective than spears or bare hands, fish hooks allowed humans to fish deeper water and opened the door for so many things, including, many centuries later, the thick catalogs of fishing gear I (Greg) find in my mailbox. Of course, those first anglers were crude, smelly individuals, speaking in grunts and barely capable of thought outside of what bait to try next. Oh wait, I'm thinking about fishing with my brothers.

The first hook-type devices, called *gorges,* were used during the Stone Age. Gorges were small pieces of wood or bone sharpened on both ends, with a line tied to the center. When embedded in bait, the entire gorge could be swallowed by a fish, and when the line jerked tight, the gorge would lodge across the throat of the fish. (This is handy to know in a survival situation — it's hard to carve a hook, but you can easily make a gorge.) Later, the traditional fish hook was carved from bone. The invention of metal made for better fish hooks, and after centuries of progress, today's hooks are sometimes chemically sharpened and surgical in their effectiveness. But the basic shape of the hook remains the same.

Thanks to improved hooks and hook-setting techniques, along with the growing use of circle hooks, it's now possible to release almost any fish you catch. (I don't think catch-and-release fishing was as popular in caveman days.) Whether you're using a single hook on a bait rig, or a lure with three treble hooks, your hope for landing a fish lies with that curved steel. Hooks are the key. Buy quality hooks, inspect them often, and don't cast them unless they hold your utmost confidence.

This section covers both J hooks and circle hooks, shown in Figure 9-1. Circle hooks have been used for decades in saltwater fishing but are now being used in more freshwater fishing. Circle hooks look like joke hooks — you might swear one could never hook a fish. But they work, and because they rotate around a fish's jaw, caught fish are often hooked in the corner of the mouth, making them easy to release. Most of the following information about J hooks applies to circle hooks, but the two kinds of hooks require very different hooksets.

Figure 9-1:
The standard J hook (a) and circle hook (b).

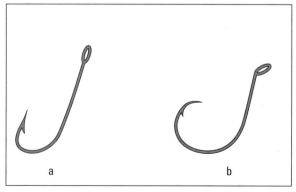

a   b

Following are the most important parts of a typical hook (see Figure 9-2):

- The *point* is where tackle meets fish. As in many situations in life, the first impression is an important one. If you don't have a good sharp point on your hook, you can have the most expensive rod in the world, but you won't catch fish.

- The *barb* is a type of a reverse point that is designed to keep a fish on the hook after the fish bites. Bigger is not better with barbs. Big barbs can make setting a hook difficult when the hook meets up with a tough-mouthed fish like a bonefish. Or big barbs can make too big a tear in the mouth of a soft-mouthed fish like a crappie. Many catch-and-release anglers fish with barbless hooks, although it is possible to release fish caught on barbed hooks, as well.

One way to help speed up the releasing process when you're fishing catch-and-release is to *debarb* (remove the barbs from) your hooks. Simply take a pair of pliers (needlenose work best) and crimp the barb against the hook's tip. Remember that you're not using a wire cutter here, and you're not trying to take the whole point off the hook. On most hooks, a small amount of pressure on the barb does the trick. Both J hooks and circle hooks can be debarbed. (Debarbing also makes it much easier to remove a hook from your skin if you happen to hook yourself. And you probably will — it happens to the best of us.)

- The *bend* is the curved part of the hook, and all those fine-sounding hook names, such as Limerick or Sproat, have something to do with the bend. Actually, such hook names have to do with two parts of the bend: the throat and the gap. Think of the *throat* as the depth that the hook penetrates. Think of the *gap* as the width of the hook, from point to shank. A relatively wide gap may be necessary to hold certain bait, to get around the snout of a billed fish, or to dig in beyond the width of a thick jawbone. The wider the gap, the easier it is for the fish to bend the hook so that it can escape. When the hook straightens out, you are using a hook that is either too light (referring to the *gauge* of the wire) or too big in the gap for the amount of pressure that you (not the fish) applied. Losing a fish this way happens to everybody; but still, developing a sense of how much pressure your tackle can take is part of becoming an educated angler.

- The *shank* connects the bend to the eye. A shank can be long or short. As with gap, a longer shank means that a hook is easier for a fish to bend. So why aren't all hooks short-shanked? The answer has to do with what goes on the hook. A short-shanked Salmon Egg hook isn't very effective for Texas-rigging a night crawler (see Chapter 13), but a longer-shanked worm hook is. A longer-shanked hook makes it easier to unhook a fish, too. Sometimes the shank has a barb or two to help hold bait more securely. These are called baitholder hooks.

> ✔ The *eye* of the hook (the loop through which line passes) may be turned up, turned down, or straight.
>
> ✔ The *gauge* refers to the diameter of the hook's wire. Heavier gauge hooks resist bending even when imbedded in the mouth of a big fish. Smaller gauge hooks are lighter and easier to hide.
>
> ✔ The *finish* refers to the coating on the hook. Some hooks wear a finish to protect them from saltwater; others are finished in bright colors. It adds to the options you have in selecting hooks.

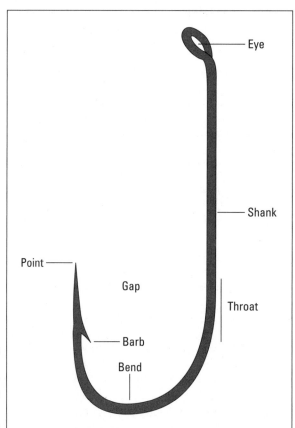

Figure 9-2:
The anatomy of a hook.

Keeping a range of hooks

Some hooks have cool names, like Limerick, Kirby, O'Shaughnessy, and Aberdeen. These are often a tribute to the people who invented them. Beginners often get bogged down when selecting hooks, but it doesn't have to be complicated. Know this: Some hooks work better than others with particular baits or plastic lures that require rigging. A nightcrawler presented to a largemouth bass excels when placed on a hook that matches the size of the bait, and the fish it's intended to catch. But you can't predict from one trip to the next exactly what hooks a situation will call for.

Suppose you like bass fishing in the community pond, and you always carry a couple of hooks ideal for rigging plastic worms. But one day at the pond, you discover a swarm of grasshoppers, and the bass are smashing them whenever one hits the surface. After finally grabbing a big grasshopper, you realize the big hooks that work so well with plastic worms dwarf the grasshopper, making your new bait look awkward and unnatural. But if you carry a range of hooks, you can easily tie on a small baitholder that presents a grasshopper perfectly. A good angler is ready for new baits or new fish.

The solution is an easy one: Buy variety packs of hooks (this is an economical way to do it), or buy a range of separate hooks that will work for your fishing location. Manufacturers often package hooks in species-specific containers, and sales clerks will help, as well. But the bottom line is this: Begin assembling a range of hooks like the ones in Figure 9-3, from tiny to large, and in a few styles, such as longshanked Aberdeens and baitholders. If you can, buy both J hooks and circle hooks. You want to be ready to fish for whatever fish presents itself, with whatever bait is available and needed. Using a hook too small will result in swallowed hooks — making the hook difficult to remove and endangering the fish. A hook that is too large will look unnatural and may be avoided by the fish.

Figure 9-3:
A typical range of hooks the general-species angler should carry at all times.

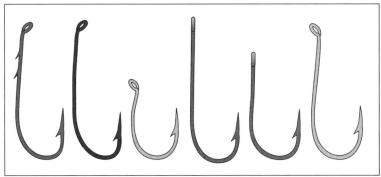

Although hooks come in a variety of shapes and styles, they also come in a tremendous range of sizes — from hooks bigger than your hand to tiny hooks smaller than the word "to" in this sentence. The classification system for hooks confuses some people, but here's what you need to know: When you use the word "size" before you give the number of the hook, you are dealing with smaller hooks (as in, "I caught it on a size 6 hook"). The *higher* the number, the *smaller* the hook. A size 6 hook is much bigger than a size 28 hook. And by the way, hook sizes are counted by twos (14, 12, 10, 8, and so on) with no odd numbers until size 1. Actually, the measuring system changes at 1 to the system called the *aughts* (written 1/0, 2/0, and the like) in which the zero is pronounced old style, as *aught*. In the aughts, the higher the number, the bigger the hook. So a size 28 is tiny, a size 1 is bigger, and a 2/0 is bigger still.

Making a point

Dull hooks rarely catch fish. Whether it's a J hook or a circle hook (both of which we cover later in this chapter), only sharp hooks get the job done.

Some anglers think they have a sharp hook as long as the hook's point pricks the skin. But a hook is more than a needle. Even though the point of a hook is relatively small, the point has some area and edge to it. That edge, just like the edge of a knife, needs to be sharp to cut into the fish beyond the end of the barb. Driving the hook home to this depth is called *setting the hook*. How to do this, when to do this, and how hard to do this are all-important elements of angling technique. But you'll never get a chance to show off all your mind-blowing techniques with dull hooks.

A hook has an edge to it, just like a knife has. So you sharpen a hook just as you would sharpen a knife, with a file or sharpening steel. Special hook hones and files are made expressly for this purpose. If your experience is like ours, you'll neglect sharpening *until* you lose a good fish. However, before you put on a lure, it's always best to run your file along the edge of your lure's hook to get it good and sharp.

Some manufacturers use chemical sharpening now, which means that hook points are honed in the factory not with a file, but with the application of various coats of chemicals. The result is a scary-sharp hook. But it's hard for you to re-sharpen chemically sharpened hooks. I've (Greg) noticed with my chemically sharpened hooks that the extra-sharp point can roll over itself when the point snags or hits a rock or something. Assuming I free the hook after it becomes snagged, I inspect the point. If the point is rolled, the hook goes into the trash. I could never get it sharp enough again with a file. It may seem like a waste of money, but I consider it part of the cost of doing business. I want confidence in my hooks, so I invest in plenty. Sooner or later, every hook gets lost or has to be replaced. Love your hooks, but be ready to let them go.

Spark plug files (which you can find in any auto parts store) make good hook sharpeners. This makes sense when you consider that spark plug points (like fishhooks) are small, have a narrow gap, and are made of metal. Fly rodders who find themselves out in a stream with a dull hook and no file may try using the striking surface on a matchbook cover to touch up their hooks. The Luhr Jensen file is a good off-the-shelf choice for sharpening most hooks.

J hooks: Some things never change

J hooks earned their name from their resemblance to the letter. J hooks work because they fit into a fish's mouth and then catch on something on the way out, and they've worked that same way for a long time. Not every J hook is the same, though, and many styles put a twist (sometimes quite literally) on the standard. Any fish that swims can be caught on the right J hook.

Buy J hooks that match your intended target. What's the typical mouth size of the fish you hope to catch? Bluegills, for example, have small mouths; even a big specimen would have to open wide to bite the tip of your thumb. So using giant J hooks to fish for bluegill will only result in hooks stripped of bait. But a fish with a big, toothy mouth, like a northern pike, calls for a larger J hook.

Setting the hook with J hooks

When a fish bites a baited hook or lure, you've been successful: You've seduced that fish into making a connection with you. But that connection — through the rod and reel, down the line, across any terminal tackle your rig consists of, and culminating in the sharp hook you've selected — is a tenuous one. You need to act quickly and wisely to ensure that the fish stays connected to you. This is called *setting the hook*, and it's the process by which the hook passes from merely being in the fish's mouth to being through the fish's mouth. When fishing with J hooks, setting the hook means pointing the rod at the fish, tightening the line, and jerking the rod sharply back toward you, driving the hook into the fish's mouth.

Different species call for different hooksets, and different baits call for different tactics. For example, it pays to let northern pike run a big livebait for a bit, to allow the pike time to turn the baitfish in its mouth. Largemouth bass striking at a plastic frog through a layer of algae need a bit of time to get the frog bait into their mouths. Some fish have hard mouths that require hard and repeated hooksets. Others, like crappies, will go free if you set the hook too hard. But the following tips should work for you most of the time, with most fish caught on most rigs:

- **Keep a relatively tight line between your hook and your reel at all times.** When fishing with a float rig, for example, slack line can form between your rod and the float. When a fish bites and the float sinks, that fish is ready to be hooked, but the slack line can prevent you from driving the hook home. By the time you furiously crank up the loose line, the fish may have spit the bait and moved away. Keep your line tight, and be ready to set the hook at any time.

✔ **Let the rod help you.** As you sweep the rod overhead, the rod should bend. This bend is providing the force that sets the hook. If your rod isn't bending on the hookset, you're not providing enough force. The other possibility is that there remains too much slack in the line. If that happens, quickly reel up the slack and set the hook again. The fish may still be on the line!

✔ **Quicker hooksets are usually better.** We don't usually advise waiting to set the hook, unless it's one of those odd situations, like catching bass through the moss. Look at it this way — if you feel a fish tap your bait, or your float goes under, that fish has your hook in its mouth. A fish can't move your bait with its hands! If the bait is in a fish's mouth, then the hook should be able to find purchase. Some folks will tell you to wait, to "make sure he has it" or something, but most of the time this pause results in a *swallowed hook*. A swallowed hook can lead to an inadvertent fish death, and is usually the result of waiting too long to set the hook. Your goal should be to land every fish that bites, but also to be able to release every fish you land, should you choose to do so.

Keeping J hooks organized

As we explain in the earlier section "Keeping a range of hooks," you really can't avoid accumulating more than a few styles and sizes of hooks. Having a good variety of J hooks on hand will find you ready for about any fishing challenge. But although you may lump all your plastic worms together or carry a sack of assorted sinkers, you should keep your hooks divided.

Separate your hooks in your tackle carrier by placing different sizes in different compartments. Sort by size and function. Put small baitholders (ideal for bluegill) and the like in one place, larger hooks for rigging soft plastics Texas-style in another. Hooks have a nasty habit of tangling together when stored in proximity, making it harder to remove the hook you need when you need it. Picking a tiny hook from a snarl of hooks is like reaching into a bag of needles.

Circle hooks: From saltwater to freshwater

Circle hooks are sized like J hooks, and available in the same wide range. Because they are so often used in saltwater, circle hooks for species like groupers and sharks could almost encircle a coffee cup. But manufacturers make small circle hooks too, and they work for many freshwater species. (And they are increasingly available anywhere freshwater gear is sold.) Greg uses small circle hooks — about a size 6 — to catch carp. And 8/0 circle hooks, which work well for a variety of saltwater species, are perfect for blue catfish. The design of the circle hook would appear to render it impotent — with the point of the hook aimed back toward the shank, how could it possibly catch fish? Well, therein lies its beauty. Circle hooks are less likely to snag, and that includes your person, simply because the point of the hook is not exposed. But they will catch fish, providing the angler can forget everything he or she knows about setting the hook in the traditional J hook fashion.

Setting the hook with circle hooks

Anglers fishing with J hooks should strike fast and hard to set the hook. Indeed, a wimpy hookset could lead to a freed fish. But circle hooks work differently than J hooks, and they require a different method.

Circle hooks work because fish often move after they pick up a bait or lure. Say a smallmouth bass grabs a nightcrawler rigged on a circle hook. The smallmouth will inhale the nightcrawler, then most likely turn away from the place where it sucked in the bait. The nightcrawler — and the hook — will be in the bass's mouth for a second or two before it swallows. As the bass turns, the hook drags across the mouth of the fish, lodging in the corner of the jaw. As the bass continues to move, the hook rotates until the gap of the hook fits around the jaw. Then the point sinks in and the bass is hooked.

I (Greg) know it sounds unlikely! I didn't believe it at first, either. Now that I have caught hundreds of fish using circle hooks, I rarely buy J hooks. Circle hooks work that well.

Here's the secret — you cannot set the hook in the traditional J hook fashion using circle hooks. If you do, you will simply jerk the baited hook right out of the fish's mouth. Instead, you need to maintain constant line pressure, and let the fish hook itself against the steady pull. A hookset with a circle hook looks like this — the angler feels the tap, then slowly raises his or her rod and holds it in a raised position. The fish will pull the rod down, and the action of the rod will drive the hook point into the fish's jaw. When the angler feels the fish has been hooked — often when the rod bends as much as it would with a J hook hookset — he or she simply commences reeling in the fish. Anglers used to fishing with J hooks will have a maddening time trying to retrain themselves, but they can do it. (At first, they're likely to instinctively jerk the hook out of the fish's mouth!) But beginners, who have never learned the hard hooksets of J hooks, will take right to it.

Using rod holders for circle hooks

A great way to learn how to use circle hooks is to go still fishing for almost any species and bring along some *rod holders.* Rod holders, often steel or heavy plastic, do just that — they hold the rod for you. For bank fishermen, rod holders are often designed to be driven into the ground or sand. (Surfcasters use them, too.) Some are made to attach to piers or fishing docks. There are many rod holders designed to be used with a variety of boats (see Chapter 18).

All rod holders work the same: They hold the rod securely, allowing the angler to fish multiple rods, or to put some distance between himself and the rod (say, so he can sit by the fire and eat fried chicken). Whereas rod holders work with all kinds of fishing gear, they are ideally suited for bank fishing with spinning, spincast, or baitcasting gear. And they work perfectly when paired with circle hooks.

When using rod holders, the angler doesn't have to fight the urge to set the hook. Simply cast the bait out, and place the rod in the holder. Keep the line fairly tight. When a fish strikes, the rod pulls down, or *loads,* against the weight of the fish. (It's important to have strong rod holders, mounted securely, or you risk losing your gear!) When the rod is sufficiently loaded, the rod is removed from the holder, and the fish is already hooked and ready for battle.

Kids, beginners, and elderly anglers may have trouble setting the hook with sufficient force. This kind of stillfishing — using rod holders and circle hooks — removes the need to "cross the fish's eyes" with a rocking hookset. And the enjoyment of fighting the fish is the same.

Experiment with circle hooks, and we think you'll find that most caught fish are hooked in the corner of the mouth, ready for an easy release. We also think you'll find that fish hooked with circle hooks have a difficult time throwing the hook during the fight. When the circle hook finds its place, the fish is quite simply . . . hooked.

Dehooking yourself

If you fish, someday, somewhere, you will hook yourself. You may reach up to pull down a tree branch where a fly has snagged. You start to disentangle the fly. Then the branch springs back, and you have a fly right in the meaty part of your finger. Or maybe you have pulled in a nice bass that you caught on a Devil's Horse. You grab the bass by the lower lip (just like the book says to do), and the bass decides to give one last shake that leaves you semi-permanently attached to a still-living bass. In both cases, you have the same reaction: You want to get that hook out of you!

You have a number of choices. First, if the lure is still attached to the fish (or anything else for that matter), clip the line to free the lure. Sometimes you can continue to push the hook all the way through the wound and out again. This action is somewhat painful, but sometimes doable.

Another method, favored by many anglers, looks as if it shouldn't work, but it does, as long as you have a J hook imbedded in you. You need to have some confidence in this method, or you may not do very well. Try practicing this on a piece of raw meat until you understand what you are doing. After you get the idea, it all makes sense.

The following steps, which are illustrated in Figure 9-4, show you how to remove a hook that is embedded in some part of your body:

1. **Take a two-foot length of at least 25-pound test line and tie the ends together so that you have a loop.**

   If you do not have 25-pound test line, then double a few strands of 10-pound or 12-pound test line.

2. **Loop the line over your wrist, and form a small loop between your thumb and forefinger.**

3. **Take this small loop and put it around the hook in the center of the hook's bend.**

4. **With your other thumb, press down on the eye of the hook.**

   This action should open the wound enough for you to gently back the barb out of your flesh. Getting the barb clear of the flesh is *very* important. If you do not get the barb clear, you should not continue with this procedure.

5. **Finally, pull on the small loop with a sharp jerk.**

   The hook should come free with relatively little pain to you.

Circle hooks, because of their shape, are harder to get out of a hand. But that odd shape also makes them less likely to end up there. If you end up hooked with a circle hook, you can either force the hook on through, pinch down the barb, and back it out, or get to a doctor pronto. Of course, prevention is the best practice when it comes to hooking injuries, and you can deflect many wandering hooks with a hat and a pair of glasses. Wear them. And bring that first-aid kit, stocked with antiseptic and bandages, that we recommend in Chapter 6! Another good tip is to have some antiseptic and bandages handy.

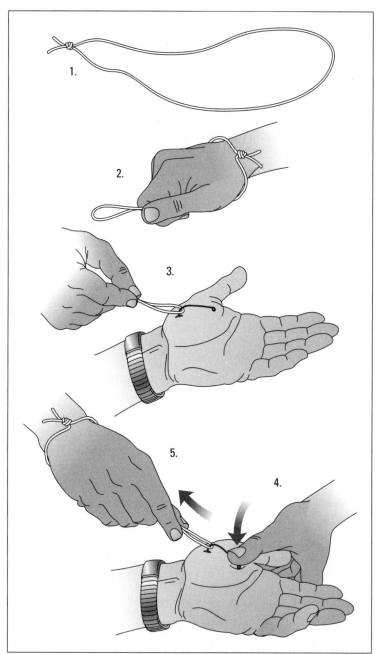

Figure 9-4:
Getting a J
hook out.

Sinkers: When You Need a Little More Weight

Sinkers are weights used to pull your baited hook down to where the fish are. Sinkers are traditionally made of poured lead, but they're increasingly being made of other heavy substances due to concerns about the environmental and health impacts of lead. Whatever they're made of, sinkers vary a great deal in shape and function. Similar to hooks, sinkers are your friends and can be used to most effectively present your bait.

When using sinkers, sometimes just a split shot or two does the trick. At other times (for example, when fishing in a moving current), you need much more lead. Peter remembers fishing for whiting one February morning off Coney Island. The fish were averaging about a pound. He started off by using eight-ounce sinkers to hold the bait on the bottom in the ebbing tide. As the day wore on, the tide raced more and more, until he was using a pound of lead to catch a one-pound fish.

Quit fishing when your sinker weighs as much as your fish. You probably won't be able to detect a bite; and when you do, the resulting fight to land the fish is about as much fun as reeling in the Manhattan phone book.

Selecting the right range of sinkers

Fish don't care about sinkers. All they care about is the bait and the presentation of that bait. So think about sinkers in this way: Their only purpose is to help you present your bait. If you can present your bait in an effective way without a sinker, by all means do it! But if your bait is not reaching the fish due to current or the fact that your bait is not sinking deep enough, employ a sinker. Sinkers are available at any store that carries tackle, and the various styles are labeled with their weight in ounces.

In sinkers, shape influences function. As shown in Figure 9-5, a number of sinker choices are available.

Following are the most common types of sinker:

- *Pyramid* sinkers get to the bottom fast and dig into sand or mud.
- *Egg* sinkers, or diamond sinkers, move over rocks and rubble a little easier than other shapes.

- ✔ *In-line* sinkers are made to slide on the mainline.

- ✔ *Bullet* sinkers are small in-line sinkers that work perfectly when placed on the line in front of soft plastics.

- ✔ *Bank* sinkers and *dipseys* work well with river rigs and dropshotting, which are explained in Chapter 15.

- ✔ *Split shot* and *twist-on* sinkers are quick to get on and off and work well when you need a little extra weight, or when using slip floats. (Notice the wings of the removable split shot sinker.)

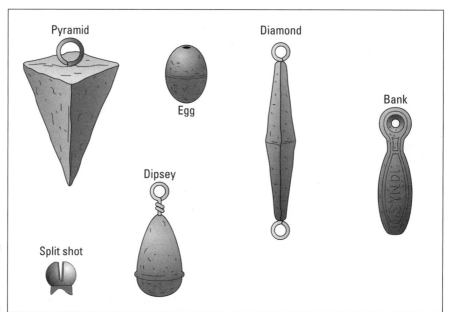

Figure 9-5:
Several
sinkers.

Start your collection of sinkers by picking up a variety pack of split shot sinkers, preferably the removable kind (look for the wings). These will serve you well in a variety of situations, and they're the kind you're most likely to need. But also pick up a few bank sinkers — especially if you intend to fish moving water. Get a range of weights in bank sinkers, all the way up to several ounces, because you never know how fast and strong the current will be. Finally, get some egg or in-line sinkers.

If you start with a few sinkers of various types and carry a range of weights, you should be ready for most situations. If you find that you can't fish the way you want to, you'll know what kind (or weight) of sinker to pick up next time you're in the store.

Storing your sinkers

A collection of sinkers can be quite heavy. As a catfisherman, I (Greg) carry enough weight to sink a small boat. (When fishing big rivers in heavy current, I might tie an eight-ounce weight to every rig.) Even though you're not likely to carry quite that much weight, any group of sinkers can be a disruptive force in your tackle box. I say, keep 'em separated. Store your sinkers in a plastic container, like the kind powdered drinks come in, or a small leather or cloth pouch. You can keep this in the bottom of your tackle box, or in a pocket in your fishing vest. Keep your split shot sinkers handy because these can be added quickly to a lure or rig as needed. (To see examples of popular rigs incorporating sinkers, see Chapter 15.)

Anglers who chew lead split shot sinkers to pass the time are asking for lead poisoning. Keep your sinkers out of your mouth, wash your hands after handling lead sinkers, and dispose of ruined lead sinkers in a trash can.

Adding On Swivels and Snaps

A *swivel* is a small metal device with two eyes designed to spin independently (see Figure 9-6a). Swivels come in different sizes and feature different materials and construction. The best swivels use ball bearings. The cheapest swivels (those with twisted wire eyes) barely work. A swivel is used when the action of the lure, bait, or sinker has a tendency to twist the line. The swivel spins instead of the line, so everything stays tidy. Some trolling or drifting rigs will mercilessly twist your line unless you incorporate swivels into the rig. Line twist is no fun, but swivels can be a weak link in the chain. They add knots to your rig, for one thing, and knotted line is always weaker than unknotted. But, again, some rigs demand them (often for adding leaders of various lengths and uses). Our advice is to buy a package of high-quality swivels. They will be rated in pound-test increments, just like line. Get swivels with a heavier pound test than your line, so they don't fail before your line does. See Chapter 15 for rigging advice, and use swivels if and when you need them. But like everything else in terminal tackle, you should keep it simple if you can.

A *snap* is most useful when you need to change lures or even sinkers quickly (see Figure 9-6b). A snap might be just a little shaped piece of wire that can be opened or closed to attach lures. When tied to your line, this can make switching lures a breeze. A snap is definitely not the way to get the best action out of your lure; however, when you are in a bluefish blitz and the action is furious and you want to change lures in a hurry because the blues have made sawdust out of your plug, you can do fine with a snap. And a few lures are shaped in such a way that makes tying them on tricky. With such lures, snaps can make life easier. Sometimes a snap incorporates a swivel into its construction, to help prevent line twist. Overall, snaps are probably a waste of your money. Learn well a few knots, and be able to tie them quickly. Your lures will move more naturally and your rig will be cleaner.

Figure 9-6:
Examples of
a swivel
(a) and a
snap (b).

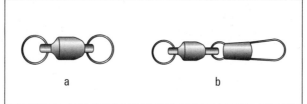

a   b

Floats and Bobbers: When You Need to Lighten Up

All anglers have, at one time or another, fished with a float. *Floats,* commonly called *bobbers,* work and are fun. Watching the little taps as a fish starts to nibble at your bait and then seeing the float go under are two of the most exciting experiences in fishing. Some fishing snobs look down on float fishing, but nothing is more pleasant than sitting on a riverbank with a friend or one of your kids and passing the time of day while watching your float. This scenario is a combination of doing nothing and doing something, which, when you get right down to it, is a lot of the fun of fishing.

The most basic float is a red and white plastic globe with a little spring-loaded button on top. To use this type of float, you push in the button and then hook your line around the hook that protrudes when the button is depressed. These floats have two obvious places to thread your line, and that's what you should do. Leave a loose end of line (about a foot or two in length) after the bobber to attach your hook. If your loose line is longer, casting gets difficult.

After your hook is on, add some bait and cast. You can't cast as far as you can when all you're using is bait and some lead weight, but this is one of the shortcomings of a standard float rig.

The advantages to floats, shown in Figure 9-7, are numerous:

  ✔ Floats keep your bait suspended, which works especially well for fish like crappies or bluegills that tend to suspend in schools.

✔ The bottom of a body of water tends to be the snaggiest place, and a float will keep your hook above the worst of it.

✔ A float can drift with the current or wind, presenting your bait to more fish.

✔ They serve as great indicators of a strike, allowing you to set the hook effectively.

✔ All this, and they're fun to watch!

Casting a standard float gets tricky if you place the bobber more than a foot or two above the hook; yet fish are often suspended in deeper water — say, 6 feet down in a pool 15 feet deep. *Slip floats* are the answer. Slip floats aren't spring loaded like standard floats. Instead, they feature a hollow core that allows the line to be threaded down through the center of the float. In this way, the line slides through the float until it hits a *bobber stop,* which you can easily place and adjust on your line. Bobber stops made of rubber can be purchased, as can pre-tied bobber stops made of thread. Or you can tie your own with a spare piece of line. The bobber stop has to be small enough to fit through the guides of the rod (so you can cast the rig smoothly), and large enough to stop the float. To facilitate this process, a *small plastic bead* is often added between the float and the bobber stop. This helps prevent the bobber stop from going through the float. The baited hook and a split shot or two help pull the line through the float until it hits the bobber stop. Now you can fish any depth you want, merely by adjusting the placement of the bobber stop. This is an ingenious way of taking float fishing to another depth. (More on rigging floats in Chapter 15.)

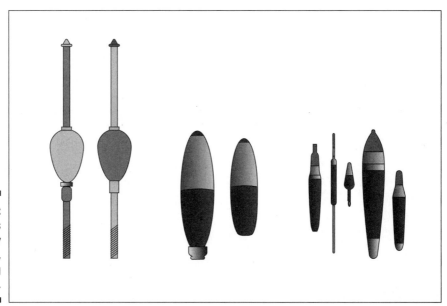

Figure 9-7:
Examples
of a variety
of floats,
including
slip floats.

To adjust to a variety of bait and water conditions, floats come in many shapes and sizes. Some floats are fat to increase buoyancy and hold up heavy baits, such as live baitfish for pike. Others are slim and take only the slightest weight to sink — perfect for light-biting fish like cold-water crappies. Some floats are built to handle heavy current. Some are tall to be seen from great distances. Others, designed for night fishing, either glow in the dark, have notches for lightsticks, or feature battery-operated lights that appear as tiny beacons on the dark water! Some anglers make their own floats out of everyday balloons. The options are endless.

Fishing with floats is a game all its own, but, like all things fishing, experience and time on the water will open your eyes to the possibilities. Know this: Every fish in the water — from the bluegill to the shark — can be taken on a float rig, if it's presented properly. And sometimes, a float allows you to present a bait in just the right way.

Chapter 10

Going Ahab: Fishing from Boats

*O*kay, so Captain Ahab probably would have been better off if he'd stayed on shore. At the very least, he might have considered staying closer to land. Maybe we shouldn't use him for a model! For a great many anglers, though, fishing from boats provides more flexibility, excitement, and success. Although boats can be expensive, affordable models exist, and even simple vessels can increase your catches.

Don't buy a boat solely for fishing if you're a beginning angler. Learn how to fish first, and see how much you like the hobby. While fishing from the shore, you can better learn the habits of fish, perfect your casting technique, and practice catching and landing fish. While you're a beginner, angling from shore allows you to focus more intently on the act of fishing.

Would having access to a boat change the way you fish local waters? For anglers fishing small streams, boating may be impossible. Even anglers fishing big water sometimes choose to stay on the bank for a variety of reasons. There's nothing wrong with that. It's quite possible the kind of fishing that best suits you doesn't require a boat.

But if you feel ready, and if your water allows it, another angling world awaits. Fishing from boats, even nonmotorized vessels, takes you into the fish's world. No longer are you observing this world from dry land — when you're floating, you become something like a fish yourself. Some things become much more complicated in boats (you have to ensure your boat is sound, watch out for obstacles, and so on), but other things are simplified (now, instead of trying to make that long, impossible cast, you can simply lower your bait . . .).

Boating isn't for everyone. And one kind of fishing isn't superior to other kinds. But knowing what boats offer anglers can help you decide if you're ready to leave the solid footing of the shore.

Taking Advantage of Boat Fishing

Fishing is fishing, whether you're leaning against a railing on a public pier or trolling for marlin. Boat fishing calls for many of the same techniques utilized by bank anglers. (There are exceptions — shorebound anglers can't troll, for example.) For more on angling techniques, turn to Chapter 17. Fishing from a boat, though — whether it's a 14-foot canoe or a deep sea charter boat — provides several advantages that shorefishing cannot.

More casting angles

Really, understanding how to fish well from a boat means visualing angles. But don't worry — no need to brush off that old geometry textbook from high school. Just think about the angles your lure and line takes as you retrieve a cast to the bank. For one thing, every cast you make from one position returns eventually to that same position. But retrieving a bait or lure to the bank means pulling that lure back to the surface near your feet — so the angle of the lure in the water looks similar, too.

When boat fishing, you can *jig* (a technique that requires lifting and lowering your offering) a lure straight below the boat, sometimes 100 feet below your shoes. You can retrieve a deep-running crankbait into the deep water below the boat, eventually cranking it to the surface. You can maneuver a boat down a bank, casting to different targets along the shore. This, too, varies the angle of the lure as it is retrieved. So boat fishing allows you to work different angles on both a vertical and horizontal axis.

Fishing places shorebound anglers can't reach

Any lake, river, bay, or inlet will have some places more accessible to foot traffic and some places that are hard to reach. For example, shore fishermen often fish rivers near public landings or ramps, which provide safe parking areas and a bank with less underbrush. But does that particular stretch of river hold a lot of fish? Maybe. Maybe not. In all these situations and more, fishing from a boat allows you to go places far from the angling crowd.

Sometimes, finding this under-fished water makes all the difference. Fish living in commonly fished areas learn quickly to avoid certain lures. (Or they get caught and taken home!) In rivers deemed *navigable* (a governmental designation meaning a river is passable to boats and, therefore, open to public boating), sometimes shore fishing access is limited to public ramps, with miles of private property blocking the rest of the river. Taking a canoe from landing to landing exposes you to thousands of fish that had been out of your reach. Even fishing the far shoreline of a bay or lake can make a difference.

When fishing from a boat, remind yourself — you're not limited to waters with easy bank access. Take advantage. Fish the areas bank anglers cannot.

Finding bluer water: Humps, points, and channels

Shorebound anglers can only fish as far as they can cast. In certain situations, the wind or current may take an offering farther offshore, but for the most part, fishermen are limited by the lengths of their casts. Anglers in boats, though, don't need to cast as far because they can move closer to the target. Boats really earn their keep when they allow you to fish offshore congregations of fish.

Many fish live near shore because that's where a lot of the cover is. But cover and structure can be found far from the bank, too.

Electronic devices like sonar and GPS units make this easier (see Chapter 11 for more on these tools), but even the naked eye can spot potential offshore spots. Islands provide structure and shoreline cover that's inaccessible to many anglers. Submerged humps draw fish, and with a boat, you can hover right over them. Often, these humps get enough sunlight to trigger weed growth, which attracts all kinds of prey.

Boats allow you to fish not only the sides of a point, but the trailing edge that tapers off into deeper water. With careful boat positioning, you can fish a point all the way from the bottom of the body of water to the shore. You could also follow the path of the *channel* — what's left of a flooded riverbed in a reservoir. Fish of all species cruise this channel like cars down a highway.

Make a beeline for these offshore hotspots every time you launch your boat. Just because you're fishing more than a cast's length from shore doesn't mean you're fishing deep water. You might be 100 yards from a bank, fishing a hump that's only 5 feet below the surface. But you'll be taking advantage of your fishing vessel.

Choosing a Boat That's Right for the Way You Fish

After you decide to get off the bank, your first choice is a doozy: Do you get a boat that's motorized or nonmotorized? Of course, cost is an issue that limits almost all of us. Beyond cost, you need to think about storage and upkeep. Safety and your overall comfort level with boating must be on the top of the list of things to consider.

But all of those things come later. First, examine your fishing water and the kinds of fish you like to pursue. What kind of boat would allow you to fish your water better? If you fish primarily small ponds for largemouth bass, even a jon boat might be overkill. That situation and species begs for a float tube, which would allow you to approach wary fish silently. If you like to fish tidal flats for striped bass or redfish, maybe your boat should be a small skiff that would allow you to cover water, looking for cruising fish. If you live near a big river, a deep-V could safely transport you for miles up- and downriver.

Check local water's regulations, too — some lakes limit the boat's horse-power. Other lakes allow only electric motors. If the water you fish most often only allows small boats, don't waste your money on Cleopatra's barge with rod holders.

The following sections look at the most common offerings in nonmotorized and motorized boats for anglers.

Great nonmotorized boats for fishing

You don't need a boat to catch fish. You don't need a motorized boat to catch fish, either. Nonmotorized boats boast qualities like affordability, silence, and ease of use. For small waters, nonmotorized boats may be the only option.

Unfortunately, nonmotorized boats usually can't cart your whole family. For the most part, boats in this category carry one or two individuals and not a lot of gear beyond that. They don't go anywhere too quickly (unless you're a champion paddler or oarsman), and they don't work well for anglers with some physical limitations.

But fish don't care about fast boats, and many of us carry too much gear, anyway. Nonmotorized boats force you to streamline your presentation, and when you couple that with a silent approach, it's no wonder anglers catch a lot of fish from boats of this type. Regardless of where you fish, the following options showcase the range of nonmotorized boats. One of them may help you fish your home water more effectively.

Rowboats

A classic that deserves mention, rowboats are *semi-V* boats (meaning that the *hull,* or part of the boat that touches the water, forms a shallow V when viewed from the front, or bow) with pointed bows that use *oars* for propulsion. Oars, unlike paddles, connect to the boat in *oarlocks,* and you use this fulcrum point to swing the oars and move the boat forward. Rowboats can be car-topped or carried in a truck bed and make for a stable fishing platform. Typically 14 feet long or less, rowboats are a bit clunkier than the other boats in this section, but they can carry more weight. A metal one is also virtually indestructible, which means there's a good chance your grandfather still has his in the garage.

Canoes

Although some canoes feature a square stern made for the mounting of a small motor, true canoes are pointed at both ends and are designed to handle current. Two people can paddle a canoe with ease after they get the hang of it, and it's possible — though difficult — to take three anglers or go it solo. Canoes can handle calm or flowing water and are at home in small rivers. A canoe can handle a decent amount of gear, but the gear should be lashed and stowed in waterproof containers because it's not the most stable vessel ever designed. Canoes transport well atop cars. Many options, such as rod holders and anchor systems, help you turn your canoe into a more efficient fishing machine.

Kayaks

Kayaks are the faster, sleeker siblings of canoes (see Figure 10-1a). Kayaks primarily carry one angler, and he or she can sit atop or inside the hull, depending on the design. Kayaks love fast current and are common on swift rivers all over the United States. Saltwater anglers enjoy kayaks too, and some amazingly large fish have been hooked by anglers pursuing saltwater fish from their relatively tiny vessels.

Similar to canoes, kayaks are easy to customize and transport. Kayak fishing is a rapidly increasing hobby, and manufacturers offer a range of models and angling options to meet the new demand. Kayaks are typically propelled with a two-bladed paddle, but some fishing kayaks feature feet-pedaled flippers for propulsion, and a few use a small electric trolling motor. These options free the hands for fishing.

Float tubes and kick boats

You paddle canoes and kayaks with paddles, for the most part, but you propel float tubes with your feet. Also called *belly boats,* float tubes originated as innertubes (yes, like the tire innertubes you used to float in at camp as a kid) rigged with a seat in the middle. (And models like that still exist.) Most float tubes now feature two parallel inflated tubes, which allows an angler to move around, half submerged, and cast to fish quite literally at his or her feet (see Figure 10-1b). Kick boats are evolved float tubes, and some allow the angler to fish with dry feet. They have floats (called *pontoons*) rigged to a frame that supports the seat. Anglers provide propulsion with paddles or oars.

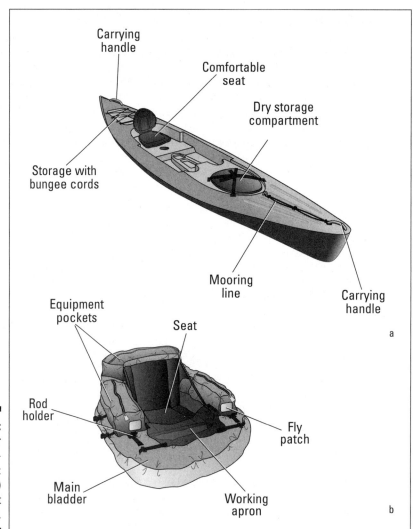

Carrying
handle

Comfortable
seat

Dry storage
compartment

Storage with
bungee cords

Mooring
line

Carrying
handle

a

Equipment
pockets

Seat

Rod
holder

Fly
patch

Figure 10-1:
Popular
nonmotor-
ized boats:
Kayak (a)
and the float
tube (b).

Main
bladder

Working
apron

b

Unlike canoes or kayaks, which you can use for fun or sport, kick boats and
float tubes are simply miniature fishing boats, and come in a range of styles
and with a variety of options. Although you can use them in small creeks and
streams with light current, kick boats and float tubes work best in lakes or
other sources of still water. Strong current or heavy winds could be disastrous in a float tube.

Ideal motorized boats for fishing

The motors on some boats move them across the water at speeds more typical of cars on the interstate. Some anglers, primarily those fishing in tournaments, see speed as a necessity. For millions of other anglers, though, motorized boats offer them the chance to pursue fish in a quiet, leisurely manner that offers dependability and safety. Whereas some might think small, nonmotorized boats are inherently safer, going on big water in a small boat is much more dangerous than going in a properly equipped large boat. And although some motorized boats are blazingly powerful, most are powered by simple two-stroke outboards generating less than 40 horsepower. Motors aren't cheap (think $100 per horse), but small motors make a good investment. For elderly anglers or those with disabilities, motors allow them to get out on the water more easily.

Electric motors can complete a boat. Although almost every bass boat uses a bow-mounted trolling motor to ease into casting position, most boats can be outfitted with either a bow- or a stern-mounted trolling motor. You can buy these electric motors in different sizes, and, depending on the size of the motor, they run on either one, two, or three 12-volt marine deep cycle batteries. Even though the motors and batteries aren't cheap, they're reliable, long-lasting, and quiet. Think of it this way: You move with your gas motor, but many times you fish with your electric motor. Whether you use your trolling motor to ease down a bank, casting as you go, or to troll lures along a drop-off, trolling motors move the boat without spooking the fish.

Jon boats

Jon boats are small, aluminum, square boats that look like floating matchbooks (see Figure 10-2). Square across stern and bow, jon boats don't slice through the water. Rather, they float along on top of it. (They're called *flatbottoms* for a reason.) What they lack in grace, though, they make up for with stability and *draft,* which is the amount of water a boat needs to avoid hitting the bottom of the river or lake. Jon boats work well in shallow water and for this reason are good choices for small rivers, ponds, and tidal flats. Because jon boats don't really cut through the water, they don't do well in choppy conditions. Deep-Vs (covered later in this chapter) do better when facing big waves.

The open floorplan of a jon makes it ideal for carrying lots of gear. Because they're aluminum, jon boats are easily customized: You can bolt rod holders to the *gunnels* (the edges of the boat), fasten lights to the bow, add soft seats to the benches — the options are endless. Jon boats can be trailered or carried on a car or in a truck. They come in small sizes — like 8 feet long — all the way up to more than 20 feet. Manufacturers design them for a variety of waters and uses.

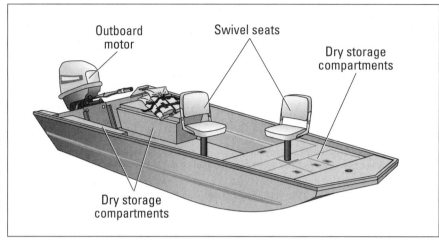

Figure 10-2:
The jon boat
is a common
motorized
boat.

Bass boats

Bass boats were born to meet the demand from the increasing interest in bass fishing. These boats are low sided, with stable platforms where you can stand and cast from bow and stern. Many models feature pedestal seats so you can sit and cast from an elevated position. Not just for bass fishing, these boats work for pursuing any fish in reservoirs, lakes, and big rivers. Not considered a big wave vessel due to the low sides, bass boats are often paired with strong outboards to increase speed. Many also use electronic trolling motors mounted on the bow to approach fish quietly after the boat is in the general vicinity. Bass boats are typically 14 to 22 feet, and vary widely in price (the motor has a lot to do with this). Because of their weight and size, bass boats are trailered to the water, where you need a decent launch ramp to get one floating.

Pontoons

The ultimate in comfort, pontoon boats are the equivalent of fishing from your family room. They ride on long, air-filled tubes, called *pontoons,* which support a flat, wide platform. Many pontoons boast comfortable seating, and some even offer such amenities as gas grills. Ideal for anglers with disabilities, and perfect for situations where the boat doesn't have to be towed long distances or at all (say, having one tied to the dock at the lake house), pontoons range from basic to quite fancy. While the most luxurious cater to families more than to anglers, pontoons can be modified into real fishing boats. In fact, on Santee Cooper, a giant reservoir in South Carolina, fishing guides take clients out for catfish aboard large pontoon boats.

Pontoons aren't especially fast, and they need quite a bit of room to turn. Heavy winds or current can really grip them. But if your home water stays calm most of the year, you may be able to fish from the comforts of home aboard a big pontoon boat.

Deep-Vs

These traditionally shaped boats earn their name from the shape of their hull. When viewed from the front, the bow forms a V shape, and a deep-V features a hull with high sides that offer wave protection (see Figure 10-3). Deep-Vs can handle rough water and are ideally suited to big lakes and rivers. You could pursue any species from a deep-V, but these are often heavy, expensive boats best matched with big-water fishing. Deep-Vs are usually 16 to 22 feet long, and are paired most commonly with an outboard motor (although an inboard motor is also a possibility). Again, the size of the motor greatly influences the price of the boat.

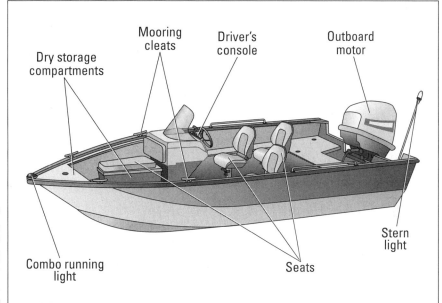

Figure 10-3:
The deep-V is suited to bigger water.

Skiffs

Skiffs work well in both freshwater and saltwater applications, as they feature a center console, lightweight construction, and a relatively open floorplan (see Figure 10-4). But they are ideal for anglers fishing shallow coastal inland flats targeting tarpon or bonefish. For that application, some skiffs feature raised casting platforms and even observation decks where fishermen can spot cruising fish. A skiff is a good all-around choice for serious anglers fishing mostly calm water, although some do have raised sides for wave protection. Skiffs get their power from outboards, and those can range from 25 horsepower motors pushing 15 feet skiffs to giant outboards for 22 feet models.

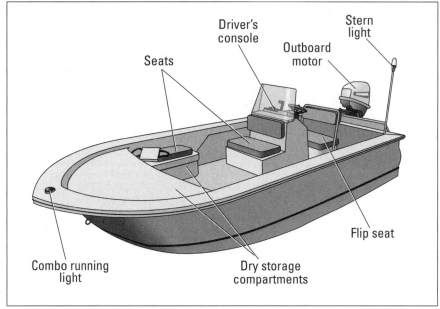

Figure 10-4:
The skiff
is a good
choice for
fishing calm
water, such
as shallow,
coastal
inland flats.

Considering the Costs of Watercraft

The old adage goes like this: The two happiest days of a boat owner's life are when he buys his boat and when he sells it. Bah — Greg says the two happiest days of a boat owner's life are when he buys his boat and when he buys his second boat. Millions of people invest in watercraft and never regret the decision. A little forethought will help you become one of those people.

As with anything, research before you buy. Shop around and look for deals. Timing matters too — some say the best time to buy a boat is in winter, when manufacturers are looking to secure sales to get the factory churning out units. Talk to dealers, attend boat shows, shop online — but don't be pressured to buy. Make sure you know exactly what you want — and what's a reasonable price for it — before you sign on the line.

Used boats appear along roadsides and in want ads every day. Certainly good deals are possible. As with buying a used car, check out any boat before you buy it. If you're buying a motorized boat, know that most of your investment is in the motor. You can check the *hull* — the outer part of the boat that touches the water — pretty easily, and you can inspect the interior, as well. But have a mechanic check the motor if you're not sure what you're looking for.

Start small. Your first boat probably isn't your last. My (Greg's) first boat was an inflatable dingy. A canoe came later. Before long a jon boat with an electric motor followed me home. Then I added an outboard motor. Then a bigger outboard. Finally, I bought an 18-foot deep-V with a four-stroke outboard delivering 115 horsepower. I researched every purchase beforehand, bought high quality for the lowest price I could find, and enjoyed every day with every one.

Some added expenses to owning a fishing boat are detailed in the next sections, but let us start by offering a mild caution: Like any hobby, boating can get expensive if you let it. Look at it this way: When you buy a tackle box, your expenses don't end. You still need to add some tackle to your tackle box! New lures become available. Your fishing style changes, and your tackle needs shift. Buying a boat is similar. Countless attachments, available from a wide range of manufacturers, allow you to customize your rig, whether you have a canoe or a 21-foot deep-V. But, remember the tackle box — you don't have to fill it all at once. You can accumulate lures and tackle over time. Boating is the same way. After you have a working vessel, you can slowly acquire the additions your kind of fishing calls for. This process of acquisition is also called getting through the winter months.

Licensing, plating, and fees

Check your state laws concerning the registration of boats. Often, boats smaller than 16 feet without motors don't have to be registered. Other states will require you to purchase an annual sticker if your boat (of any size) gets launched in public waters. If your boat has a trailer, the trailer will need a license plate and its own registration. Check with your local license branch and Department of Natural Resources (DNR) to see what you need for your particular boat.

Although these expenses add to the overall cost of boating, a portion of the funds collected by your state DNR should go toward the upkeep of boat ramps and resources management. In other words, you'll get some of your money back through fish and facilities.

Upkeep, storage, and maintenance

The bigger your boat is, the more work you have to do to keep it in running order. Big boats call for bigger motors, which require periodic service and can be costly to repair if something breaks. Small, nonmotorized boats, though, will cost almost nothing in maintenance. Keep a fiberglass canoe clean with a little elbow grease and it should last about forever.

All boats require storage space, however, and that can vary from the rafters in a garage to rented space. Before you buy, think about the boat you have room for, and think about the annual costs of maintenance and possible storage fees.

Trailering

Some boats come with fully rigged trailers. Other small boats, like jon boats, are often priced for the boat only. Of course, the best advice is to know exactly what you're buying. Some boat dealers have trailers for sale as well, and they'll often adjust it to fit your new boat. Whereas some small boats can be car-topped or truck-bedded, a decent-sized vessel needs a trailer. This means another expense for you, and additional maintenance. However, a good trailer lasts a long time without a lot of upkeep, and you won't miss having to muscle your boat onto the top of your car.

Don't cut corners on the trailer. You need one that's adequate for the weight of your boat, plus any gear that stays in the boat. In fact, it's a good idea to buy a heavy-duty trailer that can handle your boat and then some. Because you will add some more gear to your boat, we assure you.

Boat trailers need license plates. For safety, they need working lights and dependable straps to hold the boat securely. Inspect the straps often, make sure the lights are in working order, and ensure the tires are properly inflated. Keep the wheel bearings greased, too.

Towing a boat takes a little practice, and I (Greg) recommend you do that in your driveway or a big parking lot, as opposed to the ramp at the lake on Sunday. You can learn how to back a boat trailer — a lot of us do it, and we're not all geniuses — but you will need to practice. And learn to rely on your side mirrors, too, instead of having to twist your back to look over your shoulder. They even make little stickers you can place on your side mirror that read, "Did you put the plug in?"

Before launching at a busy ramp, load your boat with your gear first and attach a line to the bow. Back your boat trailer into the water (usually, until the tops of the trailer tires are at the surface of the water), set the parking brake of the vehicle, and push the boat from the trailer. Using the bow line, guide the boat away from the ramp and attach it to the bank or a dock. Park your vehicle and return to the boat. Having a partner along helps — he or she can board the boat before you launch and motor the boat off the trailer. However you choose to launch from a trailer, be courteous to your fellow boaters and don't dawdle on the ramp.

Chapter 11

Gadgets Galore: Fishing in the 21st Century

....

In This Chapter

▶ Fishing with high-tech equipment

▶ Exploring fish finders

▶ Using GPS to find you and your fish

▶ Choosing a trolling motor

▶ Viewing the fish's world with cameras

....

*T*he technology that shapes our daily lives has accelerated in recent years. For proof, look no further than the cellphone in your pocket. In the span of a few short years, cellphones evolved from small, reliable phones (you know — just phones, like in the old days) to smart phones with touch screens capable of taking decent pictures and video while surfing the Web at blazing speed. That kind of technology forged into the world of fishing, as well.

But first, a disclaimer: You can catch fish without using a single tool mentioned in this chapter. You might even be able to outfish someone with a boatload of these tools, and you certainly can have as much fun. So, if you want to keep your fishing simple, forever or just for now, by all means, cast away.

On the other hand, the new technology available really amazes most anglers, and almost all agree that it helps them catch more fish. Underwater cameras capture the lives of fish in clear, real-time video. Global positioning system (GPS) units allow you to mark structure and cover as well as chart return paths and drift patterns. The latest trolling motors can position a boat over a school of fish and keep it there, regardless of wind or wave patterns. Innovative technology continues to open the door into the underwater world of fish.

The technology helps only if you know how to work it. As with any new gadget, until you figure out how it functions, you probably spend more time messing with the buttons than you do benefiting from its features. The devices described in this chapter represent some of the most exciting forays into the fishing world, and most of the items discussed here come in a range of prices. Some of them cost more than a decent used car; others can be found for less than $100. One thing about technology — the longer it's out there, the cheaper it gets. Even the least expensive fish finder available today is better than some of the best from ten years ago.

One more thing about fishing with technology — it's there to help you fish, not distract you from fishing. We know some guys who hit the water only to spend more time watching their sonar unit displays than they do wetting a line. This is a problem. Even the best technology can't make fish bite. It might help you find them, but it won't hook them for you. And if you get so obsessed with your gadgets that you're no longer fishing, you might as well stay home and play video games. If you choose, own and know how to use these gadgets, but don't let the gadgets own you.

Fish Finders: Can They Really Find Fish?

Yes, they can. And they can do it amazingly well. Anglers who fish small ponds and streams will find no use for a fish finder — your eyes will serve you better while fishing smaller waters than any electronic device ever could. As a rule, if a body of water is too small to fish from a boat, it doesn't beg for a fish finder. But for anglers fishing big water — say, the Great Lakes or the Mississippi River — the hundreds of acres of water defy mere visual inspection. Although no electronic device will ever supplant the need to pay attention while fishing, fish finders will help you locate fish in the deepest, nastiest, murkiest water. And even small lakes reveal more secrets when fish finders are employed.

As you can imagine, fish finders are primarily used in boats. As anglers in boats move around a lake or inlet, their fish finders show them what is under the hull. Most fish finders are permanently mounted to boats, but portable models allow you add a fish finder to small vessels like canoes and float tubes. There's even a castable model on the market for those fishing from the bank.

How fish finders work

Fish finder is a common term applied to *sonar units,* and sonar stands for SOund, NAvigation and Ranging. Sonar units are used by millions of anglers today, but the technology first had to find something more important than a big northern pike: enemy submarines during World War II. Any sonar unit has four components: transmitter, transducer, receiver, and display. The transmitter sends out an electrical impulse, which the transducer converts into a sound wave. These sound waves are sent into the water, where they bounce off of objects and return to the transducer as echoes. Those results are converted back into electric signals, amplified by the receiver, and shown on the display.

On boats, the transducer is often mounted on the lower hull of the transom. The transducer often rides in the water, and the display is mounted somewhere in the boat where the angler can see it. The transducer has to be near the water, but certain models are designed to read through boat hulls made of material other than aluminum (allowing you to mount it inside the boat) or even through ice. Portable units might combine all the components, allowing you to hang the one-piece unit off the side of a small boat, with the transducer on the lower end and the display near the top. The castable fish finder lets you attach the small transducer to your line while you keep the display on your person (often wearing it as a watch). You can read the depth and look for fish under the spot of your cast!

Transducers emit these sound waves in a cone shape, spreading out as they leave the transducer. Usually this cone is broadcast directly beneath the boat. The bottom is shown as a line near the bottom of the display, and as fish move into the cone, they appear on the screen, as well. Some units allow you to project this cone to the side of the boat, too. All objects that enter the cone — fish, schools of baitfish, tree branches, sunken cars, a rocky bottom — show up on the display. Learning how to interpret the marks on the display takes practice, but every object in the cone should appear. The display will show the current depth and often the water temperature, as well.

All of this probably sounds confusing. It is! What you need to know: the biggest sonar manufacturers (Lowrance, Humminbird, Garmin) have great, interactive Web sites, and tackle shops often have displays of live units that feature tutorial modes. You can examine fish finders closely before you buy, and the best tackle shops will boast an employee or two with superior knowledge and advice.

I (Greg) have fish finders on both of my boats, and I'd be a little lost without them. But I'm not someone who believes I mark every fish before I catch it. (When it comes to fish finders, *mark* is a verb meaning "to show on the display screen"; it's also a noun referring to a fish on the display.) Some anglers fish for marks — fish they see on the display. In my experience, I catch a lot of fish I don't think I mark first. How does this happen? Perhaps the fish is so close to the bottom so as to be indistinguishable. Or perhaps the fish just approaches the lure without swimming into the cone under the transducer.

Do you really need a fish finder?

If you're bank fishing or fishing from a small, nonmotorized boat in shallow water, you probably don't need a fish finder. While small, portable sonar units help you interpret the water around you, they don't add much to the picture your other senses can paint for you. Any electronic device can serve as a distraction if you let it, and in my experience, time spent messing with portable fish finders would be better spent fishing and observing your surroundings.

Having said that, fish finders are amazing tools. People often assume sonar units find fish only. While they do that, they can also tell you important things about the water body in general: the depth, temperature, constitution of the bottom (whether it's hard or soft, rock or sand), presence of cover, and the appearance of structure — things like channel drop-offs and ledges. That information is crucial to your fishing success, and it might help you even if you never mark a fish.

If you own even a small fishing boat, one that allows for the permanent installation of a sonar unit, you should probably invest in a fish finder. You don't need a top-of-the-line model, however. There are very good $100 fish finders on the market. (With fish finders, more money gets you a more powerful transmitter, a sharper display, color screens, and more features.) Even a small fish finder will give you important details regarding the water under your hull. You may well find that after you use one, you won't feel completely at ease without it. The more expensive options, like the one featured in the color section of this book, call for tough decisions. Color screens are easier to read than black and white versions. More pixels provide crisper displays. More powerful transmitters reveal more. How much can you spend?

Large boats need sonar units for safety, if for no other reason. Vessels running in big water need the information sonar units provide to avoid running aground.

Where to find fish finders

Our best advice is to push the buttons on a fish finder unit before you buy it. Although you can order them online (along with everything else), you probably want to interact with the various models before you choose one. Research fish finders online, and maybe even purchase one online, but visit a tackle shop to examine the units before buying.

Most stores that sell a decent selection of rods and reels will also sell electronics. They probably have a display case with all of their sonar unit models connected to a power source and in display mode. Spend some time browsing the different units and ask questions of the sales staff.

If you buy a boat from a marina, often they will install a unit for you. Other stores may or may not be able to install units for you, but they should be able to recommend someone who can, and every unit will come with installation instructions. Installing a basic unit isn't too difficult, but the more advanced the unit, the more complicated the installation.

GPS Units: Finding Yourself

GPS operates on this rock-solid, easy-to-understand system: there are 24 satellites positioned 12,000 miles above the earth, rotating the planet twice in 24 hours and moving at 7,000 miles per hour. Built by the U.S. Department of Defense, these 24 satellites were originally designed to protect us from attack. They still do that, but now they can also help you find fish or the closest Pizza Hut.

Your GPS receiver, whether it's in your car, boat, or hand, needs to find at least three satellites to acquire your position, in terms of latitude and longitude. With four or more satellites in view, a receiver can also chart altitude. Modern GPS receivers can pinpoint your location to within a few feet. So how can GPS help anglers?

Well, GPS can help you find your way to and from a fishing hole. It can also help you mark fish or likely locations of fish. You can begin to take advantage of GPS while fishing in one of two ways: You can either add a GPS unit to your boat (many fish finders now come with built-in GPS; refer to the previous section for more on fish finders), or you can purchase a handheld unit (to be used either from the boat or while bank fishing). Either can help you fish more safely and effectively, regardless of where or how you're fishing.

Waypoint fever

A GPS unit will show your location and a trail of where you've been. Anglers, though, tend to find great value in the *waypoints* — saved spots that remain on your GPS map. Suppose you're fishing a remote lake in Canada from a canoe. You can save a waypoint for your base camp. With that saved, you can always make your way back to that point. Boaters can waypoint a ramp or marina and then find the easiest path back. (Most units will let you change the waypoint symbol as it appears on the screen, allowing you to use a launching boat symbol for the ramp, a tent for your camp, and so on.) You can always delete waypoints you no longer need.

But those are more obvious waypoints. While wading upstream, you could waypoint every spot where you catch a fish. Eventually, you'd have your favorite stream pockmarked with waypoints — spots where you know you've been successful in the past. You can also make obstacles or hazards into waypoints to help you avoid them in the future.

Boating anglers also find a great many uses for waypoints. You can save permanent structure features with waypoints such as deep holes, drop-offs, or large rock piles. Even particular schools of fish or solitary gamefish that appear on the fish finder can be waypointed. Those waypoints won't be accurate on the next trip, perhaps, but they can always be replaced with fresh ones. (And some units let you save *event markers,* which temporarily mark these things that shift, like schools of fish.)

When drifting or trolling, a GPS unit lets you record the exact trail or path you've taken on a particular pass. You can then retake that path, or one slightly near it. (This kind of drifting or trolling is the equivalent of fan casting — spreading out your presentation incrementally until you locate fish.) You can make a waypoint for each fish caught along a pass, too.

Look for patterns in your waypoints. As with any kind of fishing, by paying attention to the fish you catch, you can begin to ascertain a pattern. Seeing a pattern allows you to tighten your approach, leading to more caught fish. If you drift along a shoreline and make a waypoint for every caught fish, and then notice that most of your waypoints are clustered near a drop-off, you know where the most active fish are feeding.

As with any other technical tool, the better you know your GPS unit, the more you can do with it. For example, some anglers waypoint a rockpile and then anchor upriver from that rockpile. Using the unit's navigation tools, they can then determine precisely how far away that rockpile waypoint is. Taking into account the depth of the water, they then understand how far to cast behind the boat to reach the rockpile. (Okay, it seems like your high school geometry teacher was right — you really will need that stuff about measuring triangles in your real life.) GPS is another tool that can help you locate — and find again and again — fish.

Updating your maps

You can customize your GPS unit to your home area by ordering specific, more detailed maps that can be uploaded into your unit. For anglers, this often means acquiring specific lake maps. Your GPS unit will come from the store loaded with maps, but these more specific maps can show your favorite lake in incredible detail, such as how much the lake bottom changes in one-foot increments. More lakes are added to the list all the time, so if your favorite lake doesn't have a detailed map available yet, be patient.

These maps are not just effective for the water, but for the land surrounding the water. They can help you find the nearest hospital, the closest roads, the best parking spots. My (Greg's) brothers and I once ordered a map for a stretch of rural, lonely river, and with the enhanced map we could choose our campsite beaches before we even launched the boats.

Trolling Motors: Quiet Power for Boats

Trolling motors aren't new gadgets — these battery-operated electric motors have been silently pushing boats around for decades. And you can still buy basic models that are largely unchanged from the trolling motors your grandparents used on their rowboat. But today's trolling motors have many new features that combine the traits of both sonar and GPS units.

Trolling motors vary in *thrust,* which is the rating, given in pounds, of the motor's power. The more powerful the motor is, the higher the cost. For example, a 55-pound thrust trolling motor is powerful enough to move an 18-foot boat, but it requires a good-sized marine battery and costs about $250.

And every motor is only as good as its battery. You don't use car batteries for trolling motors — you use marine batteries, which are designed to hold a charge a long time and then withstand being recharged over and over again. New technology allows for maintenance-free and long-lasting batteries. Some trolling motors are made to run off of one 12-volt battery, but others run on a 24- or even 36-volt system. These motors call for two or three batteries, respectively, to be rigged together. This requirement adds to the overall expense, but these systems move bigger boats faster, and the charge lasts longer. You might add on an onboard charger for your batteries, so all you have to do after fishing all day is plug in the charger.

Mounting a trolling motor

For small boats, an inexpensive transom-mount trolling motor will move the vessel across calm water silently and steadily. There's usually plenty of room for a battery near the stern, and you can remove the motor and battery when the boat is loaded into the truck bed or atop the car for the trip home. This is a convenient way to avoid having to paddle across the lake.

Many anglers, particularly those fishing for bass, often mount a trolling motor on the bow of their boat, leaving the outboard alone on the transom. This arrangement allows them to use the bigger motor to get across the water, before lowering the quieter trolling motor and silently gliding into casting position. For this reason, a bow-mounted sonar unit can come in handy, so the angler in the front of the boat can watch the display and react accordingly as he steers the trolling motor. Trolling motors can be controlled by hand (through a tiller), a foot pedal, or a wireless remote about the size of a car key fob. These wireless remotes allow you to operate your trolling motor from anywhere in the boat.

Combining trolling motors with sonar and GPS

Today's best new trolling motors allow you to buy a trolling motor with a transducer for your sonar unit already installed in the nosecone of the motor. This way, with the trolling motor deployed in the water, the transducer transmits back to the receiver of the sonar unit. Even more amazing are the trolling motors that utilize GPS, allowing you to record a path and then retrace it with a push of a button. You can also tell the motor to keep you in one spot, and it will adjust itself accordingly to stay there. (Think of it as an anchor that never leaves the boat or touches the bottom.) These innovations aren't cheap, but for the serious angler, a new wave of electric motors has arrived. These fancy units probably aren't your first trolling motor, though. Start simple and work your way up as you gain experience. Understanding how and why you position a boat to fish structure or cover is tantamount to owning a trolling motor that can try to do it for you.

Underwater Cameras: Seeing Is Believing

As amazing as good sonar units are, they can't show you the actual fish below your boat, swimming around. You'll see an arc, or a computerized fish shape, but not the fish. Underwater cameras show you the live fish. A camera is lowered into the water with a cable that connects to a monitor. These cameras are small enough to fit in your hand, and many of today's models hide the camera in a realistic-looking fish replica. That way, when a camera suddenly drops in on a school of fish, it's not too disruptive. You view the fish from the monitor above. Some models have cameras pointed in four directions, allowing you to see in all directions at once, whereas others show one view, and you need to rotate the cable to see in another direction.

Aqua-vu is the most popular manufacturer of underwater camera systems, and their Web site (www.aquavu.com) shows clips of many species of fish recorded in their natural habitat. So yes, underwater cameras work — even in cloudy water, anglers can see fish. But you can see a lot more than fish, and that's what makes underwater cameras so valuable.

What you can learn by viewing

Suppose you lower your camera to the bottom of the lake and see not one fish. But wait — what else can you learn? Look at the bottom composition. Is the bottom sand, rocks, or gravel? Are weeds present? Is that a stump or a barrel? A sonar unit will have trouble distinguishing among these things, but a camera will leave no doubt. In that way, a camera is a great teaching tool to accompany a fish finder. You can study both your fish finder and the camera and learn how to interpret what you see on the fish finder display.

The best fish finder can find fish, but it won't identify species. What you think are a school of walleye might turn out to be carp when the camera is lowered. On the other hand, if they are indeed walleye, you might be motivated to stay a bit longer, trying to convince reluctant fish to bite. You'll know they're there!

Some anglers, particularly those fishing stationary presentations, have been able to set up a camera to watch while a fish inspects or bites a lure. If several fish approach a lure, but all fail to bite, the angler has learned something about his presentation. A different lure might make the difference.

What cameras can't do for you

All electronics can tempt you — they make you think the fish are right there, and certain to bite at any moment. But cameras can really mess with your mind — the fish are indeed right there, and cameras don't lie! Most experienced anglers will tell you that it's hard to fish and watch the camera at the same time, especially if you're moving while fishing. Again, for a stationary presentation like ice fishing, anglers can easily sit, watch the camera monitor, and wait for the fish to hit. But anglers fishing from moving boats often have too much going on to watch the camera steadily. Think about it — how do you cast, watch out for other boats and obstacles, maneuver the boat, keep an eye on the fish finder, and lower and raise the camera, too? For that reason, some camera companies now offer devices that lower camera cables with foot controls.

Even so, many anglers prefer to use cameras on scouting trips — inspect likely spots carefully, probe with the camera, and then return with the camera off, ready to concentrate on fishing. Or perhaps anglers will fish a spot for a while, then lower the camera to confirm or deny what they think the sonar shows them (verifying a species of fish, for example).

Anchormates, Lightning Detectors, and What's Coming Next

When I (Greg) purchased my Lund deep-V, I ordered it brand new. I got to choose the color, motor size — even the number of seats. I was in heaven. Wifey, though, made the biggest choice — she said I had to order an Anchormate. The Anchormate I got lowers and raises a 40-pound anchor without difficulty at the push of a button. (Thanks for asking, but I'd rather not tell you why this option was so important to my wife and beloved fishing partner.)

Gadgets, not gimmicks: Trinkets to avoid

The tools covered in this chapter might not be necessary, but they work. Too often, people will try to take advantage of the angler's nature: her drive to catch more and bigger fish. For that reason, enterprising companies are always offering a new trick or tool sure to help you catch a whopper. Well, buyer beware. Reputable tackle shops sell quality products, and often the staff have used a lot of the gear themselves. Funny, you see fewer talking lures for sale on their shelves. Buy your gear wherever you want, but check it out first. If it seems too . . . well, gimmicky, to be true, it probably is.

The point is, there are gadgets out there designed to make your fishing life easier. Anglers with hand disabilities can find reels with electric motors that do the cranking. There are lights, drift socks, outriggers, downriggers, bells and, yes, whistles that customize your fishing gear. Some of it won't work for you, but a lot of it will. Some of this gear is costly, and could be accumulated slowly, whereas other tools are inexpensive and will reward you many times over your investment.

One of the fishing magazines I subscribe to recently touted a personal lightning detector. Does it work? I don't know, and I don't think enough tests have been done to tell conclusively. But I bring it up to remind you that nothing stops when it comes to technology, and fishing gear is no exception. By the time this book goes to press, some new items will have found their way onto the market. It's impossible to predict where the technology will take us. But enterprising anglers will always find a way to make the latest gadgets work to catch more fish.

Take, for example, the smart phones we mentioned at the beginning of this chapter. Already many anglers have found apps that help them fish better. You can check river forecasts, weather warnings, and tides — all from your phone!

This cutaway view of a typical river or stream shows a classic riffle-hole-run pattern. As the current goes over a harder bottom, a 1) riffle is formed, and fish gather to feed on incoming food. Below a riffle, a 2) hole forms, which is the deepest part of a river, where fish both rest and feed. After a hole, a 3) run forms, which is a fairly featureless (and often fishless) stretch that continues until the next riffle forms.

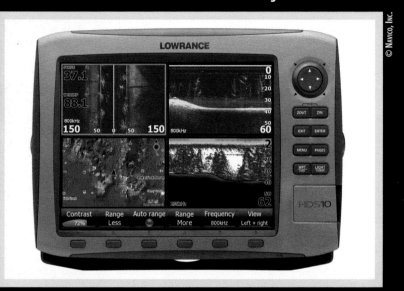

© JOSEPH R. TOMELLERI

The beautifully marked rainbow trout, one of the world's most popular gamefish, prefers water cooler than 70 degrees.

© NAVICO, INC.

Fish finders have come a long way, as this HD Lowrance unit shows. This split screen reveals what lies under and to the sides of the boat, and it includes GPS mapping as well.

© JOSEPH R. TOMELLERI

Found in freshwater across the country, the pugnacious bluegill is adored by anglers for its willingness to bite and its great taste.

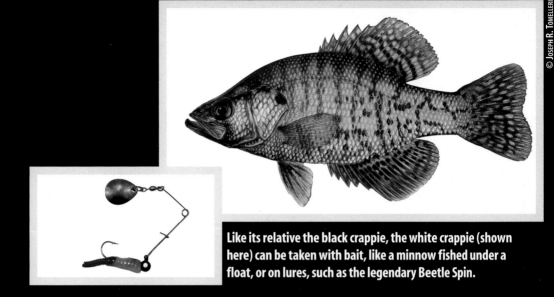

© Joseph R. Tomelleri

Like its relative the black crappie, the white crappie (shown here) can be taken with bait, like a minnow fished under a float, or on lures, such as the legendary Beetle Spin.

© Joseph R. Tomelleri

The channel cat is a hard-fighting gamefish widely stocked in ponds, reservoirs, and lakes everywhere. Its barbels (whiskers) help it locate food even in clouded water.

© Joseph R. Tomelleri

The walleye makes a challenging, worthy opponent for many anglers, who pursue this cool-water fish with livebait rigs or lures, like the XCalibur One Knocker.

The yellow perch tastes great, so anglers pursue this schooling panfish with livebait and lures like the Mimic Minnow Shad.

The largemouth bass ranks as one of the most-recognized and prized gamefish the world over. A largemouth will take livebait, but it's usually caught on a wide range of lures, including the soft plastic Yum Big Show Craw.

The fierce northern pike swims primarily in cooler waters, where it chases baitfish and lures like this Rapala. Caught on lures and livebait, the pike is a worthy adversary.

Gaining popularity as a hard-fighting gamefish, the common carp can be found everywhere in freshwater, where it can be caught on flies or bait such as canned corn.

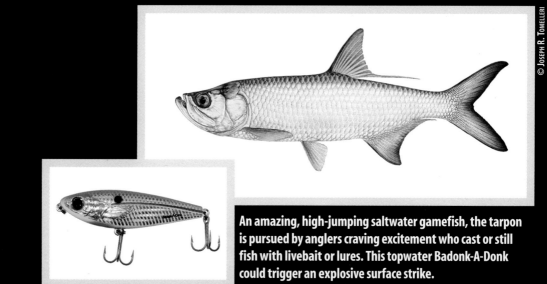

An amazing, high-jumping saltwater gamefish, the tarpon is pursued by anglers craving excitement who cast or still fish with livebait or lures. This topwater Badonk-A-Donk could trigger an explosive surface strike.

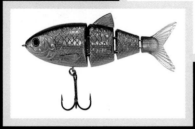

Found in both fresh- and saltwater, the striped bass reaches weights in the triple digits. Anglers troll or cast lures or livebaits for stripers. This Spro Shad Swimbait mimics a common forage fish.

Sharks, like the abundant blue shark, are sought by anglers for their hard, fast fight and feisty dispositions. Anglers often take them with livebaits like whole or cut fish.

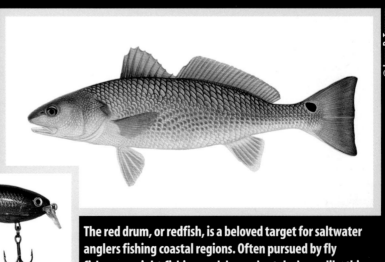

The red drum, or redfish, is a beloved target for saltwater anglers fishing coastal regions. Often pursued by fly fishermen sight-fishing, red drum also take lures, like this Rapala X-Rap Shad.

The halibut is a massive saltwater gamefish caught in the Pacific Northwest, where it prefers cool water. Caught on bait fished near the bottom, a halibut might fall for this Berkley Gulp! Saltwater Peeler Crab, made with natural, biodegradable ingredients.

The Pacific cod, like its relative the Atlantic cod, prefers cool water and can be found feeding near the bottom. Fished commercially for food, cod eat small fish and crabs, and maybe this Berkley Gulp! Shrimp.

© RON HILDEBRAND

In this cutaway view of a typical lake, you can see features that are likely to concentrate gamefish. Look for visible clues, such as 1) places where streams enter or leave the lake, 2) weedbeds or stands of cattails, bulrushes, or other plants, and 3) shade, which can attract fish during high-sunlight periods. Also seek out cover and structure hidden beneath the surface, such as 4) submerged logs, 5) drop-offs and ledges, and 6) points where land trails into deeper water.

Part III

The End of Your Line: Enticing Fish with Bait, Lures, and Flies

The 5th Wave   By Rich Tennant

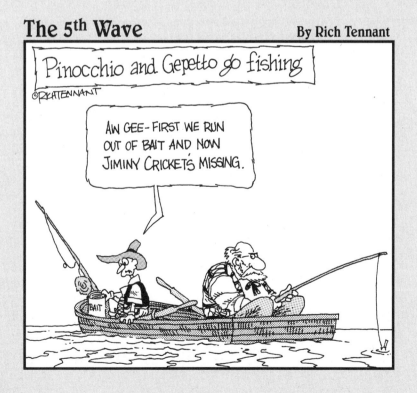

In this part . . .

You'll find three chapters covering the three basic kinds of offerings you'll present to a fish: bait, lures, and flies. Here you'll get advice on gathering and storing livebait, choosing the right crankbait, and matching the hatch on a trout stream. Each kind of offering has its advantages and disadvantages, and that's all covered here.

Chapter 12

Real Food for Real Fish: Using Bait

Think about it this way: Fish still eat when you aren't there fishing for them. As they go about their fishy lives, they seek shelter and protection, reproduce when the time is right, and look for something to eat. All fish do some combination of those three activities year-round. So, when you show up at their home with a fishing rod in your hands, you're simply stepping into a world in progress.

When you offer fish a hook baited with something they're used to eating, presented in a way that looks natural, you're almost certain to catch some fish.

Over decades of trial and error, anglers have discovered that fish will also eat things that don't exist in their natural habitat. We don't know who discovered that fish will eat chunks of Ivory soap, but apparently some will. Fish have also fallen for such things as Spam, cheese, and bread. Some species of fish fall for hot dogs. In other words, fish eat a lot like you do when you're watching television.

Part III of this book covers what you can offer on your hook in an effort to catch fish, and it makes sense to start with bait. After all, bait is easy to obtain and use, and it often works more effectively than anything else. Some species of fish (like blue catfish) can be caught reliably only with bait. Every gamefish in the world can be caught with some kind of bait.

Assessing Your Bait Options

Bait, by popular definition, is any natural (think worms) or processed food (say, cheese) used to catch fish. Over the years, the term *lure* has come to mean any artificial offering. Lures, covered in Chapter 13, often imitate natural baits, and they come in a dazzling variety of styles. But bait, too, can be divided into different categories and styles:

- ✔ **Natural baits:** Anything that a fish finds and eats in its habitat is considered natural bait. Minnows, crabs, frogs, insects, crayfish, snakes, mice, eels, worms — you name it. Fish eat what's available, and using the same natural bait is an effective technique.

- ✔ **Livebait or cutbait:** Livebait most often refers to fishing a natural bait while it is still alive. (For example, hooking a minnow through the lips and allowing it to swim freely.) However, anglers also use the term livebait to refer to baits that were recently alive, such as a smashed grasshopper pulled off the bumper of a car. Finally, cutbait is just that: livebait (mostly fish) that's been cut up in strips or chunks. Popular in both salt- and freshwater, fresh cutbait offers the scent and taste of real baitfish, but in sizable portions.

- ✔ **Commercial baits:** Manufacturers produce a variety of baits designed to attract fish. Often made with real or processed foods (ground fish or cheese, for example) commercial baits are sold alongside fishing tackle in convenient packaging.

- ✔ **Food baits:** Many foods that humans eat also take fish. Corn, bread, cheese, and meats of all kind can be used to catch fish. The most convenient of all kinds of bait to use, food baits are accessible, cheap, and often less messy than other kinds of bait.

Gathering and Keeping Bait

Some anglers have a gift for fishing; some anglers have a gift for bait. Catching natural baits like grasshoppers or crabs takes skill. Figuring out what baits to use on what days also requires some thought. Greg's younger brother, on most days a mediocre fisherman, is a dedicated baithound. He would rather pursue bait than go fishing. You don't have to be great at bait, but it helps if your fishing partner is.

Support your local baitshop

Some gas stations sell nightcrawlers. Big box stores often stock a refrigerator with cartons of worms, often in the aisle with the hooks. Some even keep a minnow tank running. There might be a guy in your neighborhood who sells bait out of his garage. Anywhere anglers gather, someone will usually offer bait for sale.

For best results, seek out a baitshop. You can usually count on finding interesting characters who know the local waters. Not only can you buy baits that work in the surrounding areas, you can gather advice on how to use them and where to fish. Most baitshops will sell maps, gear, and tackle. The more you visit (and the more regularly you spend) the more tips they offer.

Forget your checkbook: Gathering free bait

You need quality bait, but you don't have to go broke obtaining it. The enterprising angler can find any style of bait for minimal cost. With natural baits, you can fish with bait you caught with your own hands. You can gather nightcrawlers from lawns at night; trap or *seine* minnows using a net pulled along by two poles rigged on either end; and net crayfish and crabs. In a sense, gathering natural baits becomes its own fishing expedition. Sometimes anglers targeting striped bass or catfish often pursue bluegill first, using them as bait for the bigger predators. (Be sure and check your local laws before gathering any kind of natural bait.)

Ideally, the bait you gather should come from the area immediately surrounding the area you intend to fish. Crayfish caught in a stream will smell, look, and taste just right to the smallmouth bass in that stream. A small pinfish hooked under a pier will be familiar bait to the snook waiting farther out.

Remember to look on dry land, too. Grasshoppers can be hard to catch, but the price is right. Worms and grubs often reside under rotting logs. Cicadas, particularly those that explode in a swarm every 17 years, trigger quick strikes from all kinds of fish. Be observant and seek out free bait. You'll save money and often outfish those using more expensive lures.

Grocery store baits

If the baitshop is closed and you don't have the time or energy to gather your own natural bait, you can buy effective bait right where you buy your groceries. Canned sweet corn, bagged frozen shrimp, tubs of chicken livers — many groceries can go from your cart to the water. You could even buy fresh or frozen fish and make your own cutbait. If you have a little more time, hundreds of recipes exist online for doughballs, often made from cereal and bread.

What you need depends upon the fish you're after, but many species of fish, from rainbow trout to carp, will take corn. Catfish love chicken livers. Both saltwater and freshwater fish love shrimp. Experiment and try out different recipes. We don't know why fish like corn — it's not likely they could ever find it in their habitat — but someone discovered that it works.

Storing and transporting bait

Different kinds of baits call for different storage and transportation techniques. Generally, though, most baits should be kept cool, and they shouldn't be kept for long. If you're married, allow us to save your marriage with this nugget: Don't forget your carton of nightcrawlers in the trunk of the car. Or this one: Don't put nightcrawlers in the fridge in a container without a really good lid — and don't forget to label it as a courtesy to anyone else who may be scouting your fridge for a snack.

When transporting bait of any kind, make sure the container is securely packed and airtight, if possible. (Of course, some baits, like crickets, require airholes.) Check to ensure the lids are on tight. Many a fishing trip has been derailed after a tube of crickets released themselves, one by one, into the darkness under the car seats.

Common Natural Freshwater Baits

At one time or another, somebody, somewhere, has tried just about everything to catch a fish: peaches, candy corn, leftover lamb chops, dead (and sometimes not dead) goldfish from the aquarium. But for the most part, fish like to eat things that they find in their natural environment: insects, worms, other fish, and fish eggs. And, through centuries of trial and error, anglers have narrowed their bait choices to a few reliables. This section covers the most popular natural bait for freshwater fish.

Nightcrawlers: Great bait by the dozen

Earthworms make great bait. They're small, easy to thread on a hook, and panfish love them. Nightcrawlers, though, are a different breed of worm. King of all worms, nightcrawlers can be longer than a pencil and twice as thick. A healthy, juicy nightcrawler draws strikes from just about anything that swims in freshwater.

The most common livebait in the country, nightcrawlers should accompany you on your next fishing trip for several reasons:

- ✔ You can buy a dozen almost anywhere bait is sold.

  Make sure to check the contents before you pay. Open the carton carefully and look for dead crawlers. If things haven't gone well in that container, you'll smell it pretty quickly.

- ✔ With practice, you can gather your own. See the next section for advice on catching your own nightcrawlers.

- ✔ They catch fish. Fish that have never seen a nightcrawler will attack one when given the opportunity. Many other creatures that look like earthworms appear in the fish's environment: eels, snakes, and other kinds of aquatic worms, and fish feed on them readily. Not to say that earthworms don't get washed into the water as well: A big mud-producing rain can wash a decent number of worms into the water, where it's fair to say that "a worm in a stream is like a fish out of water." In other words, it's easy prey.

Get him! Grabbing nightcrawlers

Unless you have access to a big compost pile (lucky you!) or a pile of rotting leaves, nightcrawlers can be hard to find during the day. (Their name tells us something about that.) They live in tunnels that run quite far beneath the ground. However, a deep, soaking rain can bring them to the surface, even during the day. When that happens, you can often gather them easily from driveways and sidewalks. Store nightcrawlers in a cool, dark place in a container with loose soil mixed with some peat moss, leaves, or grass clippings. Commercial worm bedding is also available.

Even without rain, you can catch nightcrawlers at night (although rainy nights are even better). On a warm summer evening, look for a lush lawn that hasn't been overly treated with chemicals. Using a flashlight that isn't super bright (if your light is too garish, cover the lens with a red balloon skin or a thin cloth), step softly and scan the ground for nightcrawlers. (Some bait hunters like to use headlamps, which free up both hands.) When you see one, odds are good that part of the worm is still in its burrow, and with a jerk, the nightcrawler can disappear back down its tunnel. So you have to be quick, but soft at the same time. Holding the flashlight in your nondominant hand, crouch and position your other hand near the nightcrawler. Grab it as close to the tunnel as possible, pinching the worm firmly, but not so firm that you break the nightcrawler in two. Holding the worm firmly, wait until it relaxes, then slowly pull the nightcrawler from its hole.

Yes, it gets easier with practice. But, as with all forms of gathering bait, some people are just naturals. Our advice? Teach your kids to grab nightcrawlers and then pay them a penny a worm.

Hooking a nightcrawler

There are four standard ways to put a nightcrawler on your hook. Be sure to use a hook large enough to hold the bait, but small enough for the fish you're targeting:

- ✔ The simplest method is to push the hook through the smooth or *collar* section of the worm, as shown in Figure 12-1a.

- ✔ It takes a little more finesse, but another method is to put the point through the top of the head and then out through the collar, as shown in Figure 12-1b. It gives the worm great action when you move it through the water.

- ✔ *Texas rigging* is just like the preceding method, except that you turn the hook around and bury the point in the collar so that the worm doesn't hang up in weeds or rocks. Refer to Figure 12-1c.

- ✔ It doesn't look as natural, but you can thread the nightcrawler on the hook, as you see in Figure 12-1d. The flavor and the scent remain, and fish can't jerk the crawler from the hook as easily.

Figure 12-1:
Four ways to hook a night-crawler.

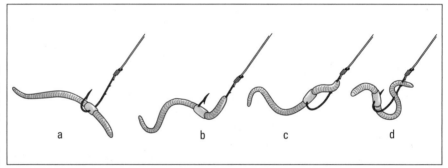

a   b   c   d

Minnows and other baitfish: Little fish catch big fish

When people refer to minnows, they are usually talking about a whole range of small baitfish. In addition to true minnows, some of the fish lumped into this category include chubs, shiners, herrings, suckers, smelt, sculpin, alewives, and gizzard and threadfin shad. Big fish love to eat little fish. If you open the belly of most trophy-sized fish, you'll find that small fish account for most of the food in their stomachs.

There is something very exciting about casting a minnow into the water and watching your line as the minnow swims around. Because gamefish often feed on baitfish, you're offering a natural bait that triggers a wholehearted strike.

Where to get minnows

Most baitshops sell minnows by the dozen, and if you need it, they'll sell you the bucket to carry them in, too. Most of these minnows are fathead minnows, and they're a small minnow popular with crappie anglers. They catch other species of fish, too, and they're usually not too expensive. The best baitshops carry minnows in a few sizes — either larger fathead minnows or suckers, chubs, or goldfish.

Although you pay more for bigger minnows, the larger sizes are better bait for fish like largemouth bass, catfish, pike, and walleye.

If you want to catch your own minnows, buy a *minnow trap,* which is a wire contraption that looks like a large can with cones built into either end. When submerged in a likely spot and baited with bread or dry dog or cat food, minnows swim into the cones, but can't find the exit. Another option is to master a *castnet,* a weighted net that you throw like a blanket over a school of fish. It's not easy, but when you get the hang of it, you'll never need to buy bait again. Check your local regulations before trapping any kind of fish for bait.

Live baitfish are hard to keep alive for very long. Usually, the water heats up and runs out of oxygen. If you put a trayful of ice cubes in the bait bucket before you set off on a long drive, you improve the chances of your bait surviving. Put the cubes in a plastic bag so the chlorine in the tap water won't poison the fish. Also, go easy on the ice. You want to keep the fish active and spry, not flash freeze them. Minnows keep better in cooler seasons, and small, battery-powered air pumps that clip to the sides of bait buckets will help your bait stay lively in any season.

Hooking a small baitfish

Two of the most common ways to hook a minnow are to run the hook through both lips (bring the hook out the upper lip), or to pass the hook through the top part of the body just behind the dorsal fin (see Figure 12-2).

Rattlin' worms, Cajun-style

Of all the ways I (Peter) have seen for catching bait, the most surprising was shown to me by two Cajun fishermen in the little town of Washington, Louisiana. I was going to a catfish dinner with Herman Biedstrop and Reynard Soileau when they said, "Wanna see us rattle up some worms?" I was a guest, so I said, "Sure," and they pulled their pickup truck to the side of the road. Reynard grabbed two sticks from the back of the truck. One of them had a line of notches running up its whole length. He rubbed the smooth stick over the notches and it made a rattling sound. Within seconds, the ground erupted with hundreds of wriggling worms. Something about the vibration of the notched stick just drove them to distraction. So if you know a place where there are worms, this trick is a pretty foolproof way to get a mess of 'em.

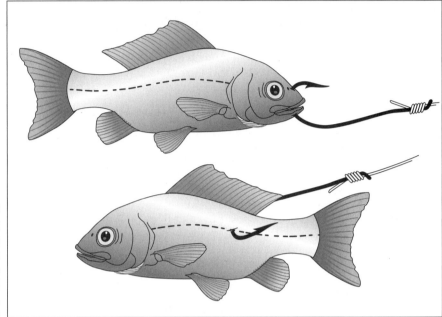

Figure 12-2:
Two ways
to hook a
minnow
or small
baitfish.

Be careful when you cast. If you really muscle it, you'll rip the minnow off the hook and watch it sail out over the water.

Crayfish, also called *crawfish* or *crawdads,* may be the best smallmouth bait. But other species of fish target them as well, despite their hard exoskeleton and threatening pincers. Look for crayfish under flat rocks in the riffles of a stream. You can catch them with a seine or net and some quick handwork. A good technique requires placing a net or seine just downstream from a rock, and then flipping over the rock. This will stir up the bottom where the crayfish live, and when the debris floats down to your waiting net, with luck a crayfish or two will accompany it. They can also be grabbed by hand, but you must be fast and careful to avoid getting pinched. Crayfish keep well in damp moss or in oxygenated water.

Hook a crayfish through its tail, as shown in Figure 12-3. Hooking it in this location allows the crayfish to move around freely so that it can attract the attention of foraging fish.

Grasshoppers and crickets: Hopping good bait

Crickets and grasshoppers make terrific bait for bass, trout, and all kinds of panfish. They struggle mightily when they hit the water, causing ripples and attracting attention from gamefish below. In late summer, when the fields are abuzz with jumping grasshoppers, fish are particularly keyed in on them. You can fish them on the surface, under a float, or on the bottom.

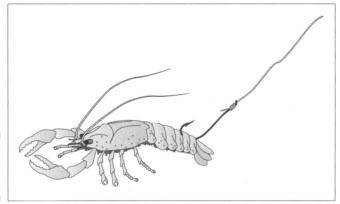

Figure 12-3:
A hooked crayfish.

You can load up on crickets at most baitshops, but you'll probably have to catch your own grasshoppers. Using a dipnet helps, and you can use the same net you'd use for catching crayfish. Going out first thing in the morning increases your odds, too, as the dew and chillier temperatures will slow grasshoppers. Store them in a jar (poke some holes in the lid) or in a cricket tube. Add some grass for them to chew on.

You hook a grasshopper through the collar just behind the head, as illustrated in Figure 12-4. You need to cast delicately because a hard cast may rip the collar away from the body.

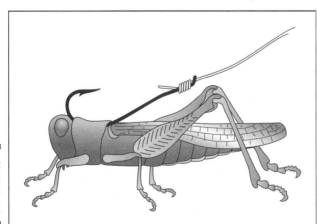

Figure 12-4:
Hooking a grass-hopper.

Leeches suck, but fish like them

Dark and slimy, leeches are pretty ugly and guaranteed to turn off small children and sensible adults. Having said that, they make good bait for many species, including walleye. Don't worry about them attacking you and sucking out all your blood. They won't be that interested in you.

More popular in northern waters, leeches can be bought at baitshops just like minnows. Like minnows, leeches come in different sizes (or *grades*). Some baitshops even sell leeches online and ship them to you. You can catch your own by placing a perforated can of dog or cat food or a piece of bloody meat on a rope. Hang it from a dock and check it often. Leeches will be drawn to the scent and attach to the meat. You can keep them for days in the refrigerator. (You might label the container, though.) When storing or transporting leeches, make sure their water is clean and cool. If the water starts to appear milky, change it.

Hook a leech through the sucker in the tail, as seen in Figure 12-5, and it will try to swim away. This is a good thing. Its body stays fairly straight when it's trying to swim, which helps counteract the leech's tendency to ball up on your hook. Leeches have a sucker on both ends, but hook the tail end.

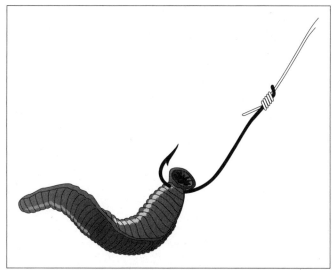

Figure 12-5: A leech hooked through the sucker.

Salmon eggs

When the great runs of Pacific Salmon make their spawning journey up the rivers of the northwestern United States, both the grizzly bears and the rainbow trout are very happy. The grizzlies love it because the streams are full of spawned-out, weak, easily caught salmon. The rainbows love it because the streams are full of delicious, easy-to-catch salmon eggs. (Of course, those rainbows that get eaten by the aforementioned grizzly bears are probably not that happy.)

It's not easy to gather your own eggs, so you'll need to buy your preserved salmon eggs at a local baitshop.

The eggs of salmon are delicate, and casting them requires the kind of soft touch that you use for crickets and grasshoppers. Figure 12-6 shows how to hook one. You should use a special hook, a short-shanked, rounded-gap brass hook, which you bury completely in the egg to give the hook maximum holding power and castability.

You can also prepare a *spawn bag* by placing a few eggs in mesh nylon netting. Your hook holds better in the mesh.

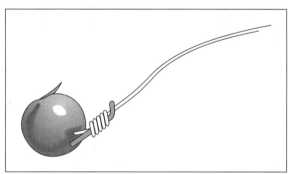

Figure 12-6:
Hooking a
salmon egg.

Common Natural Saltwater Baits

If it lives in the ocean, something else in the ocean eats it. Saltwater fish are opportunists, which means that if they get an opportunity, they eat. Like their freshwater cousins, however, saltwater fish do have preferences, and the biggest tarpon or striped bass might prefer, at times, a tiny two-inch worm to a big juicy herring.

As with freshwater fishing, you have choices when it comes to baiting up for saltwater fish. You can either offer a general bait, such as shrimp, or a specific bait meant to match exactly what your gamefish is feeding on. Either way, get fresh bait, keep it cool, and present it as naturally as possible. (See Chapter 15 for more on livebait rigs.)

Buy your bait from a baitshop or catch your own. Saltwater baits are often exposed when the tide falls. Just remember to follow all local laws concerning the capture of bait.

Clams and mussels on the half-shell

Fish, like people, find shellfish easier to eat when the shells are removed. Cut the bait into bite-sized pieces, particularly for flounder or fluke. Using a big piece of soft bait allows the fish to pull the bait off the hook without alerting you. You'll have to remove the meat from big clams, but smaller clams can simply be crushed and baited that way.

You can find clams and mussels during low tide. Cutting them open and leaving them in the sun for a bit will harden the meat inside, making it easier to hook.

Marine worms: Salty nightcrawlers

Fishermen use a number of worm species for bait, including sand- and clam-worms, but bloodworms are the most popular. Cut off a piece of bloodworm and the liquid that squooshes out looks like blood. These many-sectioned, pincer-headed worms give freshwater hellgrammites a run for their money in the ugly department, and they can be very effective bait. As with mussels and clams, use small pieces for small fish. For bluefish and stripers, use a whole worm hooked right behind the head.

Bunker: Bait school

Bunker, or *Atlantic menhaden,* are a prolific baitfish off the east coast of the United States. They arrive in huge schools, and you can often see equally large schools of bluefish and striped bass slashing through them as they feed: a sight that never fails to excite anglers. When the bunker are in, you can snag them with weighted treble hooks expressly manufactured for this purpose. Heave your hook into the middle of a school of bunker, then reel in while really hauling back on your rod, and you might snag a bunker. Put it in a livewell or cooler, and when you have a half a dozen or so, you are ready to fish for stripers and blues, weakfish, and even tuna.

Squid: Easy and effective

It's hard to fish a squid incorrectly. Fresh or frozen, whole or in pieces, they are a preferred food for everything from tuna to striped bass, sea bass, and flounder. You can buy squid at baitshops, and it can be trolled, bottom fished, or cast under a float.

Shrimp and crabs: Fish like them, too

In many tidal flats, grass shrimp thrive in the underwater vegetation. When they get swept up in moving tides, they become a very good bait for striped bass, weakfish, redfish, bonefish, and just about anything else that feeds around beds of seagrass in shallow water.

You hook a shrimp by carefully threading the hook through the tail (see Figure 12-7). With this rig, the shrimp can still move about, attracting the attention of feeding fish. You can also hook them through the shell on top of the head. (No need to peel first.)

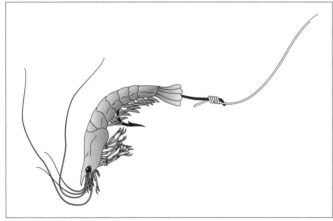

Figure 12-7:
Hooking
a grass
shrimp.

Crabs, both blues and fiddlers, make good baits for fish like grouper, tarpon, snapper, and redfish. Some anglers use big blue crabs when fishing deep water, and smaller fiddler crabs when fishing coastal waters. Hook crabs through the shell, once, in the corner. Some anglers believe it helps if you remove the claws. Crabs can be netted in tidal pools, caught in a trap, or lured out of hiding with a piece of meat on a string.

Mullet: More than a hairstyle

These good-sized baitfish run in huge schools. They make quite a distur-bance and never fail to distract me (Peter) from concentrating on what's on my line. You'll be standing there on some jetty and a school of mullet will break the surface with a loud whoosh. You think it's a big fish breaking water and you turn to see all these little rounded mullet snouts sticking out of the water like seals in the zoo begging for a snack. Many fishermen capture their mullet by throwing a castnet into a school. Insert a hook into a live mullet the way you would a minnow. Redfish, bass, blues, marlin, and tuna all take mullet.

Ballyhoo: Funny but effective

These small fish are in the halfbeak family, named for their elongated bottom jaw. Ballyhoo look odd but work well as bait. You can catch them with castnets, but until you learn how to throw one, you can buy frozen or fresh ballyhoo in baitshops.

The baitfish are often trolled for marlin, but you can use them in coastal waters, as well. Hook a strip of cutbait once on the edge of the strip so the bait flows naturally from the hook.

Eels: The ultimate slime

On the east coast of the United States, especially in the northeast, eels are about the best striper bait going. They move about and make a lot of commotion. And they're big enough to make a nice meal. They are also the slimiest thing since Jiffy Lube. If a live eel drifting in the tidal current doesn't call up a striped bass, there might not be any around.

To hook an eel, while holding it with a towel or rag, insert the hook through the jaw and nose, as shown in Figure 12-8. You can fish them on jigs or bottom rigs.

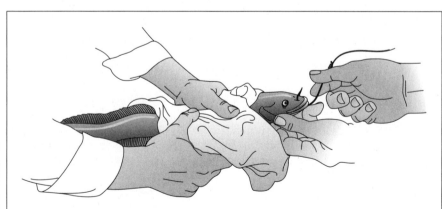

Figure 12-8:
Hooking
an eel.

Stay put, you little bugger! In addition to being slimy, eels are very strong, and they wriggle like crazy. Put some ice in the bucket with your eels, enough to keep the water chilled in the bottom of the bucket. The cold calms them down so that they don't squirm out of your hand and wriggle all over the boat.

Why You Can't Take It with You: Disposing of Leftover Bait

You never want to run out of bait while fishing. If you do, it often means the fish are biting better than you expected, and suddenly you reach into the bait bucket and realize you're out of bait. You'll find you never run out of bait on the slow days, when you're probably ready to head home, anyway. Instead, you'll run out of bait in the middle of a dream fishing adventure. So bring enough bait to last for your entire trip.

But what if you overestimate your bait needs? Greg's younger brother, the baithound, has to be physically pulled away from bait-gathering. He'll throw the castnet until his arms fall off. He never wants to run out, so instead he tries to bury us in slimy shad. But what about leftover bait? Sadly, it's not wise to simply dump your baitbucket into the water after you're done fishing. In fact, it may well be illegal to do so.

Dumping extra bait into other waters carries many risks. For one thing, minnows bought in a baitshop might be diseased or otherwise unhealthy for the local fish population. You don't want to spread diseases in your favorite lake, do you?

More importantly, carrying bait from one body of water to another can help the spread of *invasive species,* an organism introduced outside of its natural range to disastrous effects. In short, return any unused bait back into the place where you got it. If that's not possible (baitshops won't buy back unused bait), kill any bait you have left. It's the only responsible thing to do. However, many kinds of bait can be frozen. When thawed, it may work nearly as well as fresh bait. So, to sum up: Store fresh, live bait in the refrigerator and dead bait in the freezer. (And good luck with your housemates.)

Chapter 13

It Only Looks Alive: Tricking Fish with Lures

In This Chapter

▶ Figuring out what makes a lure a lure

▶ Understanding how plugs work

▶ Catching up with spoons, spinners, and spinnerbaits

▶ Grasping the benefits of jigs and soft baits

*W*hen fishing with bait, you're offering fish a chance to eat something they can digest. Sometimes you're fishing with something they eat all the time, anyway, like using gizzard shad for stripers. Fishing with a *lure,* though, means fishing with a device intended to merely trick a fish into think-ing it's found something to eat. Fish bite for different reasons: to eat, to defend a territory, or out of predatory instinct. Lures come in many shapes, and offer a wide variety of actions, sounds, and appearances, but each one is designed to trigger a fish's willingness to bite, whether it does this on the surface of the water, a few feet down, or on the bottom. Either the lure already looks like something to eat, or you fish it in such a way that it looks good enough to eat.

Although fishing with bait works for obvious reasons, there are many advan-tages to fishing with lures. Lures can be reused many times, whereas bait is often done after one fish chomps it. Lures can be cast repeatedly more easily than bait. And bait can be messy, inconvenient or costly to buy, and hard to gather — lures allow you to head right to the water without worrying about getting bait first. This chapter introduces you to most of the lure categories and also helps you figure out exactly how to choose the right lures for you.

Picking Perfect Plugs

A *plug* is a lure, often made of plastic or wood, that looks like a baitfish or other creature that fish want to eat. Also known as *crankbaits,* plugs can swim, dive, pop, or burble, but they are all alike in that they look and act like prey. (A few are molded to look like crayfish or even insects, but most look like baitfish.) Plugs cast well and come in an array of shapes and sizes. Some are colored to look like fish, whereas others come in every color of the rainbow. Most use treble hooks, and some incorporate rattles to attract fish. Plugs are built to fish specific areas of the water column: Some remain on the surface; others dive to several feet; and still others dive nearly 20 feet below the surface.

You should acquire a variety of plugs, and it's a good idea to have a couple of plugs for every "layer", or depth, of water. The following sections explain the different kinds of plugs, moving from surface plugs to deep divers.

Popping and chugging plugs: Designed for surface explosions

Popping and *chugging plugs* are designed to imitate frogs, mice, little birds, insects, and other nonaquatic creatures who find themselves out of their own element and in the fish's world. Because predatory fish often watch the water's surface for their next meal, these plugs attract fish by disturbing this plane. Poppers and chuggers have concave, hollowed-out faces, and this scoop pops and chugs against the water when you jerk the lure. (You don't retrieve poppers and chuggers steadily — they call for more of a jerk, pause, jerk retrieve.) Fish hit these lures with abandon, and anglers love the excitement of seeing a fish strike. Sometimes a popper (like the one in Figure 13-1) can pull a nice fish from its lair even at high noon on a sunny day. They tend to work better in warmer water and when fish are actively feeding.

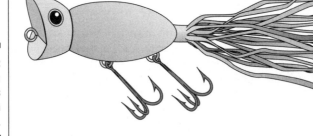

Figure 13-1:
The Hula Popper is great in freshwater.

Plunking a Hula Popper, a classic popping plug, beside a lily pad and giving it an occasional pop or chug has lured many bass (and quite a few pike) over the years. Let the Hula Popper (or similar lure) hit the water, and wait until the concussion rings subside. Then give it another pop. Wait again. By using the plug that way, the Hula Popper stays in the fishy zone longer.

Pond fishing often calls for restraint with a Hula Popper, but casting an Atom into a wolf pack of marauding bluefish calls for a different understanding of fish psychology. When a great deal of bait is in the water, you want to draw attention to your plug so that the fish keys in on it and ignores the thousands of other baitfish all around. A loud, splashy plug, fished very fast with a jerky motion, often works in this situation.

When fishing with all poppers and chuggers, sometimes the excitement of the surface strike of a large fish can rattle you. You'll be watching the plug, resting calmly on the surface while the rings of your last pop dissipate, when suddenly a fish will rocket to your lure from below. But wait! Don't set the hook until you see that the plug has disappeared, meaning the fish has the lure in its mouth. Sometimes fish miss the plug on the first attack, and setting the hook too early might jerk the lure away, preventing the fish from taking another whack at it (which they often do).

Wobblers: Great if you lack finesse

Not as common as poppers and chuggers, a *wobbler* is a surface plug meant to be retrieved steadily, allowing it to produce a constant chugging sound. A Jitterbug, a classic wobbler, sounds like an old car engine sputtering far in the distance. This plug catches fish without requiring a great amount of finesse on the part of the angler. We recommend the Jitterbug (shown in Figure 13-2) right up there with the Rapala (see the sidebar "If Peter had only one lure" for more on this particular lure) as a newcomer's tool: The appropriate action has been designed into wobblers like the Jitterbug — all you have to do to attract a bass or pike to it is reel it in at a few different speeds. The wobble will take care of the rest.

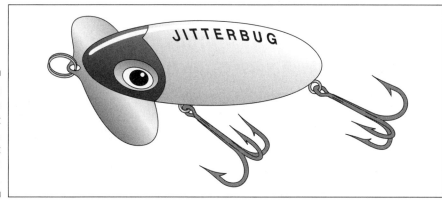

Figure 13-2:
The Arbogast Jitterbug, a great American wobbler.

Stickbaits and propbaits: Some take some skill, and some do the work for you

A *stickbait,* until you do something to it, just lays there on the water like — you guessed it — a stick! Usually cigar-shaped, a stickbait needs to be jerked, twitched, and popped by the angler before it has any action. For this reason, it takes a little practice to master the back and forth pattern they call "walking the dog." Really, you just need to jerk and pause, jerk and pause, while holding your rod tip low and to the side. This will make the lure dart left, then right. Bass and other predatory fish can't resist this wandering lure. The Zara Spook is a popular stickbait.

Propbaits, short for propeller baits, look like stickbaits with little propellers on one or both ends. Propbaits, like the Devil's Horse shown in Figure 13-3, *chug-plop-gurgle* and wobble around, all of which are good features that gain the attention of predatory fish in the neighborhood. The propellers move in two different directions, so they don't twist your line.

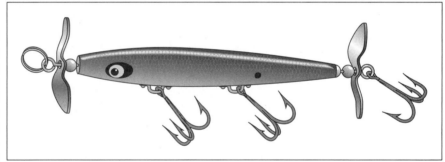

Figure 13-3:
The Devil's Horse is a stickbait with fore and aft propellers.

Floating/diving plugs: Classics that work, even for beginners

Floating/diving plugs float until you begin to reel them in. With many of these plugs, the faster you reel, the deeper they dive (although even deep-running plugs have a cutoff depth beyond which you cannot fish them). A number of fine plugs swim at or near the surface. The Rebel Minnow is one of these, and the Mann's 1-Minus is another. Some plugs are designed to suspend in the water when paused, and a few sink, but most plugs fit into this floating/diving category.

If Peter had only one lure

My favorite lure is the Rapala, which is a plug made by the Rapala company of Finland. I love the way this plug lands in the water; and even more, I love the way that it moves in the water. I've caught bass, trout, pike, bluefish, and even tarpon on the Rapala. *Outdoor Life* once sent me to Finland to research the story behind these phenomenal plugs that had become so popular all over America. What I found was an unusual story for a sport-fishing lure.

At the turn of the twentieth century, Americans began to make a plug called a *wobbler*. The wobbler was a little wooden fish that wobbled like a distressed minnow. Some of these plugs found their way over to Finland where a woodsman and fisherman named Lauri Rapala began to fish with them. You have to be a pretty fair fisherman to keep your family fed and clothed on your take from the lakes of Finland. These lakes are not very rich, and the fish — mostly trout — are few and far between. A good lure meant more to Lauri Rapala than a nice fishing trip. The plug that he devised, the one that came to be known as the Rapala, was designed for trolling behind a canoe-like boat paddled by Lauri. After a great deal of trial and error, Rapala's wobbler minnow began to wiggle and wobble behind him in a very tantalizing way. It caught fish better than anything ever had in those hard-fished northern lakes, and the Rapala went from being a commercial fisherman's preferred tool to one of the most effective weapons in the sport-fishing arsenal.

When buying floating/diving plugs, you'll find that the packaging informs you of the running depth of that lure. Sometimes the depth is incorporated in the name, such as the Rapala DT, or "Dives-To." The model DT04 "dives-to" four feet, and so on. A Mann's 1-Minus (great lure!) runs under 1-foot deep.

Some plugs dive deeper than others. In many cases, this deep diving is a function of the angle and size of the *lip,* the angled piece of plastic on the head of the plug. The sharper the angle of the lip and the faster the retrieve, the deeper the plug dives. With this in mind, you might cast your plug over a submerged weedbed that you know lies three or four feet below the surface. Weedbeds provide a number of food sources, and gamefish know this. As your plug travels over the weeds, you want to get it down to the level of the fish. If they don't see or sense the plug, they won't bite it. By experimenting with a few different retrieval speeds, you can see (and eventually feel) the depth at which your plug runs. Plugs in this go-a-little-deeper category include the Cotton Cordell Big O, the Rat-L-Trap, and the Rebel Wee-R (shown in Figure 13-4).

Many diving plugs dive only when you retrieve them. When you stop the retrieve, they float to the surface (which is a good thing to bear in mind when your plug is passing over submerged rocks and stumps). Instead of reeling furiously, let the plug rise to the surface, and you will avoid hanging up on underwater hazards.

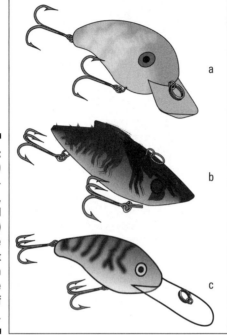

Figure 13-4:
The Big O (a), Rat-L-Trap (b), and Rebel Wee-R (c) are three plugs that work in the middle range of depth.

Deep divers: Good for hitting the bottom

Deep diver plugs are designed to dive deep quickly and stay down there. When fishing open, deep expanses of water, deep divers allow you to cover a lot of water, targeting fish near the bottom or suspended deep in the water column. Like other plugs, deep divers can be cast or *trolled* (pulled behind a boat to cover the maximum amount of water).

Depending on design, deep diving plugs work well at different depths, although no lure runs very well beyond 20 feet deep when cast unless the lure is weighted. Plug design allows them to move well through weeds and around obstacles, because the hooks tend to trail behind and under the plug. Shown in Figure 13-5 are two typical deep divers.

Suppose that the fish in the lake are *suspended* (or hanging out) at seven feet below the water surface. So you run to the tackle store and buy a lure that says that it runs at seven feet below the water surface. Next year, you return to the lake, and you have no idea which lure in your box is the seven footer. The solution is simple: Take a laundry pencil and write the optimum running depth on the belly of the lure.

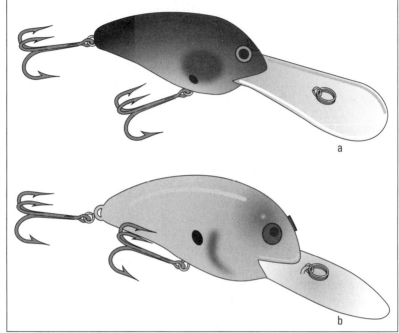

Spoons: Heavy Metal Time

In the old days, people fished with real tablespoons with hooks attached. If that's tough to picture, just take a look at the business end of a tablespoon. See how it's shaped somewhat like a fish? It also has some metallic sheen, and (by the nature of its design) it has shaded portions as well, so it presents that contrast between light and dark that is characteristic of many successful lures.

Today, fishing spoons and kitchen spoons share only the material they're made from. Spoons come in all sizes and colors, but almost all are metal and designed to sink. Spoons are built three different ways, to be used three different ways: cast, trolled, or jigged. Casting and trolling spoons look the most like a traditional "spoon." They wobble when retrieved and often feature an eye for your line at one end and a treble hook on the other. Jigging spoons are more elongated, and almost rectangular in shape. These are meant to be jigged — raised and lowered — vertically (done when fishing from a pier or boat).

Spoons can be fished different ways, and even topped off with a piece of bait or soft plastic. The appealing wobble and flash of all spoons make them a great lure for about every kind of fish that swims.

The champ came from Detroit

Back at the turn of the century, kids in the working-class neighborhoods of Detroit would take a trolley car to the end of the line and fish in the Detroit River. One of those kids, Lou Eppinger, grew up to run a small taxidermy and tackle shop. In 1906, he went on a fishing vacation in Ontario and brought a new spoon that he had designed. It was heavy — two ounces — so he could cast it with the clunky baitcasting rods that most anglers used in the days before spinning made light lures a possibility. Eppinger hammered out the metal so that it was thinner in the middle and thicker at the edges. This imbalance gave his spoon a pronounced wobble. The lure *almost* turned over when it was reeled in, but it *always* righted itself. Eppinger caught a lot of fish with the spoon, and when he returned from his vacation, he began to sell the lure that he first called The Osprey.

When World War I came along, the United States Marines made quite a name for themselves and began to be known as daredevils. Eppinger admired the Marines, but being a God-fearing man, he couldn't bring himself to write the word *Devil*. So, in honor of the Marines and in keeping with the teachings of his Lutheran pastor, Eppinger called his new spoon the Daredevle. Shown in the following figure, the Daredevle is one of the most successful lures for all kinds of fish. Midwestern pike fishermen swear by it, but so do Ozark smallmouth anglers, Louisiana redfishers, and even tropical bonefishers.

Spinners: Easy to Fish, Hard to Miss

Your basic in-line spinner is a metal shaft with a hook on one end, an eye on the other, and a blade rigged so that it spins around the shaft. The blade spins, and the lure spins and wobbles as well as it's pulled through the water. Quite often, a piece of animal hair, pork rind, or rubber is attached to the spinner to give it some extra length and wiggle. A basic spinner is shown in Figure 13-6. Most spinners are small — perfect for trout and panfish. But giant in-line spinners make popular lures for muskies and pike. Spinners can be cast and retrieved quickly, allowing you to cover a lot of water in a hurry, seeking out active fish.

Spinners spin, and a spinning lure that spins the way it was designed *always* twists your line. This line twisting can lead to all kinds of casting problems. The solution to these problems is simple: When using a spinner, always use a swivel tied several inches above your spinner (requiring three knots), or use a snap swivel (with one knot). (See Chapter 9 for information on snaps, swivels, and other terminal tackle.)

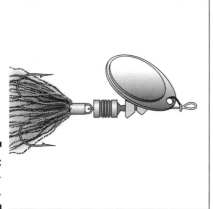

Figure 13-6:
A typical in-line spinner.

Spinnerbaits: The Masters of Bass

If spinnerbaits had mothers, even they would be hard pressed to say their little ones were good-looking. Made from a piece of bent wire, dressed with a few blades, some lead and a skirt, the *spinnerbait* (see Figure 13-7) is one of the most gizmo-like lures. But remember: It's not how a lure looks to you that's important. What's important is how a lure looks to a fish. A spinnerbait moving through the water looks like a baitfish or other animal doing its best to get away in a hurry. The vibrating blades also attract fish by sending out tiny shockwaves. This rapid action often triggers an attack response in *gamefish*, the predatory fish that go after fleeing prey.

Figure 13-7:
A spinnerbait attracts fish by creating flash and vibration.

A spinnerbait can be retrieved fast or fairly slow (as long as there's enough speed to spin the blades). Some anglers will *buzz* a spinnerbait by retrieving it quickly, so the blades create a disturbance on the surface. The idea of buzzing is to retrieve a lure so rapidly that it skims along the surface of the water, creating a great deal of commotion and leaving a bubbly wake. The advantage of this technique is that you can use it to cover a large amount of water, and fish are often attracted by all the fuss. This technique led to the *buzzbait*, a type of spinnerbait meant to be fished on the surface. With a rapid, steady retrieve, buzzbaits plow across the surface like a speedboat. Until a fish hits them, that is. (A typical buzzbait has a giant blade, as shown in Figure 13-8.)

Spinnerbaits typically use some of three kinds of blades: willow, Colorado, and Indiana. Colorado blades are round and produce more thump and vibration. This makes them a good choice for dark or cloudy water. Willow blades are narrower, giving them less thump but more flash. They work well in clear water, where fish are more likely to rely on sight to find the bait. Indiana blades are teardrop-shaped and somewhere in the middle. Any spinnerbait may use more than one blade, and may be a combination of these blade types.

Figure 13-8:
A buzzbait has turbine-like blades.

Jigs: The Ugly All Star

A *jig* is a piece of metal, usually lead, with a hook attached. Jigs cast well in the wind, and they sink rapidly. A jighead by itself could be just a weighted hook, but with the addition of feathers, plastic tails, and pork rinds, jigs (such as the Hammertail shown in Figure 13-9) can imitate all kinds of bait. In fact, sometimes jigs are tipped with a piece of real bait. Sometimes fish take a jig as it drops to the bottom. Or more commonly, the angler *jigs,* which means raising and lowering the rod tip to bounce the lure off the bottom. This motion stimulates a response in many fish. Jigs come in a wide range of sizes, both in terms of weight and hook size, and in a variety of styles. Some jigheads are round, others flat or football-shaped — each design works a different way. Any jig could be dressed with an added attractant on the hook: a plastic jig trailer, a pork rind, or a piece of livebait.

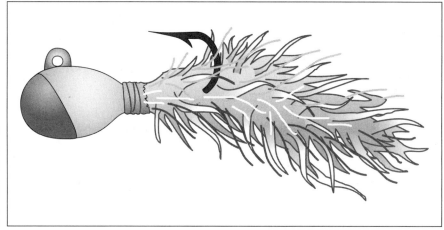

Figure 13-9:
The Hammertail, a typical bucktail jig.

The real advantage of jigs is that the weight is part of the lure, eliminating the need for a separate sinker. Thus, when choosing jigs, weight matters. Pick jig weights that match the conditions you're fishing. In still water, say a lake, a crappie jig weighing ¼ of an ounce will be effective for panfish. In a big river, jigs over an ounce could be used to cut through the current. In saltwater applications, jigs may weigh several ounces or more.

A whole family of jigs (universally used in saltwater but also popular in freshwater, too) look a bit like spoons but are fished like jigs. Lures like the Hopkins, the diamond jig, and the Kastmaster (as shown in Figure 13-10) are all jig-like in that they are heavy metal, they cut through the wind, and they sink fast. However, on the retrieve, they are fished more like spoons, where their shine and bait-fish-like motion attracts gamefish.

The Hopkins is a descendant of the old tin squids (so-called, I guess, because somebody thought they looked like squids). The Kastmaster is great for bluefish and the occasional striped bass. The diamond jig, especially when fished with surgical tubing, is a very effective surf lure if you fish it slow and hop it along the bottom. The tubing is soft on the fish's mouth, has the outline of an eel or a small fish, and comes in fish-attracting colors.

Figure 13-10:
Spoon-
like jigs: A
Hopkins
(a), a
Kastmaster
(b), and
a Diamond
jig (c).

Soft Baits: Plastic Worms and Beyond

Soft baits are no longer just another name for the classic plastic worm, a lure that has ruled the fishing world since Nick Crème poured the first plastic worm in his house in 1949. *Soft baits,* generally plastic, are all the baits that aren't hard plastic like plugs, or metal like spoons. These lures now look like crayfish, crickets, lizards, frogs, and mice. And they're not just made out of plastic anymore: Some companies have created formulas that look like plastic but are actually biodegradable and made of real food. Berkley, for example, has the Gulp! Alive! brand, featuring creatures that look like crayfish, shad, and lizards, among other things, and the lures are made with natural scents and tastes. Soft baits are fished the same way, whether they are totally synthetic or biodegradable. The sections that follow outline a few soft plastic baits and show you how to rig them.

Experiment with different types of soft plastic baits (like the ones shown in Figure 13-11). Depending on the kind of fish you pursue, you can probably find a soft plastic bait molded to match its prey. Soft plastic grubs and tubes dominate smallmouth bass rivers, for example, because they nicely imitate the crayfish of the smallmouth's diet.

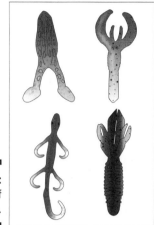

Figure 13-11:
A range of
soft plastics.

There are many kinds of soft baits available today, with more coming on the market every day. Most, though, fit into one of several categories. (And more importantly for you, they are rigged and fished primarily in one of several ways.) The following sections walk you through the three main kinds of soft baits:

✔ **Plastic worms:** Especially dynamite for bass, plastic worms come in many lengths and colors, and although some could pass for nightcrawlers, others have crazy twisted tails and metal-flake coloring! Like a jig (which we describe earlier in this chapter), a plastic worm can be taken as it lands, as it drops, or while it is bounced along the bottom. It can also be slithered off a lily pad or pulled off a log. In short, if you can think of a new way to fish a plastic worm, try it: Some fish somewhere may like it.

Soft baits and crankbaits are getting married these days, too. Some lures feature a molded plastic crankbait head, but a soft plastic body. The idea is to get the deep-diving swimming of a crankbait, but the natural feel and taste of soft prey.

Every angler needs a bag of plastic worms. They work well for bass, but other species, too, and can be rigged to be almost entirely snag-free. Black is a good color to start with — it's not too eye-catching to humans, but fish seem to love it, and it works in any water, regardless of clarity or time of day.

✔ **Jerkbaits:** Soft plastic lures, or *jerkbaits* (like the one in Figure 13-12), get their action from the way that the user retrieves them: fast jerks, erratic jerks, or trolling. Many anglers think that the action of these lures resembles the action of a distressed or injured baitfish, the kind of bait that predatory fish like stripers, bass, muskies, and pike find very attractive. Jerkbaits made of soft plastic are fished on jigheads, weighted hooks, or just rigged with an exposed hook.

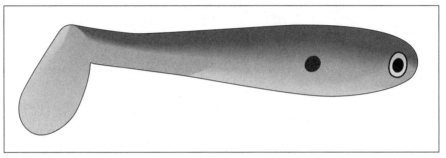

Figure 13-12:
Strike King
Shadalicious:
a great soft
jerkbait.

✔ **Swimbaits:** A few years ago, anglers in California started catching giant largemouth bass with *swimbaits* — big lures handcrafted to look almost exactly like baitfish (often the little trout that big west coast bass love to eat). Now swimbaits like the one shown in Figure 13-13 are popular, and the latest technology has created baits that look eerily alive. These baits are often made of soft plastic, although they are sometimes hard-bodied, too, and so detailed that every scale and fin is distinct. They are often hinged for lifelike swimming action. For serious fishermen only: A good swimbait might cost nearly $30! If your swimbait doesn't come pre-rigged with hooks, make sure you buy the right hook for it. You may need a weighted hook, for example, to ensure the bait swims correctly.

Figure 13-13:
The
amazingly
detailed
Lucky Craft
swimbait.

Narrowing Your Lure Options by Asking Some Key Questions

Literally thousands of lures are available. From dual-propellered, double-jointed rattlers as big as a Hummer (or at least they seem that way) to tiny leadhead bucktail jigs, and from little scale models of trout that look absolutely lifelike to floating salads of rubber legs and metal blades that look like something that came to life in the junkyard of a toy factory — so many lures are available that you could go bankrupt buying them all. (Some of the newest lures might cost more than 20 bucks . . . apiece!) But many are just endless variations on a theme. Others have been improved upon by new technologies. Know what to buy so you don't have to buy them all.

The following sections present eight questions you should ask when buying and using lures.

How deep does the lure run?

If you want your lure to catch fish, you need to make sure it goes deep enough to attract the fish where they're hanging out. If the fish you're hoping to catch are suspended five feet below the surface, you're probably going to have to go to them (that is, you must fish at their level) rather than have them come to the surface. On the other hand, if they are busy feeding on the surface, a deep-running lure won't be very effective. And if you're fishing in shallow water, or over a weedbed, a deep-running lure will continually snag the bottom or the weeds — not a very effective presentation.

Where's the action?

When you retrieve the lure, think about how the lure moves. Does it wobble and shimmy, does it dive and surface, does it burble and pop, or does it chug and sputter? Any of these characteristics can serve either to excite a fish or to turn it off. The same noisy lure that may entice a bass out of its shadowy hole on a hot day is guaranteed to send a bonefish on a beeline for the continental shelf. Different actions suit different fish. Different water also dictates different action. (The pronounced action that spurs a bite in off-color water can be a real loser in clear water.)

How fast is the lure designed to move through the water?

Make sure you know the optimum range of speed for any lure you're considering so you can fish at its ideal pace. Because of the advances in reel-making technology, a few cranks of a reel's handle can move a lure through the water more swiftly than was possible in the old days. This fast response is good because sometimes a fish (like a pike or muskie) flashes after a swift-running lure while it ignores a slowpoke. However, many old standby lures act very erratically when you crank up the speed. Fish the lure at the speed the lure was designed to be fished.

How big should the lure be?

Although the general rule of "big bait, big fish" is usually a good one to follow, the optimum size of a lure is important and it may vary from place to place. In one place, for example, trout may grow fat on grass shrimp. In another, trout may be keyed in on alewives. Whatever the case, you want to use the right size lure to attract them. This rule of thumb doesn't mean that your lure must always slavishly imitate the size of a fish's food. Sometimes, a little bigger lure works well. At other times, a much bigger lure works better. I can't tell you what the right size lure is in any given situation, but fish can and do. If you're not getting any bites, switch to a larger (or smaller) lure. Experiment until you start getting bites.

Does the lure raise a ruckus?

In the sense that sound consists of vibrations, and all fish sense vibrations through their lateral lines, then all lures produce sound. The question that you need to answer is this: What sounds turn fish on, and what sounds turn them off? As with everything in angling, no hard-and-fast rule applies, although certain tendencies apply under certain conditions. For example, in the bright light of day, a big, noisy lure (such as a Jitterbug; see the earlier "Wobblers: Great if you lack finesse" section) may not do very much to attract bass. At night, however, the gentle chugging of a Jitterbug can be just the thing to attract a bass in low-light conditions. Some lures, like the Rat-L-Trap, rattle like BBs in a can when retrieved.

Does a lure's color count?

Fish respond to color, but they don't see color in the same way that you and I do. Take the color red. Red is the first color of lure that many people pick out, but after a red lure goes very deep in the water, that vibrant scarlet turns to dark gray. The thing to remember about color is that water absorbs color differently than air, so the brilliant hues of a lure in the air of a tackle shop may not even be visible to a fish in the water. Also, sunlight makes colors appear differently at different times during the day.

Water clarity matters when it comes to choosing the color of your lure. If the water is exceptionally clear (you can tell this just by studying the water near the bank), naturally colored lures work well. In other words, fish your lures that mimic real prey, like the plug painted to look like a shad (especially if the fish in that body of water feed heavily on shad). If the water is murky, try your lures painted in brighter, less natural colors. Stained or muddy water calls for bright chartreuse spinnerbaits or bright orange plugs.

Ultimately, you always want to look at color from a fish's point of view. Some years ago, I (Peter) was fishing on the Esopus Creek in the Catskills, one of the historic streams of American trout fishing. Late in the afternoon, the fish were taking pink mayflies with purplish wings. I caught one of the mayflies in my hat and held it up to the sky. Seen, in silhouette, the mayfly had no color but black. I didn't have any purple and pink flies with me, but I picked an orange and yellow fly out of my box that was the right size and shape. I held it against the background of the sky. Seen against the backlight of the sky, its color was black too, and its silhouette was similar to that of the pink may-flies. What I learned was this: If you are fishing on or near the surface, color doesn't make much difference if the fish's view is from below.

Is glittery good?

The answer is yes; so is the contrast between light and dark, and so is iridescence. All of these qualities of light reflection suggest the play of light shining through water on the scales of a moving fish. For example, the Daredevle spoon, which is probably the all-time fish taker in American waters, is nothing more than a lure (with alternating wavy bands of red and white) that wobbles like a frantic fish. The shape, the wobbling motion, and the optical effect of the contrasting colors all trigger a feeding response in many gamefish.

Do taste and smell matter?

Whether taste and smell matter depends on whether the lure is hard, like a crankbait, or soft, like a plastic worm. With hard lures, it's hard to imagine them becoming impregnated with any kind of scent. But with soft lures, some anglers swear scent makes a difference. In fact, the latest technology allows for manufacturers to produce soft lures out of natural ingredients, making for a lure that is biodegradable and similar in taste and smell to the natural prey it is imitating. Other anglers buy sprays that are spritzed onto soft lures to coat them in scent.

Chapter 14

Fish Don't Fly, But Flies Catch Fish

. . . .

In This Chapter

▶ Figuring out what a fly is

▶ Getting to know mayflies

▶ Distinguishing a wet fly from a dry fly

▶ Examining ten great flies

. . . .

*O*nce upon a time, when the only fish you fished for with a fly was a trout, a *fly* was a bit of feather and fur on a hook. It was always meant to look like an insect (specifically, a mayfly). But these days, fly fishers angle for trout, smallmouth and striped bass, redfish, bluefish, blue marlin, bluegill, tarpon, carp, flounder, salmon, and on and on. So a *fly* no longer simply means "something that looks like an insect." But anglers who use a fly rod to deliver concoctions that look like shrimp, eels, baitfish, baby robins, frogs, mice, and crabs still refer to the thing on the end of their line as a fly.

The key thing about a fly is its weight — or lack thereof. Bait and lures all have some weight to them. The minnow, crankbait, or plastic worm and sinker that you cast with a baitcasting or spinning rod is heavier than the fishing line. The weight of the thing at the end of your line bends your rod and is catapulted to where you want to fish. A fly, on the other hand, has almost no weight. Using a heavy fly line in a bullwhip motion carries the fly to your target. The fly, when properly delivered, seems to sail to the target and land as softly as a snowflake. When stealth and delicacy are required, a fly may work well when nothing else seems to do the trick.

This chapter covers many of the popular flies that work well in a variety of applications. Saltwater fly fishing often calls for heavier gear and larger flies. The flies detailed here work especially well in freshwater and for the most common quarry of the fly fishing angler: the trout.

Taking a Look at Where the Fly in Fly Fishing Came From

To best understand what anglers mean when they talk about "matching the hatch," it's helpful to understand mayflies. Figure 14-1 shows you the life of the mayfly, which begins life as a little crawler on the bottom of the stream. On the last day of its life, it sprouts wings, flies up into the bright summer sky, and, in a grand climax, mates for the first time while in midair. It then immediately dies and falls to the surface of a clear-flowing stream.

The following sections give you a look at the life cycle of the mayfly, which is of paramount interest to the trout and the fisher of trout. Why? Because terms that you come across again and again in fly fishing — wet flies, dry flies, and nymphs — all have their origin in the life cycle of the mayfly.

Immature little buggers: The nymph phase

A mayfly starts out as an egg on the bottom of a stream. Soon, the egg hatches, and out crawls a many-legged little critter known as a *nymph* — or immature mayfly. When you see trout with their noses down, rooting about on the bottom of a stream, they are often feeding on nymphs.

About one year to the day from when it began life as an egg, the nymph is ready to hatch and become a full-fledged mayfly. When fly rodders talk about a *hatch,* they don't mean what happens when the egg becomes a nymph. Technically speaking, this change is a hatch, but this type of hatch isn't of much interest to trout; therefore, it is of even less interest to trout fishermen.

Time to shed some skin: The emerger phase

The *emerger stage* begins when all the mayflies of a particular species — and millions of mayflies may be in a single stretch of a stream — shed their old skin, rise to the surface, sprout wings, dry themselves off, and (for the first time) fly. This process, which takes a few minutes for each individual fly, normally takes a few days to play itself out for all of the flies of a given type on any given stream. Usually, a hatch begins in the warmer waters downstream and moves upstream, which has relatively cooler waters.

In this period of time, between when they begin to shed their skin and when they first take flight, the mayfly is at its most vulnerable. When a hatch is on, the trout know that plenty of easy-to-catch food is around, just for the taking.

Figure 14-1:
The mayfly begins at the nymph stage and then becomes an emerger, a dun, and finally a spinner.

All grown up: The dun phase

When the mayfly has broken out of its old nymph case and is in the wriggling-out-of-the-wet-suit phase, it's often known as a *wet fly*. Many mayflies never make it to full-blown, flying-around mayflydom. For one reason or another, they cannot shed their cases and they just float on the surface as stillborns — stillborn, but still tasty to the trout. Most of the time, though, the mayfly does make it out of the case; and most of those that do rest for a while on the surface of the water, drying their wings and just generally getting their bearings. They're now known as *duns*.

You can easily tell if an insect is a mayfly in the dun phase because its two wings are folded back and stick up in the air like the sail of a sailboat. The mayfly may beat its wings every now and again in order to dry them, further attracting the attention of the trout. To the hungry trout, this is the sitting-duck phase. Because the mayfly instinctively knows that it may be gobbled up at any moment, it is in a hurry to get off the water. Because the trout knows this too, it will feed purposefully as long as there are mayflies on the water.

Ready to mate: The spinner phase

If a mayfly manages to survive the emerger phase and the dun phase, it is ready for one last change into the *spinner phase.* Shortly after becoming full-grown, a mayfly flies around for the first time and heads for a streamside bush or tree. After it reaches that sanctuary, its tail grows longer and its wings lose their milky translucence and become clear. Then, that evening or possibly the next day, the spinners fly over the stream and mate in midair. The male, having done his assigned job, drops to the surface of the stream and dies. The female deposits her eggs in the stream (where they cling to a rock, hatch, and start the nymph cycle all over again). Following this, the female joins her husband-for-a-day on the surface of the stream. At this time, a trout sees a huge amount of delicious mayfly meat that has no chance of escaping.

At this stage of the mayfly life cycle, known as a *spinner fall,* an angler can encounter some amazing fishing. In the case of some mayflies — particularly one of the biggest mayflies, the Green Drake, and the smallest mayfly, the *tricor-fithydes* or *trico* — the best fishing in the whole hatch is during the spinner fall.

Figuring Out Which Fly to Use

During any hatch, the trout may be keyed in on one phase of the mayfly's life cycle. If you can figure out what the trout are taking, you have a fighting chance to "match the hatch." This match-the-hatch principle is one of fly fishing's deeply held articles of faith: You try to give the trout a fly that looks like the food that it is currently eating.

Just as mayflies have different stages of life, different artificial flies represent each of those stages. We help you determine which fly to use and when in the next sections.

Opting for the dry fly

For most trout anglers most of the time, the *dry fly* — any fly that stays on the surface film of water and resembles a dead or hatching insect — is the preferred method of taking trout, likely because when a trout eats your dry fly, you get to see the whole thing. If and when the trout takes your fly, it engenders one of angling's great feelings (just as the plug fisherman gets a happy jolt when watching a largemouth slam a popping plug; we cover plugs and other types of lures in Chapter 13). Fish won't always take a dry fly, and you need to adjust if they're feeding, say, on the bottom of a stream. But most fish, sooner or later, are susceptible to dry flies.

However, a dry fly (shown in Figure 14-2) is not always the most effective method, and it doesn't always pull up the biggest fish (although there are times when it does both). The traditional dry fly has the following features:

- The tail is as long as the body.

- The tail is usually made of stiff fibers from the *hackle* (neck feathers) of a rooster. The hackle is what allows the traditional fly to float high and dry — just like a real mayfly.

- The body is made of fur or synthetic material wound around the hook with silk thread.

- The wing is traditionally made from the soft body feathers of a wood duck, but many other materials, from deer and elk hair to synthetics, work.

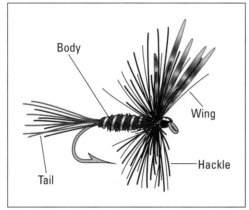

Figure 14-2:
The classic
dry fly.

Body

Wing

Hackle

Tail

Not every dry fly is tied to imitate a mayfly, and not every dry fly mayfly imitation has all of the parts in the picture. For example, I (Peter) often use the Comparadun on flat clear water. This mayfly imitation has no hackle, but it floats just fine. In most of the world most of the time, however, when people talk about a dry fly, they are talking about the classic mayfly tie illustrated in Figure 14-2. This is the dry fly that spawned a whole school of fishing and fly fishing techniques.

The spinners fall at the end of the hatch; and for the next few hours, you may have excellent dry-fly fishing. In this case, you can use a special kind of dry fly made to imitate the spinner; this type has a less-bushy hackle and wings that lie flat out rather than upright. (I fill you in on the spinner phase of the mayfly life cycle in the earlier related section.)

The whole idea of a dry fly is that is floats on the surface just like a natural fly. But fur and feathers and other fly-making materials have a tendency to get wet in the water (no surprise here). When you also consider the weight of the hook, you are dealing with something that naturally wants to sink after a while. So you have to do something to help the fly float. You can do three things to give your fly a fighting floating chance:

- ✔ **Use a floatant.** Some *floatants* (materials designed to waterproof flies) are gloppy and some are liquid, but all floatants are designed to keep the fly on top of the surface film. You don't need to heap floatant on, but you should use it. I find that rubbing the stuff between my thumb and forefinger and then rubbing my fingers on the fly avoids saddling my fly with a large gob of goo on top. Scotchguard wasn't designed for flies, but it really works well as a floatant, especially when you forget your regular floatant and are nowhere near a tackle shop.

- ✔ **Use a drying substance.** Also useful are commercial powders that work on the same drying-out, or *desiccant,* principle as cat litter. Use a commercial desiccant powder after you catch a fish, when the fly is wet and slimy, or when your fly starts to sink prematurely. Simply take the fly — no need to clip it off the leader — and put it in the desiccant bottle; then close the bottle and shake it. When you take the fly out, it is covered with white power. Blow off the loose powder. Give your fly a few false casts to remove any residual powder, and start fishing again.

- ✔ **Use the air.** Sometimes you run out of floatants and desiccants, or your floatant may have fallen out of your vest or you just plain forgot it. In these cases, swishing the fly in the air with a few crisp false casts usually dries out all but the most waterlogged fly for a reasonable float. In heavy, choppy water, however, you are simply not going to get much of a float without using a floatant or a desiccant.

Discovering when you may want a wet fly

Wet flies are called *wet flies* because, since they're submerged, they get wetter than dry flies. Back in the old days of fly fishing, wet flies served for everything: duns emergers, nymphs, and spinners. Figure 14-3 shows a classic wet fly, which has the same parts as the dry fly we describe earlier in this chapter but with a differently positioned wing. Instead of riding high and dry, a wet fly lays down on the water. Also, the hackle is softer (or *webby*) so that a wet fly rides in or under the film.

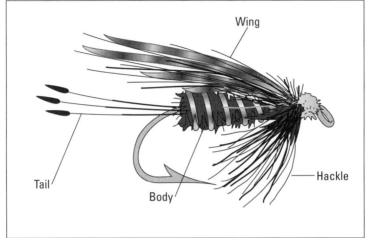

Wing

Tail

Body

Hackle

Figure 14-3:
An old-time
wet fly.

With the wet fly, the question always is, "How does an angler fish it?" The wet-fly fishing technique is more fully discussed in Chapter 16.

Going the nymph route

A *nymph* imitates the nymph stage of the mayfly life cycle and usually looks more like a natural nymph than a wet fly does. The wing is gone, replaced by a wing case and nubby fur that often imitates the gills that run along the side of a nymph's body (as shown in Figure 14-4). Fished free-floating, or with the purposeful action of a live nymph rising to the surface and hatching into a dry fly, the artificial nymph is a versatile fly that often scores when nothing else does. Remember, even during a blizzard-like hatch, more nymphs are in the water than drys are on the surface, and trout frequently continue to feed on nymphs through the hatch.

Of all trout flies, the artificial nymph looks most like the natural product (at least to the human eye). The wing case, thorax, abdomen, and tail all correspond to a stream-borne nymph.

Use the flies and methods that you are most comfortable with. In fact, this tip goes for bait fishing and lure fishing, too. If you have no confidence in a certain lure, fly, bait, or a certain technique, you cannot catch many fish. On the other hand, sometimes the "wrong" fly, fished with style and confidence, takes the fish. Or (put another way) it isn't always *what* you fish with, but the *way* that you fish with it that counts.

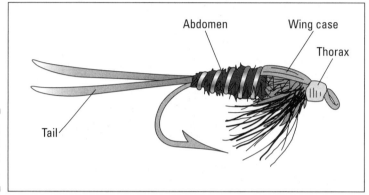

Figure 14-4:
A typical
artificial
nymph.

Labels in figure: Abdomen, Wing case, Thorax, Tail

Picking the meatier streamer fly

Trout, especially large trout, like to eat small fish. Whether the fish is one of their own kind or just a forage fish, such as a minnow, sculpin, or alewife herring, is not that important. To a trout, a baitfish (compared to a dry fly) provides much more meat on the hoof — make that meat on the fin. Anglers have long known this, and their attempts to imitate this favored food source resulted in the *streamer fly,* which looks like a feather held on its side (which also happens to look like a minnow).

A sideways feather has the rough outline of a fish: for this reason many streamer patterns started out as a pair of feathers tied lengthwise along the shaft of a hook. And many fish were caught, and continue to be caught, with simple streamers. Some more developed streamers have hackle feathers wound around the head of the hook to give the fly more lifelike motion in the water. In addition to feathers, bucktail has long been used as streamer material. I (Peter) think that deer hair (like much of the fur and hair of land-dwelling animals) works so well in flies and other lures because it behaves like living material. Marabou feathers also work well when attached to streamers, as do a whole range of synthetic materials that shine, sparkle, and wave seductively.

The Gray Ghost shown in Figure 14-5 is a classic feather-based streamer first tied by Carrie Stevens (one of the founding mothers of American fly-fishing) in the Rangeley Lakes region of Maine at the turn of the century. Decades later, Don Gapen revolutionized streamer fishing with his deer-hair sculpin imitation, The Muddler Minnow.

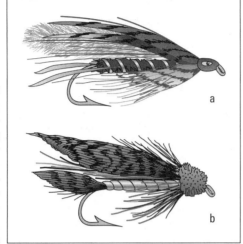

Figure 14-5:
A Gray
Ghost
streamer
fly (a) and
a Muddler
Minnow
streamer
fly (b).

Choosing the caddisfly

A *caddis* is a type of insect found in most trout and smallmouth streams. Trout and other fish prey on caddis in addition to the mayfly, which makes a caddisfly another alternative for you. However, using a caddisfly, which can be fished like a dry fly, is like traveling in coach class compared to fishing with a mayfly imitation (that's considered first-class trout fishing).

Pick up a rock from the river bottom, turn it over, and chances are you can see some immature mayfly nymphs scurrying for safety. You may also notice a number of little cocoons made of twigs or small pebbles. These little cocoons are *caddis cases.* Inside the cocoons, the caddis larvae grow to their next stage, *the pupa stage,* which is sort of the booster rocket for the mature caddisfly. When the caddis pupa is ready to hatch, it often moves very swiftly to the surface, emerging from the water like a Polaris missile going straight up. Unfortunately, a caddis doesn't usually do as well as a Polaris missile on its first flight attempt. The fly often falls back to the water and tries to take off again. It keeps flapping its wings, bouncing and skittering on the surface. All this activity, both above and below the surface, can excite the trout into feeding. Later, when a swarm of caddis descends on a stream to lay eggs, the trout are on the lookout for these *ovipostitors* (egg-laying insects).

You can tell a caddis from a mayfly when they are on the water because caddis wings don't stick up like little sailboats (which is how many anglers traditionally describe the upright wing of mayflies). They lay flat.

Look at the water

You come down to a stream and see a bunch of rising fish. "Oh, boy!" you say to yourself as you tie on a mayfly imitation. You float a dry fly over the trout a dozen times. The trout continues to rise in a very splashy way, sometimes leaping clear out of the water. You are excited, but nothing happens with your fly. "Must be taking emergers," you say. You tie on a wet fly (or maybe you use a special pattern that looks like an emerger). You fish with great concentration, looking for the slightest twitch in your line. The trout keeps rising. You're starting to dislike this trout. It really is thumbing its nose (or maybe "finning its nose") at you. "Hmm, Mr. Trout must be taking a really teeny fly that I can't see," you tell yourself as you give up on that fish and go after another splashy riser.

What went wrong? Very often a splashy rise means *caddisflies*. As the caddis pupa rockets to the surface, the trout follows it, trying to get up a head of steam that results in an attention-grabbing rise.

Remember: Next time you get to the stream, rather than casting blindly to a rise, you should study the water to see what's *really* happening.

Anglers aren't as finicky or precise about caddis imitations as they are about mayfly imitations. A typical artificial caddis has a body like a mayfly, but the caddis wing is tied in a down position, and the hackle is often wound through the body (the flytier's term for this winding technique is *palmered*). This kind of hackle breaks up the light pattern on the surface of the water and, from the trout's vantage point, gives the fly a skittering kind of appearance.

Getting bigger with stoneflies

The biggest insects in most trout streams are *stoneflies*. You will find stoneflies most commonly in riffles because they seek highly aerated water. A stonefly nymph looks like a big mayfly nymph. When stoneflies hatch and sprout wings, they crawl up on rocks and climb out of their cases while perched on these rocks. That's why you can see many of their dried cases on exposed rocks in midstream.

Trout usually take live stonefly nymphs, and they rarely see examples of stonefly dry flies, except for the spectacular salmonfly hatch in the Rockies. This early season hatch was made for duffers. Things like delicate presentation and light leaders, which count for a lot with the hatch of smaller flies on placid water, don't matter so much as long as you can plop a really big dry fly on the water and give it a decent float.

The Montana nymph in Figure 14-6a looks like a large mayfly. Its palmered hackle suggests the gills that run along a stone fly's abdomen. Like a mayfly nymph, the artificial Montana nymph has a bulging wing case, a tapering body, and a tail. The salmonfly imitation, shown in Figure 14-6b, is also big and bushy.

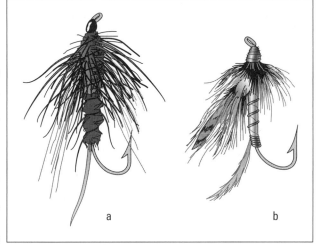

Figure 14-6:
Two stonefly patterns: the Montana nymph (a) and the salmonfly (b).

a

b

Usually just a bass thing: Popping bugs

The popping bug shown here is usually made out of molded plastic or carved cork. It has a concave face that makes a burbling *pop* as you retrieve it. When fished correctly, you just know that a popping bug is going to catch fish. Of all kinds of bass fishing, this technique is my (Peter's) favorite, and it may be right up there as my favorite overall fishing technique. However, popping bugs are not confined to bass fishing. I once caught a six-pound brook trout from under a lily pad in northern Quebec while using a popper, and I have taken both snook and tarpon on poppers.

Extra: Terrestrials

Sometimes, no mayflies are hatching, no spinners are left over from yesterday's hatch, and no nymphs are getting ready to hatch (you may see trout feeding). You may be able to interest them in feeding by using a *terrestrial,* which could be an imitation of an ant, a beetle, a grasshopper, and the like. They're called terrestrials because their natural environment is on land, not water. When a passing breeze or a sloppy jump deposits one of these land-lubbers in a stream, the terrestrial insect is (in a manner of speaking) a fish out of water. And the fish know it.

Late in the season, when most of the big hatches are finished (but grasshoppers are plentiful), terrestrials can make up a large part of the trout's diet, especially on windy days when many insects are blown out of the bushes and trees. And when the grasshoppers are hopping, a big Muddler or hopper imitation can lure a trout from its lair, even when no natural flies are on the water.

A Rundown of Flies That Work Everywhere

Zillions of pages have been written about flies. Every fly angler has an opinion, a favorite fly, a neat little trick. Although I (Peter) have no doubt that every situation has a best fly, you can spend years learning these situations and I would much rather spend my time fishing. If you want to learn a great deal about a great number of flies, don't take this as a warning not to learn. Your continuing study can pay off. Still, as the years go by, I find that I catch more fish with a smaller selection of flies. I really believe that a well-presented fly that gives the *impression* of the real thing is often just as effective as a fly that *duplicates* whatever it is that the fish are eating. And sometimes, the best strategy is to go against the hatch and give the fish something that stands out from the crowd.

So this section contains a list of ten flies that I always carry. In time, you may make up your own slightly different list; but I guarantee that your list will have a good number of the flies I'm recommending here because they are tried-and-true fish catchers.

The Ausable Wulff

This member of the Wulff series of flies is named after the most famous angler of the twentieth century, Lee Wulff, who was born in Alaska in 1896. One day in 1934, Lee, who was a commercial artist, was quite upset when a friend of his was fired just a few weeks from retirement. So he told his boss what to do with his job. "I never wanted to compete for money again," Lee later said. He spent that summer camping out on the Esopus Creek in the Catskills. One night, during a hatch of the mayfly known as the Dark Hendricksen, he tied a fly using bushy deer hair for the wing instead of the less-buoyant wood duck feathers of the standard Hendricksen pattern. The new fly, the Gray Wulff, worked well in the high and roily water, and a new style of dry fly was invented. The Ausable Wulff, a variation on the same theme, is lighter in color than the Gray Wulff, and I (Peter) find it to be an excellent *prospecting fly* (one you use to search the water when no fish are rising). It works especially well in riffly pocket water. I usually carry an assortment of these Wulffs in sizes 12, 14, and 16. (See Chapter 9 for more on hook sizes.)

Clouser's Minnow

This lead-eyed bucktail streamer may be the most versatile fly to come along in the last 30 years. It was invented by bass angler Bob Clouser for his home-waters on the Susquehanna River. It has proved effective for many freshwater species (as well as such saltwater species as bluefish, redfish, and striped bass). To a fish, a Clouser's Minnow (shown in Figure 14-7) can look like a small bait fish, a large shrimp, a sand eel, and probably many other things. The lead eyes give the Clouser's Minnow a kind of dipsy-doodle motion that often provokes gamefish. Carry it in sizes 2, 4, 6, and 8.

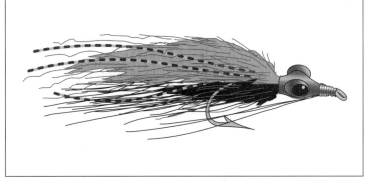

Figure 14-7: Get a bunch of Clouser's Minnows in a bunch of sizes.

The Comparadun

Al Cauicci and Bob Nastasi, two buddies who fished the very challenging waters of the West Branch of the Delaware, devised these no-hackle, deer-wing flies so that they would float flush in the *surface film,* the thin layer of stuff floating on the water's surface. I (Peter) have found that Comparaduns really score well with highly selective fish. I especially like them when the little yellow mayflies known as Pale Morning Duns are hatching, which they do with great frequency on the blue-ribbon waters of the Rocky Mountains. The Comparaspinners, also no-hackle with *spent deer hair wings* (that is, wings that lay flat and to the side, like outriggers) are the best spinners I know. Size varies depending on what's happening, insect-wise, on the water.

Dave's Hopper

In late summer, in the grass-bordered streams of the Rocky Mountains, a late-afternoon wind can be counted on to deposit a number of big grasshoppers on the streams. You can rarely see a more-explosive strike by a trout than when it attacks a struggling hopper being carried along in the current. There are many hopper flies, but none have worked better for Peter than the one devised by the great bass-and-trout angler, Dave Whitlock. As for size, catch a hopper in your hand and that's your size.

Elk Hair Caddis

Although elk hair gives this fly extra buoyancy, it still has a sleek and delicate profile. The Elk Hair Caddis is a very good prospecting fly when you see a few splashy caddis rises. I usually carry sizes 14, 16, and 18.

Gold Ribbed Hare's Ear

The Gold Ribbed Hare's Ear is a general impressionistic nymph that picks up flash from gold wire coiled around its body. The fur used to tie this fly comes, as its name suggests, from the ear of a hare. It is gold, brown, white, and black in color, and its texture is stubby and filled with many short hairs that stick out at all kinds of angles. To a hairdresser these short hairs would be thought of as unsightly split ends. To a fish, this unkempt look is very buglike. In recent years, some anglers have been fishing the Gold Ribbed Hare's Ear with the addition of a shiny metallic bead head that gives it both a jigging action and some more flash. Carry this one in sizes 8, 10, 12, 14, and 16.

Griffith's Gnat

This little all-purpose fly, invented by John Griffith, the founder of Trout Unlimited, is the one I (Peter) go to when there is small stuff on the water. The hook of the Griffith's Gnat is wrapped with a body of peacock herl (fibers of peacock feather) and a palmered small hackle from a grizzly rooster (which has multicolored feathers of white, black, and gray). To the fish, I think that all those neck fibers sticking out must make Griffith's Gnat look like a buzzing little bug. I've used this fly for gnats, tricos, midges, and ants. It is one of those flies that fish often take even though it may be bigger than the natural insects on the water. Carry this fly in sizes 16 through 22.

The Muddler Minnow

Many of the great flies are kind of like folk songs or legends: They're really good, but nobody knows where they came from. Quite often, many people had a hand in the fly's creative process. Not the Muddler Minnow. Don Gapen observed that sculpin (a bait fish) make up a large part of the diet of game-fish. To imitate this bait, Gapen took some deer hair and tied it in long strips. He spun it into a ball and then gave it a crew cut to create a bulbous head. Voilà! The Muddler Minnow was born. Fished under the surface, it looks like a sculpin. Fished another way, we're sure that it's taken as a crab. Greased, it's often taken as a hopper. And you can fish all three ways on any cast simply by adjusting your retrieve. Carry Muddlers in sizes 2 through 12.

The Variant

A Variant is a dry fly with no wings. Instead, you rely on the hackle to give the impression of the buzzing appearance of insect wings flapping at great speed and breaking up the light that shines through them. In his later years, Lee Wulff fished for trout almost exclusively with Variants. And the great Art Flick, a famous fisherman and fly-tier, was a major fan of Variants. When Variants are tied the way that Flick tied them (with oversize hackle and a slim body made from the center quill of a hackle feather), they're the most deli-cate of dry flies. For some reason, I (Peter) have always thought of these clas-sic Variants as the fly fishing version of the simple but beautiful designs of the Shakers who lived just one mountain range over from the Catskill Mountains where Wulff and Flick fished. Carry the Variant in sizes 8 through 18.

The Wooly Bugger

When you can only have one fly, many fly rodders will tell you that the Wooly Bugger is probably the one fly to have. With its simple body and a long supple feather tail, this fly catches fish everywhere. Depending on what size of Wooly Bugger you use, it can be taken for a stone fly, a leech, a minnow, or a worm.

I (Peter) will never forget a day on a slough full of enormous rainbow trout in Argentina. Nothing was hatching, and there was no visible sign of fish. I tied on a Wooly Bugger and stripped it in six inches at a time (that is, I retrieved it in short pulls). I caught fish after fish, up to an unbelievable 11 pounds. When one fish struck, I pulled back to set the hook with such violence that the hook pulled out of the trout's mouth, and my momentum carried the fly over my head and into the water about 20 feet in back of me where another five- or six-pound rainbow took the Wooly Bugger on my backcast! This was the ultimate case of using the right fly at the right time. Carry this fly in sizes 4, 6, 8, and 10.

Part IV
Now You're Fishing

In this part . . .

You'll find straightforward advice and clear illustrations on how to tie effective rigs, cast all kinds of rods and reels, and even set the hook and fight a fish. Here, too, is a chapter dedicated to the techniques you'll use to pursue all kinds of fish in all kinds of water. In this part, the world of fish and angler come together.

Chapter 15

Tying Popular Fishing Knots and Rigs

- -

In This Chapter

▶ Practicing basic knot-tying techniques

▶ Knowing a handful of super knots

▶ Understanding how to use fixed and slip-float rigs

▶ Using standard bottom rigs and river rigs

▶ Adapting all rigs to meet your water's conditions

- -

*R*eading about the fish you can catch in Chapters 4 and 5 will get your blood pumping, and it's exciting to look at Part III of this book and think about the various ways to fool those fish using bait, lures, and flies. Chapter 9 covers the all-important terminal tackle like hooks and snaps, and Chapter 8 tells you what you need to know about line. What's left? The crucial link in the middle of this chain — the knots and rigs you use to connect your offering to the line.

Knots are a compromise. Some knots weaken your line, but you need them to attach all your lures, hooks, and sinkers. You couldn't very well go fishing without tying on a hook! Every fisherman loves a particular knot or two, and you'll find your favorites, as well. Some popular fishing knots have been around forever, whereas others were developed in laboratories within the past year. (As new lines are developed, new knots often follow — knots designed to work best with particular lines, like braided or fluorocarbon, for example.) Some are easy to tie; others seemingly require four hands and a magnifying glass.

A knot's goal is to connect your line to something without failing in the heat of battle. A rig's goal is to present your offering to the fish in a way that looks natural and appealing. In this chapter, we give you a handful of reliable, easy-to-tie knots, as well as a few basic rigs. Generally, use the simplest rig you can get away with, requiring the fewest number of knots. The simpler a rig is, the quicker it is to tie, and the less likely it is to fail at some juncture. But, with luck, the knots you tie will hold and allow you to bring a big fish to the boat or bank.

The Knots You Need

The rigs that are covered later in this chapter are formed with a series of knots. Even a simple presentation — such as casting a lure or fly — requires one solid knot. Although every link in the chain connecting you to the fish — including the reel, rod, line, snaps, lure, etc. — could conceivably fail, the knots you tie are the most likely culprit when something breaks. Technicians in labs can measure the point at which knots fail, and the best knots break at close to or over the line strength. (Say, a knot tied with 14-pound line breaks at close to 14 pounds of pressure, or the line breaks before the knot fails.) But a poorly tied knot will unravel long before the line breaks, probably at a fraction of the pressure required to part the line.

The importance of practice is preached throughout this book, and knot-tying is no exception. Learn these knots well, and you'll be able to tie them quickly and efficiently, even in the rain or near darkness. Soon, your fingers will tie them without you even thinking about it.

Every knot you tie is better when you follow these basic steps:

1. **Pull the tag end of your line through the hook eye and leave plenty of room to tie your knot (maybe 12 inches or so).**

   You can always trim off the excess later.

2. **Form the knot, spit on it, and then snug it up with a firm, steady pull.**

   That's right — moisten the knot with your saliva or water to reduce friction. (The heat can harm your line.) This results in a snugger, tighter knot that holds better.

3. **After tying, wetting, and snugging the knot, the tag end will stick out. Trim this to about ⅛ to ¼ inch with nail clippers (cut the end too close and the knot will pull out).**

4. **Inspect and test the knot by pulling on it firmly before casting.**

   Better it fails on the bank than in the water. If the knot looks odd or ragged, or if the line seems nicked or kinked near the knot, cut it off and retie. Cast only what you think are perfect knots.

Rather than attempting to learn 20 knots, we recommend that you master the 6 that we walk you through in the following sections and commit them to memory. If you want to learn how to tie other knots, including the Improved Clinch knot, a simple search online will turn up many good Web sites with step-by-step instructions and even how-to videos.

Picking up on knot-tying lingo

Most knot-tying instructions use a few standard terms. These terms are pretty self-descriptive, but just to make sure that we are all on the same page, here they are:

✔ **Tag end:** The end of your line. This is the part that does the knot-tying. When you are finished tying, the tag end is the sticking-out part that you clip. (Use nail clippers for best results, unless you're using braided line,

in which case you'll need to use wire cutters or scissors designed to cut braided line.)

✔ **Standing line:** The rest of your line that runs up toward your reel.

✔ **Turn:** Sometimes called a *wrap*. A turn occurs when you pass the tag end completely around the standing line.

The Arbor knot: It helps if the line is tied to the reel

Actually, you should finish fighting your fish (or the fish should finish with you) a long time before you get to the knot that connects your line to your reel. But even if you never get into this extreme predicament, you need to tie the line to your reel. (For more info on putting new line on a reel, see Chapter 8.) We suggest that you use the Arbor knot, which is shown in Figure 15-1.

Here's how you tie one:

1. **Pass the tag end around the center post of the reel spool and tie a simple overhand knot, passing the tag end around the standing end.**

2. **Take the tag end and tie another overhand knot with it.**

3. **Pull on the standing line until both overhand knots come tight against each other and against the center post.**

The Trilene knot: Connecting your line to hook (and about anything else)

This knot was developed by the folks at Berkley, for use with their Trilene monofilament, but it works with all kinds and brands of line. Similar to the Fisherman's knot or Improved Clinch knot, the Trilene knot ties easily and holds up well in harsh conditions. I (Greg) have used this knot for decades and I can't recall when it last let me down. The line will often break before this knot fails, making it a 100-percent strength knot when well tied.

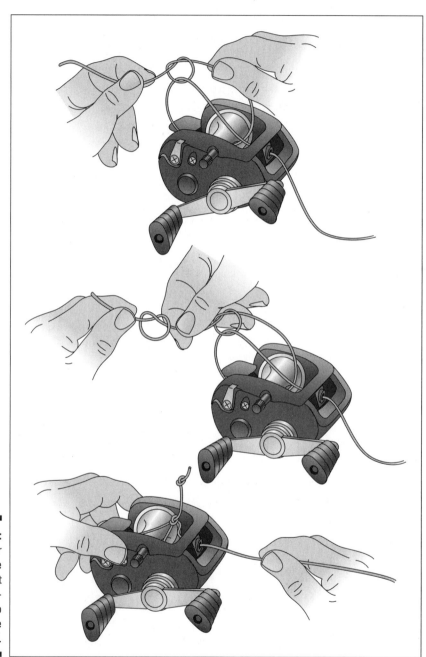

Figure 15-1:
The Arbor knot is one of the best and easiest ways to attach line to a reel.

Use this knot to connect your line to a hook, lure, or fly, as well as when using swivels to form various rigs.

To tie the Trilene knot, as shown in Figure 15-2, follow these steps:

1. **Run the tag end of the line through the eye of the hook and pull 8 to 12 inches of line through the hook eye.**

2. **Pass the tag end through the eye a second time, forming a small, double loop you can maintain with your forefinger and thumb of your nondominant hand.**

3. **Wrap the tag end around the standing end for three to five wraps or turns.**

4. **Now pass the tag end through the double loop next to the hook eye.**

   You will have formed another loop by making your wraps.

5. **Wet the loops with some saliva to lubricate the knot.**

6. **Hold the bend of the hook and standing line of the line in one hand, then pull with steady pressure on the tag end with your other hand.**

   If you are not sure about safely holding the hook, grip it firmly with needle-nose pliers.

7. **Tighten slowly.**

8. **Clip the tag end so that only ¼ inch is left.**

The Palomar knot: An easy classic

The Palomar knot is a bit of an oddball because it requires you to double a length of line before you pass it through the eye of your hook or snap. You can use this knot to connect about anything to your line, and it works well with all kinds of line, including braided. I (Greg) use it to tie sinkers to river rigs, as it's easy to tie and can be quickly whipped together in the dark. Like the Trilene knot, the Palomar retains more than 100 percent of the line strength, and can be tied with all kinds of line. (In fact, in some tests with some lines, the Palomar outperformed the Trilene. But both are excellent knots.)

To tie the Palomar knot, as shown in Figure 15-3, follow these steps:

1. **Double the tag end of the line and run the double line through the eye of the hook and pull 8 to 12 inches of looped line through the hook eye.**

   If the eye of the lure is too small to easily allow the double line, run the line through once, pull through 12 inches, and then run the line back through the eye before you proceed to Step 2.

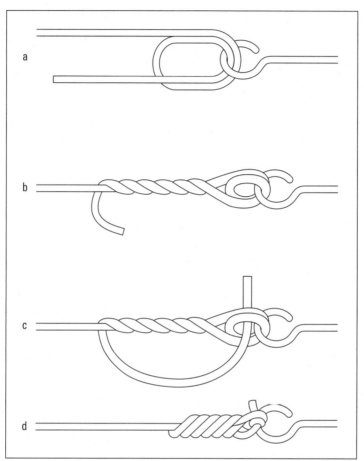

Figure 15-2:
The Trilene
knot.

2. **Form an overhand loop in the double (looped) line.**

3. **Pass the hook or snap (whatever it is you're tying on) through the small loop formed beyond the overhand knot.**

4. **Wet the loops with some saliva to lubricate the knot.**

5. **Hold the bend of the hook in one hand, then pull with steady pressure on both the tag end and standing line with your other hand.**

   If you aren't sure about safely holding the hook, grip it firmly with nee-dle-nose pliers.

6. **Tighten slowly.**

7. **Clip the tag end so that only ¼ inch is left.**

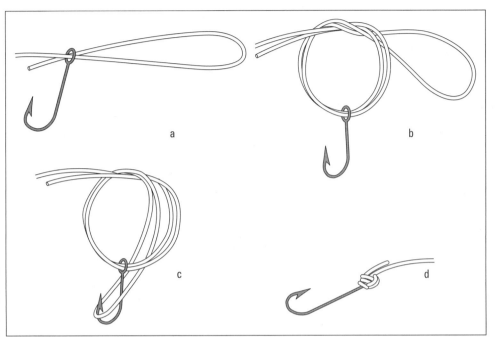

Figure 15-3:
The Palomar
knot.

The Surgeon's knot: Easy for tippet to leader

The well-known fly fishing author Doug Swisher uses a Surgeon's knot to join the last length of his tippet to the leader, and he convinced Peter to do the same. (See Chapter 16 if you're unfamiliar with the terminology of fly fishing gear.) This knot got its name because it's the same one that surgeons use to close up their handiwork. I (Peter) use it to join two pieces of line that are similar in diameter. More than one fly fishing buddy has turned his nose up at my scraggly looking Surgeon's knot. Hey, it may not look great, but it works great. And if a surgeon feels that this knot is dependable enough to close up a wound, I am willing to trust it to haul in a trout.

To tie the Surgeon's knot, just follow these steps:

1. **Lay about 10 inches of tag end on top of your standing line, as shown in Figure 15-4a.**

2. **In one hand, hold about four inches of standing line and the tag end and make a loop. Pinch the loop together between thumb and forefinger (see Figure 15-4b).**

3. **Take the other end of the tag end and the end of the standing line and, passing it through the open loop, wrap them twice around the two strands of your loop (see Figure 15-4c).**

4. **Using both hands, pull evenly on all four strands (see Figure 15-4d and e).**

5. **Wet the knot with saliva when you're just about ready to finish pulling the knot tight.**

6. **Clip the tag ends, as shown in Figure 15-4f.**

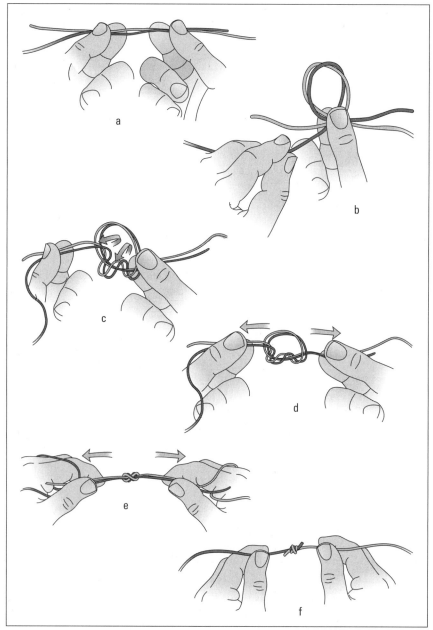

Figure 15-4:
The
Surgeon's
knot.

After a little practice, you'll see that the Surgeon's knot is easy to tie. After you know how to tie this very well, practice tying it in a dark room or step into a closet and tie it. Knowing how to tie a simple knot in the dark can be a handy skill. (I leave it up to you to explain things when someone opens the closet door and finds you standing there with two lengths of fishing line in your hands.)

The Perfection Loop knot: For leader to butt in fly line, among other things

The Perfection Loop is another of those less-than-gorgeous-looking knots. I (Peter) use it to connect my leader to the butt of the fly line. I also use this loop to make droppers for 8-ounce sinkers when I am fishing live eels for stripers 80 feet down in the currents of Hell Gate on the East River in New York. In other words, the Perfection Loop is a versatile knot. It is very fast to tie, and (like the Surgeon's knot) you can do it all by feel in almost total darkness.

Check out Figure 15-5 and follow these steps to tie a Perfection Loop:

1. **Create a 1½-inch loop and pinch between thumb and forefinger.**

2. **Repeat the action, creating another smaller loop around the first loop and pinch again (see Figure 15-5a).**

3. **Run the tag end between the two loops and continue to hold everything pinched together (see Figure 15-5b).**

4. **Pull the second loop through the first loop, as shown in Figure 15-5c, and start to tighten the knot (see Figure 15-5d), providing the final tightening with a pair of pliers.**

Will snaps save you from knot-tying?

Snaps, covered in Chapter 9, are designed to make it easier to change lures. Instead of tying on every lure, you simply tie on a snap, and then clasp and unclasp the snap to change lures. Easier? You bet. Some snaps incorporate a swivel, as well, which helps eliminate line twist. Snaps can make your life easier, but they come with a price. Not only are they one more thing you need to buy, but their weight can deaden the action of some lures and make your hooks appear more obvious or garish in the water. For that reason, many experts advise you not to use them at all. Depending on where and how you're fishing, though, you might be able to get away with using a snap.

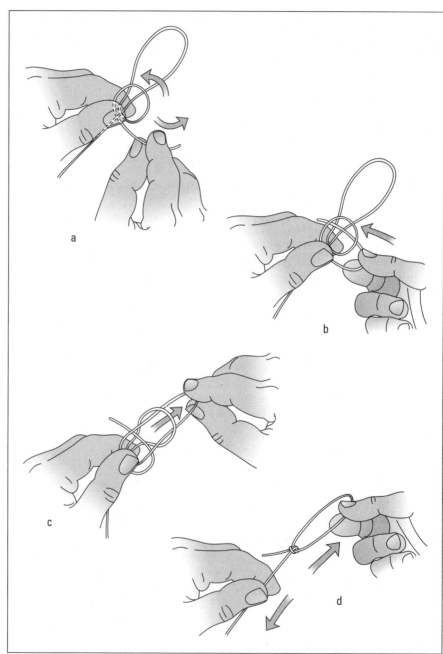

Figure 15-5:
A perfect
Perfection
Loop.

The Albright: Joining fat line to skinny line

When joining wire to leader or backing to fly line, I (Peter) use the Albright knot. This knot works well even if the two pieces being joined are very far apart in diameter.

Here's how you tie an Albright:

1. **Make a 3-inch loop in the heavier piece, as shown in Figure 15-6a.**

2. **Pass the tag end of the lighter line through the loop for 7 to 8 inches, as shown in Figure 15-6b.**

3. **Pinch the loop and the light line together and take the tag end and wrap it six times, trying to include the new wraps in your pinch (see Figure 15-6c).**

4. **Pass the end of the line you have been using for wraps back through the loop on the same side that it entered (see Figure 15-6d).**

5. **Pull gently on both ends of the lighter line so that the wraps slide up against the end of the loop, as shown in Figure 15-6e.**

6. **When everything is lined up and fairly snug, give a good firm pull (not a yank) to finish the knot.**

The Albright knot sounds and looks a little complicated, but as you tie it, you see the logic to it. It really isn't hard to make.

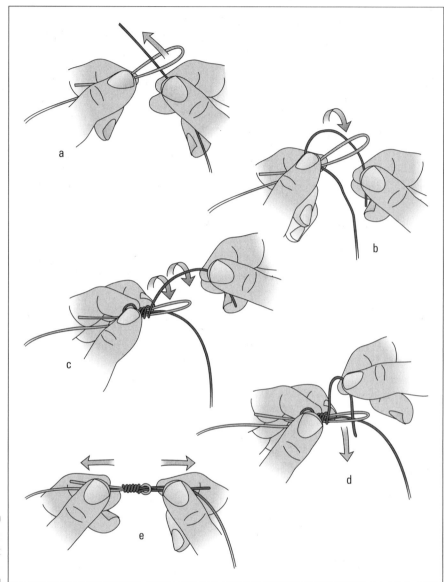

Figure 15-6:
The Albright
knot.

Using the Right Rig to Present Your Offering

After you know how to tie a handful of knots, it's time to master a few basic rigs. At its simplest, fishing only requires one knot on the tag end of your line:

the one tying on a hook, lure, or fly. Sometimes that's all you need. You might walk to a pond, tie on a Hula Popper, and start casting.

Sometimes, though, an angling situation will call for a more complex presentation. *Rigs* are methods of presenting a hook to fish, often involving sinkers, floats, or swivels. Different rigs work to reach fish in different environments and present your offering in a natural way. A fish holding on the bottom of the river in strong current or in the bay during a strong tide will be impervious to most float rigs — the current will simply sweep the hook and float away. A river rig, though, is too complicated and unnecessarily bulky for slack water. Knowing when to use the following basic rigs — and how to tie them — should enable you to fish in almost any fresh- or saltwater application.

Rigging most soft plastic baits: Texas versus Carolina style

You can rig plastic worms and similar lures in many ways. The easiest would involve tying on a sizable hook (maybe a 3/0 or 4/0) and then embedding the hook into a soft plastic bait and fishing it weightless. Many, many fish have been caught using this method. The weightless method shines in shallow water, or when fish are suspended near the surface.

However, in deeper water, or when fish are holding closer to the bottom, two additional ways of rigging soft plastics will get you through most situations: the Texas rig and the Carolina rig. First, the rig from Texas:

1. **Put an in-line bullet-shaped sinker on your line before you tie the line to the hook.**

2. **Push the point of the hook through the head of the plastic worm about ½ inch.**

3. **Pull the hook point out through the side of the head of the plastic worm.**

4. **Push the hook through the plastic worm until the eye of the hook comes up against the head of the worm.**

5. **Turn the hook so that the point faces the body of the worm and bury the hook point in the worm as shown in Figure 15-7.**

   Make sure the hook point isn't buried within the body of the worm, and parallel to it, or it won't hook a fish. The point should be covered but ready to come back out of the plastic should a fish strike.

Figure 15-7:
Use the
Texas rig for
weighted,
weedless
maneu-
vering.

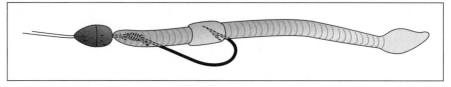

Now consider the Carolina rig, shown in Figure 15-8, which allows you to fish deeper while still allowing the worm to float off the bottom. The sinker will telegraph the bottom composition to you as it bounces over rocks and sand:

1. **Put a slip sinker up to ½-ounce on the line above a swivel, and tie on the swivel using a Trilene knot.**

2. **Tie a leader of 12 to 18 inches to the other end of the swivel using another Trilene knot.**

3. **Tie the leader to the hook using a third Trilene knot.**

4. **Thread the plastic worm on the hook in the same way that is shown for the Texas rig.**

Figure 15-8:
Use the
Carolina
rig to stay
above
trouble.

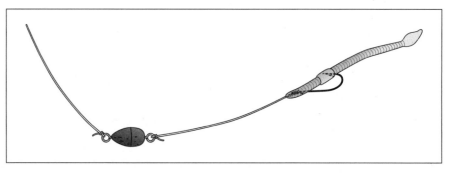

These three rigs — weightless, Texas, and Carolina — should allow you to present almost any soft plastic lure you own to fish at almost any depth. Vary the size of the sinker to match the conditions, using the least amount of weight you can get away with.

Rigging jigs

Jigs are lures that often use a hook with a weight pre-fitted around the eye. These *jigheads* vary in size and shape, and can be topped with a piece of livebait or a soft plastic. Jigs eliminate the need to add weight or a leader to a rig because the hook comes complete with a lead or steel head. For this reason, jigs are easy to fish — simply tie on one, add a minnow, bit of bait, or plastic, and cast away. Jigs are often fished by retrieving the lure in hops along the bottom.

Notice in Figure 15-9 how you can rig jigs in different ways. An exposed jig is simply tied on and fished, with or without additional toppings like bait, whereas other jigheads are meant to be buried within soft plastic lures. In that case, only the hook point shows.

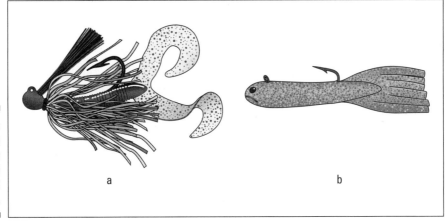

Figure 15-9:
Hooking up
plastics:
exposed (a)
and
rigged (b).

a   b

Livebait Rigs: For Presenting Bait in Any Situation

Livebait works because it's something the fish are used to eating. But for livebait to really work, it should be presented in a way that looks natural to gamefish. You need to get your bait down to where the fish are, and you may need to hold it there until a fish finds it. Livebait rigs make this presentation possible.

Livebait rigs have evolved over time, as anglers have discovered different way to present baits with rigs that are easy to tie, cost-effective, and successful. You, too, may find a new way to tweak one of the following rigs to work even better in the waters you fish. The best livebait rigs do the following things:

 ✔ Minimize the number of knots required.

 ✔ Minimize the number of swivels and other pieces of hardware.

 ✔ Present the bait in a natural way while minimizing tangles and snags.

Livebait rigs can be divided into two classes: those designed with floats to present the bait from above, and those that utilize sinkers to present the bait on or near the bottom. A few rigs use both sinkers and floats, but they are still either floating or sinking rigs.

Fixed-float rigs: Classic bobber presentations

When fish are suspended near the surface, and the bottom is particularly snag-infested and treacherous, a fixed-float rig may be ideal. The red and white bobbers you remember from the cane poles of your youth (or your grandfather's youth) work well in fixed-float rigs.

Basically, a fixed-float rig means a float is attached to the line at some distance above the hook. Often, these floats feature a spring-loaded wire that clamps to the line, or the float is pegged to the line using tiny rubber bands. If necessary, a small split-shot sinker may be added to the line just above the hook to add casting weight. (See Figure 15-10 for an illustration of this common rigging.) The rig is cast out, and when a fish bites, the float jiggles or disappears altogether. This kind of float rig allows you to wait the fish out — your bait simply hangs suspended in the water column, visible and clear of snags, until some fish decides to eat it.

Because the float is attached to the line, you must cast with the float and the line between float and hook swinging above the tip-top on your rod. If the float is tagged more than a couple of feet above the hook, this makes for an unwieldy cast. For that reason, most anglers will only fish fixed-float rigs if they intend to fish within three feet or so of the surface. Casting with more than that much line between the float and the hook is just about impossible.

Slip-floating away: How to fish a float at any depth

Because of the casting limitations of fixed-float rigs, some enterprising angler came up with a way to take advantage of the float's benefits, while still fishing deep in the water column. Enter the slip-float rig.

Figure 15-10:
Rigging a
standard
float rig.

A slip-float rig requires a more complicated rigging than the standard fixed-float rig, but it's still easy to prepare:

1. **Start with a clear tag line coming from the rod. Then, slide a bobber-stop on the line.**

   Bobber-stops are made of rubber, or can be purchased as pre-rigged knots. Or you can tie your own using a scrap piece of line. Whatever you use, a bobber-stop should be placed on the line first. Slide this up and down the tag line — this will control the depth of the hook.

2. **Slide a small plastic bead onto the line to keep the bobber-stop from sliding into the float.**

3. **Add a slip-float.**

   Usually, these are floats with a hole drilled in them from top to bottom, so the line slides through the float itself. Other floats can be turned into slip-floats, as long as they have a hole that the line can slide through.

4. **Tie a hook to the end of the line. Then add a split-shot sinker or two to the line just above the hook, to help the line slide through the slip-float.**

When you cast, the baited hook will pull line through the slip-float until the float and bead hit against the bobber-stop. When that happens, the hook stays suspended at the depth below the float. See how that works? You can adjust the depth you're fishing by sliding the bobber-stop up or down the line, as shown in Figure 15-11.

After a slip-float rig is prepared, you can easily adjust the depth as you fish different areas. If your float lies on its side, that often means your hook is resting on the bottom and not pulling the line taut to the float. Adjust accordingly until you start getting bites. Slip-floats let you fish from near the surface to near the bottom, and every depth in between.

Bottom rigs: Waiting out a bite

Although float rigs catch plenty of fish, some species prefer to feed on or near the bottom. In both salt- and freshwater, fishing near the bottom can put you in touch with some big fish that cruise there, looking for crayfish and other prey that live among the rocks and sand.

But placing a hook on or near the bottom is asking for a snag. After all, crayfish live there for a reason — they love all the rocks, logs, nooks, and crannies! A good bottom rig will allow you to fish near these snags, but still retrieve your hook when you want. No bottom rig is entirely snag-proof (no rig is, period), but a good rig will save you some snags.

Figure 15-11:
Rigging a
slip-float rig.

If your bait is heavy enough, you can simply tie on a hook, bait it up, and cast it out. It would eventually come to rest on the bottom. When making short casts or fishing shallow water, that may be all the rig you need. Most situations, though, call for more weight. More weight allows you to cast farther, lets your bait sink faster, and holds it there against the tide or current. The simplest bottom rig would require crimping a couple of split-shot sinkers to the line above the hook.

More advanced rigging calls for sliding weights. These rigs are still easy to tie, but they allow for a fish to take the hook without feeling the unnatural weight of the sinker. As covered in Chapter 9, sinkers allow you to customize your rig to fit the water in front of you. It pays to have a range of sinkers at your disposal. Always use the smallest one you can get away with. If the current sweeps your rig downstream, though, you need more weight.

For a standard sliding bottom rig, follow these steps:

1. **Slide the tag end of your line through an in-line sinker (a sinker with a hole through the center of it). An egg, walking, no-roll, or Dipsey sinker works well for this, although you could use just about any sinker.**

2. **Add a plastic bead to the line following the sinker.**

3. **You can tie the hook to the line next, allowing the sinker and bead to slide right down to the hook eye. (The bead will protect the knot.)**

If you worry about the sinker spooking the fish (it most likely will not), or if you want your bait to have more movement, don't tie the hook on next. Tie a swivel to the line next, instead, and then tie a short piece of line (called a *leader*) to the other eye of the swivel. And then tie your hook to the other end of the leader. This leader rig will still allow the line to run through the sinker, but the leader will keep the bait away from the sinker itself (see Figure 15-12). Some anglers use floating jigheads with this rig, instead of a hook. The floating jighead, sometimes brightly colored, suspends above the bottom, making it easier for fish to find.

If you're fishing from a pier, jetty or dock, or any kind of boat, a three-way bottom rig will work well for you. A three-way rig utilizes a sinker and a hook on two separate leaders, connected to the mainline with a three-way swivel, which is made precisely for this application. As you can see in Figure 15-12b, the three-way rig doesn't allow the fish to pull the line without moving the sinker. But if you maintain a snug line to the rig, you should have no problem seeing and feeling the take. Tie the sinker leader with lighter line, allowing it to break before the mainline if it gets snagged.

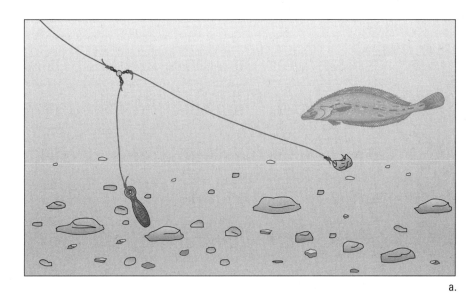

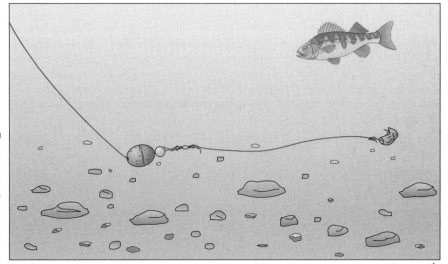

Figure 15-12: Rigging bottom rigs: a three-way rig (a) and a standard sliding rig (b).

a.

b.

River rig: For anything current

A standard bottom rig will work when fishing in current, but when fishing in rivers or tides, I (Greg) prefer to use a river rig. A river rig is similar to a three-way rig or a fishfinder rig, but with a few key differences. Rigs of this nature work best when the current lifts your bait up off the bottom. I would not use a river rig in a still water environment, simply because without current, this rig is more likely to tangle or spook fish. Again, a rig should match the circumstances, and still water bottom fishing works best (and simplest) with standard bottom rigs.

To rig a river rig, follow these steps, and look at Figure 15-13:

1. **Run the tag end of your line through one eye of a swivel.**

2. **Add a bead to the line.**

3. **Tie the tag end to another swivel using a Trilene knot.**

4. **From the first swivel, add a leader, about 12 inches, of lighter pound test line. Add a sinker to this leader using a Palomar knot.**

5. **From the second swivel, add another leader, of the same pound test as your mainline or standing line, and then tie a hook to the end of this leader using a Trilene knot.**

Your two leader lines should be approximately the same length, although you could adjust the length of either one as conditions warrant. When you cast this rig out, the sinker pulls the rig to the bottom. The leader with the hook and bait should sweep back against the current. The bait will be about a foot off the bottom, and riding in the current — just like the gamefish feeding there. The double swivel rigging allows a fish to take line without moving the sinker. If the sinker snags, the lighter leader breaks off, and you'll get your hook back.

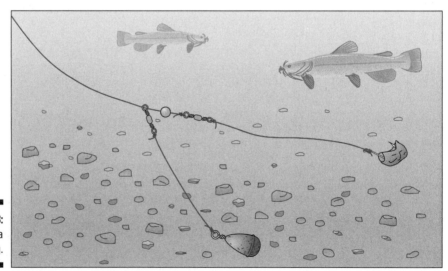

Figure 15-13:
Rigging a river rig.

The river rig is remarkably snag-resistant, all things considered. To retrieve it, lift the rod sharply and then reel quickly. Because the two leaders are the same length, the sinker and hook ride back to the rod together, and this seems to keep the hook from snagging. A fishfinder rig is similar, but it utilizes only one swivel, with both leaders tied to the second eye of the swivel. It works the same way, but the fish must move the sinker when it runs with the line.

Other anglers tie a three-way rig with a three-way swivel, again with the two leaders tied to the three-way swivel. Again, it works the same way, minus the sliding-sinker feature of the river rig.

Drift fishing with bottom rigs

All of the rigs described here can work with drift fishing, either in boats or from a bank. Slip-float rigs can be drifted with the current, and anglers can steer the float around obstacles in the stream.

Anglers in boats often drift with three-way rigs beneath the boat, and I (Greg) have had good luck drifting the simple standard bottom rig. When drifting with a three-way or river rig, you may use a walking or bottom-bouncing sinker, either of which should be a little more snag-resistant.

With any situation, adjust the size of the sinkers or floats until you reach the happy medium where your bait is presented in the most natural way. If you're snagging up excessively, you may be using too much weight. If the current sweeps your bait away, or if you cannot cast far enough, try a little more weight.

Chapter 16

Choreographing Your Cast

. . . .

In This Chapter

▶ Mastering the overhead cast with spincast gear

▶ Figuring out how to cast with spinning equipment

▶ Facing the challenges of casting with baitcasting rods and reels

▶ Presenting flies and lightweight lures with fly rods

▶ Dealing with the inevitable snags and snarls

. . . .

*I*f you could walk up to a fish and drop a lure in front of its mouth, you wouldn't need to cast. Unfortunately, fish have the funny habit of moving around. They cruise, searching for food, or they hover under or near cover that may or may not be close to the bank. The *cast* is the long-distance method you use to deliver the fly, lure, or bait to a spot where a fish may be enticed, rather than alarmed, by your offering. So in addition to *delivery,* which is concerned with where your lure lands, casting also involves *presentation,* which is how the lure appears before the fish.

The four different kinds of casting gear — spincast, spinning, baitcast, and fly — all require different casting techniques. (See Chapter 7 for more on the different kinds of rods and reels.) But all casting requires the ability to handle a rod, getting it to flex and release your cast in a controlled way, proper technique with the reel, and sometimes the direct handling of the line. Mastering the basics (say, the overhead cast) will carry over from one kind of gear to another, but we present them in this chapter in order of difficulty so that you can start at the very beginning if you need to.

As with any sport, from baseball to horseshoes, when it comes to casting, practice truly does make perfect. In fact, you should begin your fishing trip not on the water, but in the yard. Tie a small sinker or a *casting plug* (a small plastic lure without hooks designed just for this purpose) to your line and cast and retrieve a few dozen times on dry land. (Growing up, Greg and his brothers would "catch" many local cats by pulling a casting plug through the grass!) As you master the basics, you can hone your skills by placing a ring or similar object some distance away, and then cast toward it until you can reliably strike the target. Practicing on the lawn will make casting on the water much, much easier.

Casting Spincast Gear: Great for Beginners

As covered in Chapter 7, spincast equipment offers beginners an inexpensive and easy way to begin fishing. These "push-button" reels started many anglers down the road toward more specialized gear. They're popular because they're so easy to cast, and the basic motions of casting spincast gear apply to baitcasting and spinning gear, as well.

Push-button reels: Casting made easy

A standard spincast reel features a drag, a crank, and a button that releases the line (see Figure 16-1). Most reels share similar features, and you'll remember that reels are either engaged, bringing line in, or disengaged, allowing line to come off the spool (this is also known as *free spool* mode). Casting with a reel requires that you understand that basic premise. To cast, the reel must be disengaged, so line can flow out freely.

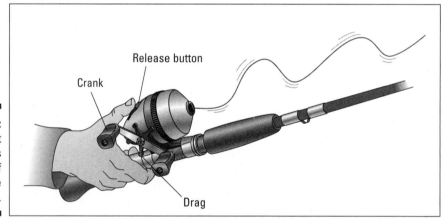

Figure 16-1: A spincast reel makes use of simple features.

Release button

Crank

Drag

On a spincast reel, if you push the button and release it, the line unspools from the reel because the reel is disengaged. Turning the crank engages the reel, allowing it to bring line back to the reel. If you press the button down and hold it down, the reel stays locked, and the line can't come off the spool. This is how a spincast cast begins.

Mastering the basics of the overhead cast

You don't need to get fancy to cast in most situations, especially when fishing with spincast gear. Follow these steps and you'll cast your lure in a smooth fashion a suitable distance away. (We use "lure" here and throughout the chapter, but understand that we mean lure, bait — whatever it is you're using.)

1. **Grasp the rod with your dominant hand with the spincast reel above the rod, as shown in Figure 16-2. Square your shoulders toward the target, and check to make sure the area behind you is clear.**

   Checking behind you not only ensures a good cast, but a safe one.

Figure 16-2: The overhead cast with spincast gear.

2. **Put the reel into *free spool* by pushing in — and holding down — the button.**

   You should have anywhere from 6 to 12 inches of line between your lure and the *tip top,* the top line guide on the rod.

3. **Point the rod at your target.**

   If you're a right-handed caster, place your left foot forward. If you're left-handed, move your right foot forward.

4. **Begin the *backstroke* of your cast by bringing the rod directly overhead until it reaches between the 12 (vertical) and 2 o'clock position (just behind you).**

   This action will put some flex into the rod, which will help you as you begin your cast. Keep your thumb on the button to keep the reel locked all through the backstroke. When casting artificial lures, the backstroke can be snappy, but using fragile livebaits calls for a softer, gentler backstroke.

5. **As soon as you stop the backstroke, begin the *forward stroke* by swinging the rod forward and toward your target, releasing thumb pressure from the button as you do (so that the lure can pull line off the reel as it travels to the target). Remove your thumb when the rod is near the 10 o'clock position, and leave it off.**

   Leaving your thumb off the button after you release it keeps the reel in free spool mode. The timing of this release — the moment you lift your thumb from the button — is crucial to a successful cast. Releasing the button too quickly during the forward stroke will send your lure high above you. Releasing too late will cause the lure to slam down right in front of you.

6. **Finish the cast by smoothly following through, ending by pointing the rod again at the target.**

   The lure should splash down with some grace near your target. If it looks like you're going to overshoot your intended spot, you can stop the lure by depressing the button with your thumb again. (Often, this causes the lure to jerk back toward you a bit — it's like slamming on the brakes.)

7. **The cast ends and the retrieve begins when you turn the crank and engage the reel.**

   Remember, the reel is disengaged until you do this, so if you cast your lure and a fish hits immediately, you cannot set the hook until you engage the reel! Most anglers find it comfortable to transfer the rod to their non-dominant hand for the retrieve. For example, a right-hander might cast with the right hand, then move the rod to the left hand for the retrieve and the fight of a fish. (This assumes the crank of the reel is located on its right side, and it usually is. Some models allow you to switch the crank to either side.)

Your overhead cast may leave some slack in the line. You should retrieve this curled line so that you can strike effectively when a fish hits. If you leave the slack, a fish may bite your lure, discover a phony, and spit it out before you have a chance to drive the hook home. Get rid of the slack by retrieving the line, but remember to apply some pressure to the line (possibly by pinching it between your thumb and forefinger of the hand holding the rod, or by pressing the line against the rod with your thumb). If you don't keep tension on the line, it will coil loosely onto the reel, and you'll be left with a snarl of line that won't cast smoothly. Your goal is to maintain a relatively straight line between you and your lure.

Casting Spinning Gear: A Little More Difficult, a Lot Smoother

Chapter 7 reveals how the mechanics of the spinning reel vary from spincast gear, but the important thing for you to know here is that spinning gear requires a different casting technique. Instead of using your thumb to press and release the button of a spincast reel, your forefinger controls the action by releasing the line from a spinning reel. Still, the timing matters. Practice helps. Instead of a push button release, spinning reels feature a *bail,* a curved piece of wire that lays the line onto the fixed spool. Casting this gear requires the bail to be opened, and on most reels, you do that by hand.

Preparing to cast

I (Peter) have handed many people a spinning rod with the mistaken assumption that they know how to initiate a cast. But if no one has shown you how to open the bail on your spinning reel to get the line ready for casting, you probably won't figure it out by yourself. So if you're one of those first-timers with a spinning rod, start here. When you prepare to cast, the reel should hang below the rod (as shown in Figure 16-3). To begin the cast, follow these steps:

1. **Hold the rod with your casting hand.**

   Know that most spinning reels allow for the crank to be moved from either the left or right side of the reel, depending on your preference. Some anglers prefer to cast with their right and reel with their left, keeping them from having to switch the rod to the noncasting hand. We both cast and reel with our right hands, so do whatever works for you.

2. **With your casting hand, grip the line with your forefinger, and hold it against the rod handle under the fleshy party of the first joint (see Figure 16-3a).**

   If you don't hold the line, the weight of the lure will pull too much line off the reel when you open the bail. Also, note that your middle finger should be on the same side of the reel stem as your forefinger.

3. **Move the reel's bail over until it clicks into the open position (see Figure 16-3b).**

   Use your free hand to do this. Your forefinger is now the only thing holding the line (and the lure), and you are ready to cast. If you forget to open the bail (we all do it), the lure won't travel very far because all it has to work with are the few inches of line between the lure and the tip top! Some spinning reels come with a trigger that opens the bail for you — these models allow you to pick up the line and open the bail with one easy motion of your forefinger.

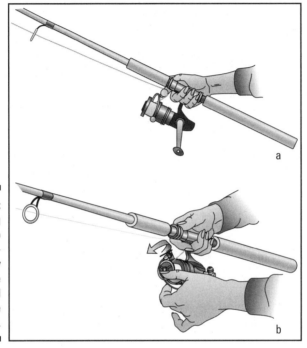

Figure 16-3: Getting ready to cast a spinning reel by gripping the line (a) and opening the bail (b).

A nice, smooth delivery: Perfecting the overhead spinning cast

Ninety out of a hundred times, the overhead cast works well. But even with the more specialized casts, the preparation remains the same. Casting, then, involves following these steps:

1. **Leave the lure hanging about 6 to 12 inches below the tip top.**

   Usually, leave no more than six inches of line for normal freshwater rods and somewhat more line with a surfcasting setup. Experiment to see what works for you with the particular lure you're using.

2. **Face the target and make sure the area behind you is clear of obstructions.**

3. **Point the rod at the target, secure the line with your forefinger, and open the bail.**

4. **To begin the cast, your backstroke should be crisp (but not overpowering) and continue until the rod points between 12 and 2 o'clock (that is, directly upright or slightly behind you).**

REMEMBER

When casting artificial lures, the backstroke can be snappy, but using fragile livebaits calls for a softer, gentler backstroke.

5. **As soon as you stop your backstroke (the rod will continue to flex behind you), immediately begin the forward stroke.**

6. **Release the line with your forefinger when your rod tip is at about 10 o'clock (or slightly out in front of you), as shown in Figure 16-4.**

7. **When the cast reaches the target, drop the rod tip, and press your forefinger against the line on the spool, which stops more line from paying out.**

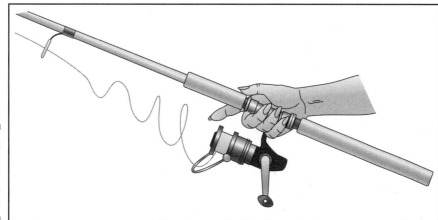

Figure 16-4:
Your forefinger releases the line as you cast.

WARNING!

Most beginners (and quite a few veterans) neglect to use their finger as a brake on the spool. And it won't work perfectly. But failing to slow the line at all often results in extra slack, all of which must be reeled in before you begin retrieving the lure. The problem worsens in high wind. As you develop a feel for this technique, you can actually slow down the rate at which line pays out (in much the same way that thumbing will slow down a cast with a baitcasting reel). This technique is called *feathering your cast*. Feathers are light, and mastering this method, therefore, requires a light touch.

Trick shots: The sidearm spinning cast

Okay, so it's not really a trick shot, but sometimes you see a nice fish, and the only possible way to cast to it is with a sidearm motion (shown in Figure 16-5). Maybe the day is too windy, or an overhang prevents an overhead cast. You'll perfect this maneuver when you truly understand that the rod has to do the work for you. Muscle this cast, and you end up casting way off target. Follow these steps for the sidearm cast:

1. **Leave the lure 3 to 6 inches below the tip top.**

2. **Face the target. Righties, put your left foot slightly forward. Lefties, put your right foot forward.**

3. **At belt level, point your rod at the target, secure the line with your forefinger, and open the bail.**

4. **If you're right-handed, move the rod with an easy stroke to the right about 45 degrees. If you're left-handed, move the rod left 45 degrees.**

5. **Snap the rod back crisply to the starting position.**

6. **As the rod tip begins to point more to the front than it does to the side, release the line with your forefinger.**

7. **Point the rod straight at the target and stop the line with your forefinger as the lure reaches the target.**

Figure 16-5:
The sidearm cast is all a matter of touch and finesse.

Mastering (Sort of) Baitcasting Techniques

Yes, you can handle baitcasting gear. As we point out in Chapter 7, most professional tournament anglers rely on baitcasters because they love the reliability and smooth cranking power of baitcasting reels. With practice, you, too, will confidently cast your new baitcasting reel with no fear of the dreaded backlash. But before you practice casting, make sure you understand how your baitcasting reel works.

Like a spincast reel, a baitcasting reel has a button or lever that disengages the reel. Unlike a spincast reel, though, the baitcaster has a spool that rotates, and you need to control the rotation of the spool. If you don't, it's likely to rotate too quickly, piling up extra line in the reel housing. Meet the backlash.

Setting the reel (and using your thumb) to cast better

Most baitcasting reels feature a *tension* knob that adjusts the speed of the spool's rotation. You want to set this so that the reel can cast freely, but not so free that you can't control it. More on that later in this section. But your thumb matters here, too — your thumb must learn to control the spool. When you cast with baitcasting gear, you need to press the spool with your thumb to stop it from spinning as soon as the lure hits the water. If you don't do this, the reel will keep spinning as the lure splashes down, and that's a sure recipe for a backlash.

The way to learn baitcasting with minimum heartbreak is to try it a little bit at a time, following these steps and referring to Figure 16-6:

1. **Before you make your first cast, hold the rod at about a 45-degree angle.**

2. **Disengage the reel and hold your thumb on the spool.**

3. **Release some thumb pressure so that the lure descends pretty freely; then, as it does, put more pressure on the spool with your thumb to slow it down so that the spool stops completely by the time the lure hits the ground.**

4. **Adjust the reel's tension. The tension should be light enough that the weight of the lure can pull line from the spool, but not so light that the spool spins rapidly.**

   If the tension is too tight, the lure won't be able to pull line from the spool at all. Find the happy medium where the lure can pull line slowly from the spool. Adjust accordingly with every lure you cast.

This test will give you an idea of how the reel's tension setting and thumb control work together to control real casts. Try short casts at first, using the thumb as a brake (better to use too much braking rather than too little when you start out). Your casts may be short of the mark this way, but you won't backlash.

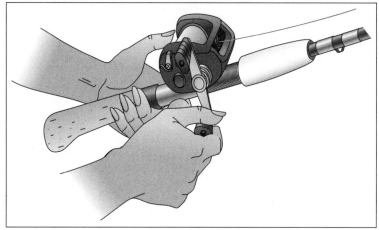

Figure 16-6:
Baitcasting gear calls for thumb control.

Casting overhead with a baitcaster

To make overhead casts with baitcasting gear, you follow the same arm motion you make when casting spincast or spinning reels. And as with casting spincast gear, your thumb helps to control the cast. But baitcasting reels are more complicated than push-button reels, and your thumb has more work to do. Following these steps will have you casting like a pro in no time:

1. **Grasp the rod with your dominant hand with the baitcast reel above the rod. Your shoulders should be squared toward the target. Check to make sure the area behind you is clear. (This not only ensures a good cast, but a safe one.)**

2. **Put the reel into *free spool* by pushing in the reel's release.**

   You should have anywhere from 6 to 12 inches of line between your lure and the *tip top* (the top line guide on the rod).

3. **Point the rod at your target.**

   If you are a right-handed caster, place your left foot forward. (If you are left-handed, step forward with your right foot.)

4. **Begin the *backstroke* of your cast by bringing the rod directly over-head and behind you, until it reaches the 2 o'clock position.**

   This action will put some flex into the rod as you begin your cast. Keep your thumb on the spool to keep the spool locked all through the back-stroke. When casting artificial lures, the backstroke can be snappy, but using fragile livebaits calls for a softer, gentler backstroke.

5. **As soon as you stop the backstroke, begin the *forward stroke* by swinging the rod forward and toward your target, releasing thumb pressure from the spool as you do (so that the lure can pull line off the reel as it travels to the target).**

   Leave your thumb lightly touching, or hovering over, the spool as you release pressure. If the spool begins to overrun the cast, you can feather (lightly brake) it to brake the spool. (If it's more comfortable for you, you can also press your thumb to the side of the spool, as opposed to the center.) The timing of this release — the moment you lift your thumb from the spool — is crucial to a successful cast. Releasing the spool too quickly during the forward stroke will send your lure high above you. Releasing too late will cause the lure to slam down right in front of you.

6. **Finish the cast by following through and pointing the rod again at the target.**

   As soon as the lure hits the water, press your thumb completely on the spool, stopping it and preventing a backlash.

7. **The cast ends and the retrieve begins when you turn the crank and engage the reel.**

   Remember, the reel is disengaged until you do this, so if you cast your lure and a fish hits immediately, you can't set the hook until you engage the reel! Most anglers find it comfortable to transfer the rod to their non-dominant hand for the retrieve. For example, a right-hander might cast with her right hand, then move the rod to her left hand for the retrieve and the fight of the fish.

Flycasting: The Beauty of Presenting Flies

Flycasting intimidates anglers, often because their only exposure to it comes from watching Brad Pitt's artful loops in *A River Runs Through It*. As with some of the more complicated things in angling, we strongly recommend that you have someone who knows how to flycast work with you in the beginning.

Peter can tell you from experience (his) that if you apply yourself, you can master every cast in this chapter in two days. You won't be perfect at these casts, but you will be fly fishing.

Presentation of the fly is the single most important skill in fly fishing. To do it well and to do it with all kinds of wind conditions requires a few more practice casts than conventional baitcasting or spinning gear. But if you master the casts, you will be able to catch fish in almost any situation. Those are covered fully in Peter's book *Fly Fishing For Dummies* (Wiley). The following sections cover the most basic casts.

Striving for the oneness of rod and line

Apologies for sounding like a wise and ancient kung-fu master, but I (Peter) would like to plant an idea in your head that may help as you approach flycasting. When flexed, the rod bends into a curve. If you're moving line at the right speed as you cast, your line will shoot off that curve in a straight path. If you hesitate too long at any point and if the arc that your rod moves through is too big, your line will no longer be able to continue the curve, and your cast will lose shape and power. Figure 16-7 shows a rod flexed properly. Note how the line smoothly continues the bend in the rod. Also note how the line curls back. This segment of line, shaped like the crook in a candy cane, is called a *loop*.

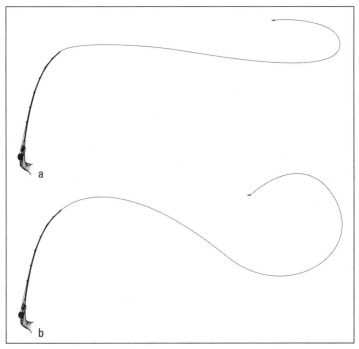

Figure 16-7:
A fly rodder with a nice tight loop (a) and one with a sloppy backcast and a wide loop (b).

a

b

Think of the loop on your rod as the bow of a boat. In the same way that a boat's bow cuts through water, the loop cuts through the air. A nice, slim v-shaped boat will move through the water with little resistance. On the other hand, if you hook up an outboard to a bathtub, you will meet a great deal more resistance to your forward motion. The same is true of the cast. A tight loop will slice through the wind. A wide loop will just hang there like a — the phrase that comes to mind in describing how it hangs there is *limp noodle*.

There is basically one right way to hold a fly rod, and it involves grasping the rod firmly above and in front of the reel, with the reel under the rod. Keep your thumb extended for more control, as shown in Figure 16-8.

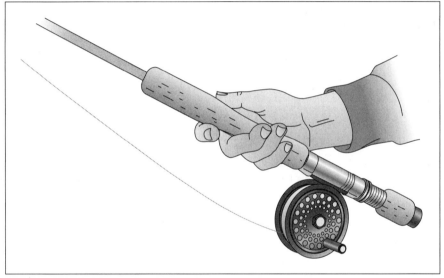

Figure 16-8:
The proper way to hold your fly rod to deliver the most power, most efficiently, is with the thumb up.

The forward (and sometimes sidearm) cast

Peter would estimate that 75 percent of all your fly-fishing casts will be a version of this basic forward cast. If you're a saltwater fisherman, make that 95 percent. Figure 16-9 illustrates this fundamental cast. To complete your first practice forward cast, follow these steps:

1. **Pull about 10 feet of line off the reel beyond the tip top guide.**

   Pulling line off the reel is called *stripping*.

2. **Stand sideways, or mostly sideways with your left shoulder in front if you are a rightie. (Lefties, point the right shoulder.)**

3. **Strip another 2 feet of line off the reel and hold it in your left hand, as shown in Figure 16-9.**

4. **With the rod held at a 45-degree angle, crisply lift the line in the air, snapping your wrist upward as you do. Your backstroke should stop when your wrist is at 12 o'clock (vertical). Momentum will carry your rod and wrist along the arc you have started and flex the rod backward.**

5. **As the line straightens out behind you, let your arm drift with it and then move the rod sharply forward. Again, stop your power stroke dead on 12 o'clock (it will drift forward); as you do so, continue to drive forward with your wrist as if you were pushing in a thumbtack.**

6. **When your rod reaches the 45-degree angle, drop the rod tip.**

If you have executed this cast well, you will feel a tug on your left hand, which is holding the extra 2 feet of line that you stripped out in Step 3, before you started the cast. Let go of the line and it will shoot out of your top guide, giving you an extra couple of feet to your cast.

Figuring out what you did wrong

With ten feet of line out of the guides, you probably performed a reasonable approximation of a cast. Now, do the same thing with 15 feet of line. This will probably begin to show some of the problems in your beginning cast. Try to keep the line in the air as you execute a few false casts. (A *false cast* is the name given to what you do when you flick the line backward and forward before finally delivering the fly.) A false cast serves two purposes:

✔ It lines up your cast with your target.

✔ It develops *line speed,* which allows you to work more and more line through the guides so that you can hold it in the air, get up speed, and shoot a longer cast to your target. With good use of line speed, you can easily add distance to your cast.

But before you worry about distance, concentrate on casting mechanics. You need to get out on the lawn with your 15 feet of line and (standing sideways) watch your line in the air as you cast. This will require you to drop your arm for more of a sidearm delivery, but don't worry about that. Sometimes a fishing situation calls for precisely that maneuver.

As you watch your line, your goal is to keep it moving in the air and parallel to the ground. If the line drops below the horizontal, you are moving through too wide an arc. You're forgetting to stop your forward stroke at 12 o'clock. We can't emphasize this enough. Stop the rod tip high, and the rod will do the work for you.

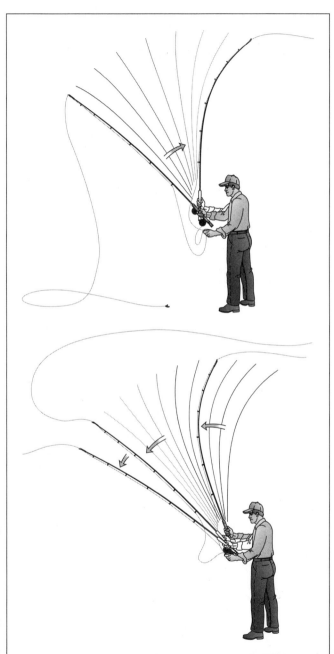

Figure 16-9:
Master the
forward
cast and
you can fly
fish right
away.

The stripping basket

During the 1960s, the otherwise forgettable film *Man's Favorite Sport* showed Doris Day and Paula Prentiss getting Rock Hudson a complete fishing outfit. With inflatable waders and a real doofus hat, nothing could possibly have looked dorkier. But that was because stripping baskets weren't around in those days. A *stripping basket* is a basket that an angler ties around his or her waist. When casting long distances from a boat, jetty, or shore, a stripping basket, which stores your stripped in line in one safe spot, can keep your line from getting tangled, falling under a rock, or getting swept out by the surge of the waves. So at the risk of looking silly, remember there are worse things in the world than walking around with something that looks like a Rubbermaid dish drainer tied to your waist — like not catching fish!

Another common error is hurrying the cast. Casting a fly isn't like shooting a bullet out of a rifle. It's not just one flick of the finger followed by delivery of the fly. In casting a fly, four things have to happen:

✔ You transfer muscle power to your rod.

✔ Your rod bends and multiplies that force over distance.

✔ Your line is set in motion by the action of the rod.

✔ The bullwhip action of the fly line develops even more speed as you finish the casting motion.

All of this action takes time. You backcast. The line straightens out and pulls on the rod. You move through the forward cast, and the line buggy-whips forward. You shoot line and drop the rod tip. A beginner's cast often falls apart at a point between the end of the backcast and the beginning of the forward cast. You need to pause just a bit at this part of the cast until you feel a little tug or, if you are not a great tug feeler, pause until you see the line straighten out.

After the fly is out there, it might interest a fish. For you to catch that fish, which is the point of all this, you need to make the transition from casting the fly to fishing the fly. You wrap the thumb around the rod and extend your index finger so that it holds the fly line against the rod shaft. This trick ensures that anytime a fish hits, you won't have unwanted slack in the line. Your other hand is now free to pull in line as required. This retrieving action is called *stripping* in line.

Caster of Disaster: How to Handle Snags and Snarls

Successful fishing is often a game of inches. Come to think of it, what sport isn't? A curveball on the outside corner, a forward pass between two defenders, a drive over a bunker — these skills require accuracy, too. The same goes with fishing. So if you want to get your cast in there where the fish are, you're going to miss by inches and hang up from time to time. Everybody does. In fact, a common angling saying proclaims, "If you aren't snagging occasionally, you aren't fishing where the fish are." With care, you will snag up less, but you are still going to snag. Sometimes you can also undo it.

With any snag, don't panic. Responding with rage will only drive the hook deeper into the snag, making freeing it impossible, or you'll slingshot the lure back at you. Most casting mistakes can be overcome as long you stay calm and reason your way out of it.

Whether you're fishing from boat or bank, one common casting miscue involves casting too far and wrapping your line around a branch. Sometimes the lure will still fall to the water (where occasionally a fish will strike it!); other times it hangs there in the tree, taunting you. My brothers and I (Greg) call this squirrel fishing, and we never mean it as a compliment. If you cast and your lure sails over a branch or limb, don't panic and jerk back on the rod. Doing that will often only spin the lure around the branch, tangling the line. Instead, follow these simple steps:

1. **Point your rod at the offending branch.**

2. **Very gently, reel up any slack until the lure comes almost up against the bottom of the limb.**

3. **With a gentle upward flip of the rod, the lure will often somersault over the limb, thereby freeing it.**

4. **Retrieve your lure normally.**

Tree branches aren't the only lure, bait, fly, and line stealers, of course. You can hang up on underwater rocks (or any other submerged obstacle); in fact, there are as many things to snag on as there are types of cover for fish to hide under and around. And as with catching fish, a number of techniques and strategies (including a couple of important don'ts) apply to getting unsnagged:

- If you're snagged on something underwater, don't rear back with your rod and put a lot of pressure on it, and don't savagely jerk it either. You'll break a rod sooner or later (which is a big price to pay, even if the alternative is losing an expensive lure). Instead, try lightly bouncing the rod upward, trying to pop the lure loose. If that fails, try pulling with steady pressure, with the rod pointed right at the snag. When you do this, don't put too much pressure on the (engaged) reel. You could harm the reel's gears. Try holding the spool of a spinning reel with your hand before you pull, or hold the line of any type of gear against the rod to take some pressure off the reel.

- If firm (but not overpowering) pressure won't free a snagged line, we often put the rod down and strip some more line off. Then we wrap the line around a stick a couple of times and pull straight on the line. (Don't wrap line around your hands or arms! Any fishing line can cut you.) Usually, if the hook has any chance of breaking free, this does the trick.

Whereas this wrap-and-pull technique is good for deep underwater obstacles far away, don't try this method if the hang-up is in a tree (or other above-water obstacle) or in barely submerged snag. You can sling-shot a lure back toward you with tremendous force, and chances are you'll be looking straight down the line at your lure. Guess what path that hook is going to take as it hurtles out of the brush — right at your face!

✔ If you're snagged in a stream, sometimes walking downstream to change the angle of pressure will free the hook. If you can't get downstream (if the stream is too deep, or if the current is too swift), some anglers put a bobber on the line and then let the bobber float downstream. This trick can have the effect of exerting some downstream pressure as you reel in. In any situation, changing the angle of the line to the snag can work wonders. Walk up and down the bank or move the boat if you have to.

✔ The final decision is to "fish or cut bait," as the saying goes. In this case, it can also mean cutting off line, lures, flies, and the like. After trying to rescue your equipment for a while, you need to consider the following: You wait all week to try and get in a little fishing. When you get right down to it, you don't spend all that much time actually fishing, even when you do get the time. Getting rigged up, in and out of waders, in and out of boats, and the like eats up a great deal of time. How much time do you want to spend trying to save the unsaveable? Sometimes the answer is "give up and get back to fishing!" You will be amazed at how good you will feel as soon as you catch a fish.

✔ Don't break your line until you're positive you're not "snagged" on a fish! Many big fish stories begin with the line, "Well, at first I thought I was hooked on a log, until the log started to swim off!"

✔ After any snag, check your hook points. Sometimes a nasty snag can dull or roll a hook point. When that happens, sharpen or replace the hook.

When using bottom rigs, in particular, you may want to wait a bit if you snag a hook. Chances are, your hook (still baited) is snagged on some cover that is probably home to a fish or two. Sometimes, a fish will bite your hook, pulling it free from the snag! Greg calls this the Whopper theory. A fish knows its environs as well as you know your living room. If you walked into your living room and saw a Whopper sandwich nailed to the wall, what would you do? That's right. You'd eat it, no questions asked.

Chapter 17

Exploring Different Fishing Techniques

· ·

· ·

*T*he first people to capture fish for food were hunters more than anglers: They used their bare hands, spears, or traps to catch fish. Today, you're more likely to pursue fish with a rod and reel, but you still have many options. After you find fishable water (see Chapter 3) and have a sense of the fish living there (see Chapters 4 and 5), you need to figure out how to get those fish to bite your hook. After all, that moment — the bite — is what separates fishing from hunting. Successful angling requires that a fish strike your offering, either through choice or instinct. (And if they don't, you go home practicing your excuses.)

Fish bite for two primary reasons:

✔ They're hungry, and they see your offering as something to eat.

✔ They're triggered to bite by instinct; they strike out of a sense of aggravation, protection, or competition.

So how do you entice fish to bite? First, you need to present something that the fish like to eat (think livebaits) or something that imitates a food source. You need an effective bait, lure, or fly, period. But that alone won't always catch fish. You must understand how to approach fish with your bait, and that's where your technique comes into play. Little about fishing technique fits neatly into a chapter because with so much of technique, experience matters. Learning how to cast takes practice. Knowing what fishing technique to use, and when, takes experience.

To simplify, whether you fish salt- or freshwater, the water in front of you is either flowing or still. Tides move water; a river's current moves water, too. Fish relate to moving water differently than they do still water. For that reason, your fishing techniques will vary as you approach the different environments. And here's another simplification: most of your fishing will fit into one of two categories: still fishing or casting and retrieving. This chapter focuses on those categories and provides you with plenty of advice for finding the best technique for you and the fish you're intent on catching.

Still Fishing (After All These Years)

Still fishing refers to methods of angling where the bait is presented, either suspended on a float rig or on the bottom, and the angler waits for the fish to find it and bite. Don't think of still fishing as lazy fishing, even though you don't cast as many times as you do while working a lure or fly. Although you can cast out a bottom rig and then do nothing but watch that line for hours, still fishing can be almost as active, or at least as mentally challenging, as casting lures or flies. Some fish practically require still fishing presentations. After all, some fish are simply too wise, too aware of their environment, to fall for artificial lures. Don't laugh, but in one test at the University of Missouri, carp and channel catfish placed near the top of an intelligence test when fisheries biologists trained fish to avoid a light source. Rainbow trout place near the bottom. (Not sure how their median SAT scores stack up.) Some fish can be caught reliably only on livebait. Still fishing presents that livebait effectively. Besides, no one says fishing has to be work. You can catch about any fish that swims while still fishing.

Bottom rigs: Waiting out the fish

Fish in both salt- and freshwater fall for bottom rigs. Such rigs are most often paired with livebait, where the scent of the bait can lure in marauding gamefish. Bottom rigs let the bait do the work for you, as the bait, either through smell and/or appearance, attracts the fish you hope to catch. Too many anglers, however, mistake this to mean that you can cast a bottom rig anywhere and expect to catch fish. Bottom rigs work best when placed in the general vicinity of active gamefish; even a lively nightcrawler or bleeding piece of cutbait can only do so much when cast into dead water.

We cover standard bottom rigs in Chapter 15, but any bottom rig should keep your bait anchored to the bottom while also allowing a fish to take it, notifying you of a strike. For that reason, many of these rigs feature a sinker that slides on the mainline, so gamefish can take the bait without feeling the drag of the sinker. As a general rule, use the least amount of weight necessary to keep your presentation as natural as possible.

Floating away

Float rigs, the term given to any rig that utilizes a float to suspend the bait from the surface, allow you present your bait (usually livebait, but occasionally a lure like a small plastic jig) suspended in the water column. This presentation keeps your bait above the snags of the bottom, and near (but not buried in) things like weedbeds. (For more on rigging float rigs, see Chapter 15.)

Chapter 9 has more on floats, but our main piece of advice is to fish them actively. Cast a float near cover like brushpiles and wait maybe ten minutes. If you don't get a bite, reel in, check your bait, and cast to a different piece of cover. Don't forget to experiment with depth, too — a slip float rig allows you to adjust the depth of your bait easily and quickly. If you know fish are in the area, change the depth of the float until you hook up.

Casting About for Fish

Still fishing has its place and works especially well for certain species of fish; however, many anglers prefer to cast. Casting allows you to cover more water actively, and your lure or fly (casting is most often paired with artificials) can be made to act as enticingly as real prey. Casting also allows you to capitalize on the aggressive nature of some fish. Species such as northern pike or marlin feed by chasing and slashing baitfish, and casting and retrieving lures can trigger that response.

Blind casting, though, is little more than exercise. To catch fish consistently, you need a solid strategy. The following sections provide some tips for effective casting.

Covering water and taking fish

Watch a professional bass angler work a shoreline. Using a practiced, polished motion, the bass pro will cast his lure to a precise spot, say by a sunken log, and work it back to the boat in a deliberate manner. As soon as the lure returns to the boat, zing, it's placed near the next target. Soon, the whole shoreline has been fished, and several fish have been caught. The pro has likely never stopped moving his lure.

Casting allows you to fish actively, and it's possible to place your lure by a lot of gamefish. The key? Cast well and cast often. Although it's certainly possible to fish too fast (and miss fish as a result), casting gives you the chance to catch the most active fish in the area — those that are hungry and looking for a good meal. Accurate casts are a must. Practice will help you land your lure precisely where you want it to go. (See Chapter 16 for more on how to cast.)

Matching your retrieve to the conditions

Lures and flies (sometimes called *artificials*) come in different shapes and sizes for a reason. As we explain in Chapters 13 and 14, they vary widely so you can use them in a variety of places and in a range of ways. Your job as an angler is to know two things:

- ✔ How a lure or fly is designed to work. Manufacturers build lures with a particular action in mind, and they'll share this information with you. After all, they want you to catch fish on their lures.
- ✔ When to use a particular lure or fly. For example, a buzzbait works well when largemouth bass hunt near the surface. But if bass lie deep, they'll tell you to buzz-off!

Carry a range of artificials (see Chapters 13 and 14 for advice on which lures and flies to buy), and experiment until you know what conditions call for which lures. With lures, you can quickly see that some demand attention: They're shiny and vibrant (if you don't believe us, just turn to the color section to see for yourself), and some are loud. Use them to find active fish, or on days when fish feed aggressively. Other lures, like a soft plastic worm, slip through the water subtly and silently. Lures like these work better when fish hang near the bottom in a lethargic manner.

Fishing Still (Nonflowing) Water

When fishing calm water, you should know that, in the absence of current, fish will relate to structure and cover. (For more on cover and structure, check out Chapter 3.) In flowing water, fish will almost always face upstream because that's where the food, in the form of floating insects or other prey, comes from. In a pond, lake, or lagoon at slack tide, fish could be facing in any direction. You must choose between still fishing or casting, livebait or lures, but start with this knowledge: The fish are usually close to cover and structure. Find the right cover and structure, and you're more than halfway home. Now you just need to use the right technique to trigger a strike.

Working the banks: A deliberate approach

When fishing a pond or lake with no current, the first thing to do is visually inspect the water and its surroundings. Think about structure — what clues are there that tell you about the bottom of the body of water? Are there points trailing from the bank into the water? Rocky shorelines? Islands? Coves or narrow stretches? Is there a dam or levy? Any of these things can concentrate gamefish. Cover will be more visible to the naked eye, and equally important. Search the banks features such as fallen trees, weedbeds, docks, brushpiles, or overhanging limbs. Gamefish use cover for protection and as ambush points, and putting your bait near cover often results in a bite.

From the bank or from a boat, move methodically around the shoreline and fish obvious points of interest. Fish the edges of the cover you can see — cast along a weedbed or along the branches of a submerged tree. Of course you'll snag some, but this means you're really trying to fish in the right spot. Whether you're using lures, flies, or livebait, keep moving. Fish the structure and cover available to you, and pay attention to your strikes. Where are most of the bites coming from? Are you catching one big fish around every sunken tree? Are fish only close to the rocky shores? Pay attention and look for patterns. Even if you're still fishing, it's usually good to resist staying in one area for too long. Usually, 30 minutes or so is enough time to allow a fish to find your offering. Keep moving and exploring.

Fan casting: Covering the bases

Occasionally, a pond or bay will have no discernible features — it looks like a bowl, uniform in appearance on every side. Stripmining pits can be like this, and so are retention ponds. In this situation, fish fast and cover water. Using a lure like a spinnerbait or a shallow-running crankbait, cast parallel to the shore to your left. Retrieve the lure and cast again, this time a little farther out. Think of your casts as an old-fashioned, handheld fan, or the spread of a peacock's tail (see Figure 17-1). Cast in a pattern until you're casting parallel to the shore on your right. Doing this will put your bait near the bank, over deeper water, and everything in between. Move down the bank (twice the reach of your previous farthest cast) and repeat. (Go far enough that your casts back toward your original location don't overlap with your initial casts.) Move down the bank and watch for patterns. This method will cover a lot of water and put your lure in front of many fish. It's a good exploratory technique.

Figure 17-1:
Fan casting allows you to cover a lot of water from one spot.

The exception to the rule: Fishing windy days

A strong, persistent wind acts like a current — it can concentrate fish in one location. I (Greg) remember approaching my grandfather's farm pond on a windy day once when I was in grade school. The strong wind made one side of the pond as smooth as glass, as a high bank blocked the breeze. Standing on that bank, with the wind at my back, I could cast my artificial worm a mile! I was having one of my best casting days ever, but I wasn't getting any bites. Only when I moved to the other side of the pond, the side whipped to a frenzy of six-inch waves (pretty big waves for a farmpond!) did I begin to catch bass. I learned a valuable lesson: When fishing on a windy day, fish the bank that the wind blows toward. It's certainly easier to cast with the wind, but you'll find more success if you cast into the wind. A strong, steady wind pushes waves against the bank, which stirs up sediment, which activates microinvertebrates, which triggers a feeding response in small fish, and so on up the food chain. You should take your place at the top of the food chain and fish that windblown shoreline!

From the bank, fan cast along the windblown shore. From a boat, move along the shoreline and work the bank. If the wind has been blowing long enough, the gamefish will be there.

Fishing Flowing Water

Flowing water can concentrate gamefish or prey as well as create eddies and pockets where fish can lie in wait. When you understand the principles of current, you can use that knowledge to your angling advantage. Saltwater fish follow the tides because the tides concentrate and move bait. In streams and rivers, fish know that the current delivers food in the form of dead or dying prey. For this reason, in everything from saltwater estuaries to mountain streams, fish tend to face into the current, waiting to see what it offers. Luckily for you, in our opinion, these places also tend to be among the most beautiful places to fish. There's something entrancing about moving water.

Casting upriver, retrieving downriver

Many smallmouth bass anglers fish streams by wading, and this is certainly the most popular way to pursue trout. Most anglers wade upstream, fishing as they go, then walk back downstream when it's time to head home. While you can catch fish on the downstream run, most of your fish will come as you wade upstream. This is because the water hasn't been disturbed yet by your passing, and you can present your lure by casting upstream and retrieving it downstream.

On popular streams, it may be hard to find unfished water during peak times. Just because you haven't disturbed the water yet doesn't mean another angler didn't work the same area an hour earlier. On small streams, there's only so much you can do about crowds, but try to fish on weekdays and be willing to walk/wade farther than others.

Gamefish will often be near the current, but slightly out of it, often hiding behind a rock or other obstacle that blocks the current. Pay particular attention to the following spots:

- **Eddies:** Places where the current swirls back upriver

- **Current seams:** Where two currents come together

- **Undercut banks:** Where the current has washed out a hole under the shore

Gamefish watching the current don't have forever to make up their minds about eating something. If they hesitate too long, the morsel will wash on downstream. This fact works to your advantage. Fish that reside in flowing water tend to be more aggressive than still water fish and are often stronger, as a result of swimming in flowing water their whole lives. Practice bringing your lure downstream in a manner that matches what the gamefish are used to seeing. In Figure 17-2, notice how the cast brings the lure right past a log where a fish lies in wait. Notice that not every upstream cast will be directly upstream — many will be at angles, often toward different targets on either side. Work upstream, but cast at quartering-upstream angles, too.

Figure 17-2:
Cast your lures upstream and bring them down-stream past likely haunts.

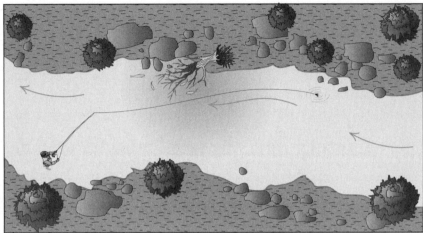

Floats: Meals au naturel

Float rigs account for many fish from streams and rivers every season. They work so well because the flowing water carries the float downstream, presenting the bait underneath in a natural manner. Because fish that reside in current get used to the speed of the flow, float rigs allow you to present a bait at exactly the same rate as the current. This looks natural to gamefish.

Using a longer rod will benefit you while fishing floats. A longer rod allows you to steer your float rig as it maneuvers downstream. As always, keep a taut line (no slack) between your rod and the float, and lift and lower the rod tip to direct the float around obstacles. Fishing streams with natural baits such as crayfish, minnows, or leeches should help you trick any fish in the river.

River rigs: This is where they shine

River rigs, as shown in Chapter 15, work when the current keeps the bait off the bottom. You can fish river rigs from a boat or from the bank, and you can either hold the rod or place it in a rod holder. For river rigs to really excel, you should cast downstream and maintain a tight line between the rod and sinker. This allows the leader with the hook to flow in the current downstream, attracting a hungry fish.

Casting upstream or cross-current makes it more difficult to maintain this taut line, as the current puts a bow in your mainline. The sinker can wash downstream toward you and snag, too. Most anglers, when fishing from a boat, will anchor above a hole and then fish river rigs off the stern, as shown in Figure 17-3. This setup allows you to fish several different spots downstream, all while maintaining tight lines. (Another reason why circle hooks work so well on river rigs: You can allow the fish to load the rod and hook itself.) Wading in a stream provides opportunities for fishing river rigs, too, and this should be one of the rare times you fish downstream while wading.

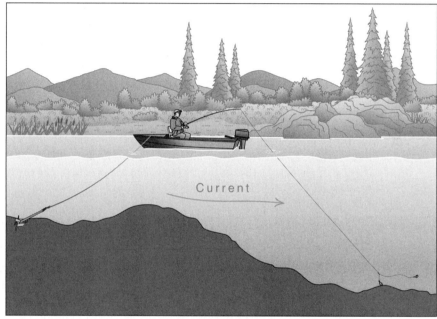

Figure 17-3:
An angler anchored above a hole, fishing river rigs.

Other Fishing Techniques

Most of your fishing will consist of casting and still fishing, but the following techniques have their place, as well. Knowing how to jig, drift, troll, and night fish will expand your possibilities for angling success, but we recommend that you try these techniques after you've mastered the fundamental art of casting and still fishing on your home waters.

Jigging

Because much of a gamefish's food lives on the bottom of a lake or ocean (think creatures like crayfish and crabs), *jigging* allows you to present a lure in a natural way right in the fish's red zone. Jigging, often done with lures called — get this — jigs, requires you to hop a lure across the bottom. If fishing from the beach, you cast a jig into the surf, allow it to reach the bottom, then sharply lift the rod tip to hop the jig back toward you. Allow it to settle, keeping the line taut, then jig it forward another step. When jigging, you can use a flashy lure like a casting jig (see Chapter 13), or a leadhead jig topped with a plastic lure, minnow, or chunk of cutbait.

This lift-and-drop jigging motion is the basis for many retrieves. A Texas-rigged plastic worm should be fished this way, and numerous other lures. The key to mastering the lift-drop technique is to stay in touch with the lure through a semi-tight line. Cast the lure and keep the line taut as it sinks — watch and feel for the telltale tap of a fish inhaling the lure. Lift the lure or jig with a sweep of the rod, then follow it back down, maintaining a semi-tight line. Fish can hit a jig at any point of the retrieve, and alert anglers are ready for the bite at any time.

When fishing from piers or boats, you don't need to cast jigs — you can simply lower them to the bottom, then occasionally give them a jerk. Keep the line tight, though, as fish will often hit a jig as it falls or rests on the bottom. This up and down motion attracts fish from far away, and often proves irresistible to fish in the vicinity. Almost any fish that swims could be taken on a jig.

Night fishing

Everyone assumes catfish are primarily nocturnal. And, indeed, catfish do often feed at night, particularly flathead catfish. So it makes sense that I (Greg) fish a lot at night. I enjoy it, but it takes some getting used to. A river at night is not like a river during the day. But even if you don't pursue catfish, you might want to think about night fishing. But there's more to fishing at night than simply staying on the water past sundown. Night fishing is its own technique.

Many gamefish — including trout, striped bass, largemouth bass, walleyes, and sharks — feed at night. There are other advantages to night fishing, too. Pleasure boaters might crowd a particular lake during the day, making fishing unsafe or at least unpleasant, but they disappear at sundown. Gamefish facing heavy angling pressure often react by feeding more at night. Many anglers find they catch bigger fish when fishing at night. Using big, loud lures like Jitterbugs or spinnerbaits, or good, fresh livebait, you can trigger explosive strikes that shatter the silence of a moonlit reverie.

Almost every challenge that daytime angling presents is amplified by darkness. You're more likely to hook yourself or your partner at night. Tangles and snags become huge obstacles. Snakes seem to come out at night — certainly mosquitoes do. Even unhooking a fish can be problematic. Any daytime danger — a fall, a dunking, a storm — becomes a bigger deal after the sun sets.

Despite the hazards, night fishing presents so many positives that you might consider it. One big advantage is that you aren't as visible to fish at night as you are in the day. Prepare yourself in this way:

- ✔ **Simplify and organize.** Take only what you need for nightfishing, and know exactly where it is.

- ✔ **Carry the right safety equipment.** I wouldn't fish without a headlamp. I carry two spotlights. My boat is rigged with the required safety lights. A cellphone is handy. (Chapter 6 looks at safety more in-depth.)

- ✔ **Don't fish an area you don't know.** Night fish only water you know well from daytime fishing. Inspect the water for dangerous obstacles during the day or ideally during low-water periods.

- ✔ **Don't night fish at all until you're comfortable as an angler.** Can you cast, tie a knot, prepare a bait or lure by touch alone? Until you can, fish with the sun.

Drifting and trolling

One of the biggest advantages of fishing from a boat is that it allows you to do everything a shorebound angler can do, but you can cover even more water while doing it. Anglers in boats often maneuver along a shoreline, casting to exposed cover. They're fishing just as bank fishermen do, but they can fish a longer stretch of shoreline, or motor across the bay to cast near the far bank. So they have an advantage, but they're essentially using the same casting tactics of the shore angler.

But bank fishermen can't *drift* or *troll* the way anglers in boats can, and these techniques are two of the most effective ways to put fish in the boat. Trolling means pulling lures or livebait rigs behind a boat, and using the boat's power (either the engine, electric trolling motor, rowing, or paddling). Drifting works the same way, but the boat moves silently with the natural power of wind or current. In the Great Lakes or offshore in the oceans, trolling from big boats might involve *downriggers,* which are devices that lower a lead ball to a particular depth. Downriggers work because the angler's line is clipped to the cable near the lead ball, allowing the lure to run at that depth. When a fish strikes, the line pops free from the downrigger, and the angler fights the fish to the surface.

Downriggers require big boats and work best on big water, but any angler with a boat can drift or troll. An in-line spinner pulled behind a leisurely paddled canoe draws strikes from pike in Minnesota. A small boat can troll nightcrawlers for walleyes. In any situation, regardless of what you're fishing for, drifting livebait vertically under a boat covers a lot of water and presents your baits to many fish. See Figure 17-4 for an example of this. Sometimes the boat will drift faster than the lure or livebait rig, so the lines trail the boat at about a 45-degree angle. This can be especially effective, as the rigs bounce along the bottom behind the boat, telegraphing the action through the rod tips.

As with any technique, drifting and trolling present their own tricks and challenges. But whether you're fishing saltwater for tarpon or freshwater rivers for blue catfish, you can learn to use your boat as a tool for presenting your offerings.

Figure 17-4:
A boat drift fishing multiple lines with livebait presented at different depths.

Chapter 18

How to Hook, Fight, Land, and Release a Fish

In This Chapter

▶ Being ready for a fish strike

▶ Getting a good hookset using circle or J hooks

▶ Fighting a fish without exhausting it

▶ Landing or boating a fish safely

▶ Releasing and, if necessary, reviving a fish

*L*earning how to cast well can be fun, and you can be proud of fishing a lure properly, with just the right touch of finesse. A beautifully crafted rod and reel is a work of art that you might someday pass on as an heirloom. The act of fishing takes you into some of the most scenic, awe-inspiring places and gives you time with people precious to you. But for all fishing is — the gear, the techniques, the scenery, the companionship — it really comes down to being able to catch fish.

A gearhound might acquire tackle, and an expert caster might be able to hit a teacup with a lure at 100 feet, but an angler catches fish. To be a true angler you need to know when to strike a fish, how to fight it, how to complete the fight and land it, and then how to kill it humanely or set it free. We walk you through each of these phases in this chapter.

Catching a fish is like riding a bike in that the best way to learn how to do it is to actually attempt it. There's only so much you can learn about fighting a fish until you get to do it yourself. Still, preparation helps in all things, and this chapter helps you prepare mentally to improve your chances of success when everything goes right and a fish actually bites your hook.

Finally! How to Handle a Fish Attack

Different fish have different takes. Whereas a pike may slaughter your top-water bait, a trout may approach your fly in a daintier fashion. A bass may inhale a lure only to spit it out a split-second later. A bluefish may slam it. Some fish will take surface lures with wild abandon but are much more deliberate with a subsurface bait.

The general rule is this: Although there's no one dictate for when to *set* the hook, or drive the hook into the fish's mouth, earlier hooksets usually result in fewer swallowed hooks. (When a fish swallows a hook, it becomes hard to remove the hook without killing the fish.) True, some fish, in some circumstances, will require you to be a bit more patient with your hooksets. For example, when fishing live chubs for northern pike, you may need to wait until the pike has turned the chub headfirst in its mouth before setting the hook. (But, even there, you should probably use a *quick-strike rig,* which involves hooking the baitfish with two hooks, one near the head and another near the tail, allowing you to set the hook on a pike without waiting.) Overall, to be an effective angler, you need to know your fish and its behavior, and this includes knowing how a particular species of fish strikes. Ninety percent of the time, you can set the hook immediately after a bite.

A savage strike doesn't require a savage response from you. Usually, all this sort of response does is ensure that you jerk your bait, lure, or fly away from the fish. You need to come tight to the fish: All the slack must be gone from your line, and you must feel the weight of the fish before you drive the hook home. Again, the more you do this, the better your feel for it will be.

This section helps you pick up the basic skills needed to properly set the hook into a fish. Whether you fish with J or circle hooks, livebait or lures, you find out all you need to know about moving from "Hey! I've got a bite!" to "Here, take my picture with this awesome fish!"

Starting out in the right (positive) frame of mind

A lot can go wrong when you're fishing — you might cast into a tree, snag a sunken log, or fall into the water and be forced to fish all day with a wet butt. All these things and more happen to all of us from time to time. Sometimes it's hard to stay positive. Greg's younger brother, a real hothead, often gets all pouty when he gets outfished (furrowed brow, big scowl, the whole nine yards).

You'll find, though, that fishing works best when your mind is clear and calm. Not to go all Zen on you, but don't take out your anger on the fish. You will miss more hooksets and lose more fish if you cast, retrieve, and set the hook like a savage. (Not to mention that you'll get fewer bites.) Hooking and fighting a big fish requires rational thought and smooth, collected action. If you get upset while fishing, take a walk until you cool off. Fishing is meant to be relaxing, and you land more fish when you're relaxed, too.

While we're on the new-agey subject of never fishing angry, think about the sports psychology of visualizing success. A poor free-throw shooter might be coached to visualize the ball going through the hoop. Well, for anglers, this means you should picture the fight of the fish going well and ending in your favor. Imagine the fish coming into the net or your hand after the struggle.

This exercise helps you to stay positive, but you also need to prepare for the negative possibilities. We talk about strategies for landing fish successfully later in this chapter, but it helps if you start with a mind that is in the right place. Much can go wrong while fighting a fish, but it seems to happen less often if you plan on things going well.

Setting the hook with J hooks

When a fish bites a baited hook or lure, you've been successful: You've tricked that fish into making a connection with you. But that connection — through the rod and reel, down the line, across any terminal tackle your rig consists of, and culminating in the sharp hook you've selected — is a tenuous one. You need to act quickly and wisely to ensure that the fish stays connected to you. This is called *setting the hook*, and it's the process by which the hook passes from merely being in the fish's mouth to being through the fish's mouth. When fishing with J hooks, setting the hook means pointing the rod at the fish (as shown in Figure 18-1), tightening the line, and jerking the rod sharply back toward you, driving the hook into the fish's mouth (shown in Figure 18-2). Setting the hook is like serving a tennis ball — it's a sweeping gesture, but one that should flow smoothly. This is true whether you're using a single J hook with bait, or a lure with three treble hooks (which are also J hooks).

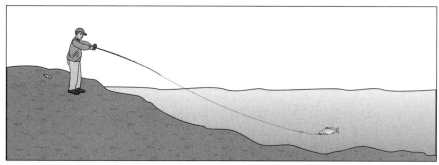

Figure 18-1:
To set a J hook, start by pointing your rod at the fish.

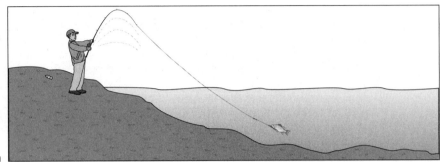

Figure 18-2:
Jerk the rod back sharply to set the J hook in the fish's mouth.

Different species call for different hooksets, and different baits call for different tactics. For example, largemouth bass striking at a plastic frog through a layer of algae need a bit of time to get the frog bait into their mouths. Some fish have hard mouths that require hard and repeated hooksets. Others, like crappies, will go free if you set the hook too hard. But the following tips should work for you most of the time, with most fish caught on most rigs:

- **Keep a relatively tight line between your hook and your reel at all times.** When fishing with a float rig, for example, slack line can form between your rod and the float. When a fish bites and the float sinks, that fish is ready to be hooked, but the slack line can prevent you from driving the hook home. By the time you furiously crank up the loose line, the fish may have spit the bait and moved away. Keep your line tight, and be ready to set the hook at any time. *Note:* If you set the hook and find that you have too much slack in the line, quickly reel in the slack and set the hook again. The fish might still be there!

- **Let the rod help you.** As you sweep the rod overhead, the rod should bend. This bend is providing the force that sets the hook. If your rod isn't bending on the hookset, you're not providing enough force.

- **Quicker hooksets are usually better.** We don't advise waiting to set the hook (unless it's one of those odd situations, like catching bass through the moss). Look at it this way: If you feel a fish tap your bait, or your float goes under, that fish has your hook in its mouth. A fish can't move your bait with its hands! If the bait is in a fish's mouth, then the hook should be able to find purchase. Some folks will tell you to wait, to "make sure he has it" or something, but most of the time this pause results in a *swallowed hook.* A swallowed hook can lead to an inadvertent fish death, and is usually the result of waiting too long to set the hook. Your goal should be to land every fish that bites, but also to be able to release every fish you land, should you choose to do so.

Setting the hook with circle hooks

Anglers fishing with J hooks should strike fast and hard to set the hook. Indeed, a wimpy hookset could result in a freed fish. But circle hooks work differently than J hooks, and they require a different method.

Circle hooks work because fish often move after they pick up a bait or lure. Say a smallmouth bass grabs a nightcrawler rigged on a circle hook. The smallmouth will inhale the nightcrawler, then most likely turn away from the place where it sucked in the bait. The nightcrawler — and the hook — will be in the bass's mouth for a second or two before it swallows. As the bass turns, the hook drags across the mouth of the fish, lodging in the corner of the jaw. As the bass continues to move, the hook rotates until the gap of the hook fits around the jaw. Then the point sinks in and the bass is hooked.

I (Greg) know it sounds unlikely! I didn't believe it at first, either. Now that I have caught hundreds of fish using circle hooks, I rarely buy J hooks. Circle hooks work that well.

Here's the secret — you cannot set the hook in the traditional J hook fashion using circle hooks. If you do, you will simply jerk the baited hook right out of the fish's mouth. Instead, you need to maintain constant line pressure, and let the fish hook itself against the steady pull. A hookset with a circle hook looks like this — the angler feels the tap, then slowly raises his or her rod and holds it in a raised position, as you can see in Figure 18-3. The fish will pull the rod down, and the action of the rod will drive the hook point into the fish's jaw, as shown in Figure 18-4. When the angler feels the fish has been hooked — often when the rod bends as much as it would with a J hook hookset — he or she simply commences reeling in the fish. Anglers used to fishing with J hooks will have a maddening time trying to retrain themselves, but they can do it. (At first, they're likely to instinctively jerk the hook out of the fish's mouth!) But beginners, who have never learned the hard hooksets of J hooks, will take right to it.

Figure 18-3: To set a circle hook, start by holding the rod still.

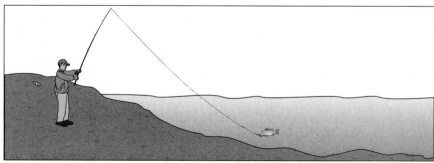

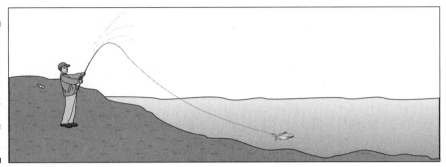

Figure 18-4:
The fish hooks itself on a circle hook against the bend of the rod.

A great way to learn how to use circle hooks is to go still fishing for almost any species and bring along some *rod holders*. Rod holders, often steel or heavy plastic, do just that — they hold the rod for you. For bank fishermen, rod holders are often designed to be driven into the ground or sand. (Surfcasters use them, too.) Some are made to attach to piers or fishing docks. There are many rod holders designed to be used with a variety of boats, as shown in Figure 18-5.

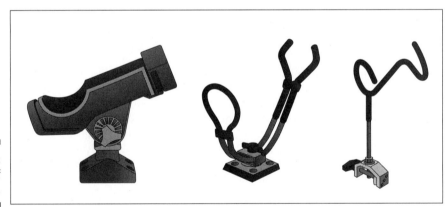

Figure 18-5:
A variety of rod holders.

All rod holders work the same: They hold the rod securely, allowing the angler to fish multiple rods, or to put some distance between himself and the rod (say, so he can sit by the fire and eat fried chicken). Whereas rod holders work with all kinds of fishing gear, they are ideally suited for bank fishing with spinning, spincast, or baitcasting gear. And they work perfectly when paired with circle hooks.

When using rod holders, the angler doesn't have to fight the urge to set the hook. Simply cast the bait out, and place the rod in the holder. Keep the line fairly tight. When a fish strikes, the rod pulls down, or *loads,* against the weight of the fish. (It is important to have strong rod holders, mounted securely, or you risk losing your gear!) When the rod is sufficiently loaded, the rod is removed from the holder, and the fish is already hooked and ready for battle.

Kids, beginners, and elderly anglers may have trouble setting the hook with sufficient force. This kind of still fishing — using rod holders and circle hooks — removes the need to "cross the fish's eyes" with a rocking hookset. And the enjoyment of fighting the fish is the same.

Experiment with circle hooks, and I (Greg) think you'll find that most caught fish are hooked in the corner of the mouth, ready for an easy release. I also think you'll find that fish hooked with circle hooks have a difficult time throwing the hook during the fight. When the circle hook finds its place, the fish is quite simply . . . hooked.

Fighting a Fish the Right Way

After a fish is hooked, the battle begins. If you maintain a tight line to the fish, the hook should remain seated in the flesh of the fish. But you still need to get the fish to you, and that process is called *fighting* or *playing* a fish.

Like playing tennis or any other sport, fighting a fish is a physical sensation. The fish is alive and working against the strange pull in its mouth. You have many tools at your disposal, including a rod and a reel with a drag, but the fish has things like its physical strength, the current, and a full understanding of its underwater domain. It will use all of these things and more to free itself. This section gives you practical advice to help you get the fish you hook into your hand.

Although it's more sporty to subdue fish on lighter tackle, you need to use enough tackle for the job. Using an outfit that doesn't let you bear down on the fish may still land you a fish after a long fight, but if the fish is totally exhausted when you land it, you didn't use heavy enough gear, or you didn't push your gear to the limit. Match your tackle to the conditions and the kind of fish you're after, so you can catch and release fish in a reasonable time. Otherwise, you may end up exhausting and killing every fish you catch, even inadvertently.

Savoring the most enjoyable part of fishing

Having a big fish on the end of your line is like any other emergency situation: If you haven't been through it before, you may get rattled. But it's only an emergency for the fish. Fighting and landing a fish is one art where you definitely learn from your mistakes, if only because you'll replay them a thousand times in your head. The better the fish, the more times you'll tell yourself, "Darn, if I'd only just. . . ."

Understand, too, that some fish are going to get away. That's part of fishing. After all, you don't really want to land every fish that bites — angling is so alluring because of its challenges. In any sport, to form a good rivalry, the other team has to win sometimes, too. And there are variables that lie (mostly) outside of your control. Sometimes the fish tangles the line around the sunken limb it was finning under when you cast toward it. Or the line will drag across a rock's rough edge and part. A jumping fish might throw the hook. It happens. It may or may not happen the next time, which is why you try again.

Having a fish hooked is the fun part of fishing. That tug. That pushing and head-shaking and throbbing. That wildness. These are the prime thrills of fishing. It's you against the fish, and the fish is in its element. That you will win is not a foregone conclusion (although the more fish you fight, the better your chances are). Win or lose, the fight is always a thrill. Enjoy it.

As wily as a fish is, and as big and strong as some fish can be, you always have plenty of tricks and tools to subdue even the largest fish. But start with this: When a fish is hooked, it takes precedence over everything else. If you've hooked a big fish, and you're fishing with a partner, he or she should come to your aid. This assistance may involve being ready to net the fish, or simply moving other rods or objects out of your way. (**Note:** He or she doesn't help you catch the fish by actually touching the rod or reel — instead your partner merely assists with the other stuff.)

Focus all your attention on the fish at the end of your line. Not only does this allow you to enjoy the experience, but you're better able to spot obstacles that could break your line and are more prepared to counter the movements of the fish. For example, if you see and feel the fish head to the right, you may need to pull your rod back to the left.

Letting the rod, reel, and line help you

A good fishing rod can be a great tool if you remember to let the rod do some of the work. It was designed to do just that. Follow the advice of Izaak Walton and keep the fish under the bend of the rod. This means that you should hold the rod at an angle that allows it to bend. (If you were to point that rod directly at the fish, it wouldn't bend at all.) It doesn't have to bend double, but it should flex. This flexing of the rod, more than anything else, will tire (and eventually conquer) a fish. No matter how far the fish runs, no matter how much it jumps or shakes, the rod will flex, keeping pressure on the hook. This constant pressure on the hook keeps the fish from coming off. So, when fighting a fish, keep the rod tip up and the line taut!

When fighting a fish, the drag mechanism on your reel serves as another ally. The drag works by allowing some line out while the reel is engaged, providing a little give and thus preventing a fish from breaking the line. When you set the drag properly (as covered in Chapter 16), the drag acts as a brake that further tires the fish. In most cases, the time to set the drag is before you cast. Adjusting the drag while you are fishing becomes just one more thing that you can mess up, and it should only be done if a big fish is on the verge of breaking off. It helps if you know where your reel's drag is located and understand how it works before you reach for it while a big fish is on the line. If the fish is able to pull line from the spool incessantly, you need to tighten the drag a bit. If the fish seems to be forcing your line to its breaking point, and the drag isn't giving any line at all, you should loosen the drag a touch. Adjust it only slightly in either direction!

When a large fish runs off a great deal of line, the resistance of the water against the line creates even more drag in the form of friction. This works in your favor if you have a sense of how much added pressure your tackle can take. Although you would never intentionally allow a fish to take line, if the fish pulls out line against your drag, don't panic. Stay calm, and let the fish tow that extra line through the water. Eventually, you'll gain it back on the spool as you work the fish toward you. If the fish takes out so much line that you're in danger of being *spooled* — or losing all of your line — then you need to do something drastic, such as move the boat to follow the fish or wade up or downstream, or you're in big trouble.

Pulling up, then reeling down

When fighting a fish, you want to recover the line so that you can eventually get the fish close enough to grasp or net. With a small fish, you can usually keep the rod tip up and reel the fish in, pausing when it makes a run. But the act of reeling, when you're hooked up with a big fish, can be the longest and most tiring part of the fight, so it pays to know how to do it right.

Most newcomers get a fish on and reel for dear life. This technique does you no good and can even harm you by causing bad line twist or stressing the line to the point of breaking. When hooked up with a big fish, pull up on the rod to bring the fish toward you; then drop the rod tip and, while you do, reel up line. Repeat as needed. Do not allow the line to go slack while dropping the rod tip!

Remember, too, that every pull up is not going to bring the fish in. Sometimes a fish will take a lot of line before you're able to recover any. Or you may have gained a great deal of line, and then the fish sees the boat and tears away on another run. Keep the pressure on — it's the only way to land the fish.

Getting the fish pointed up

If you can keep the head of the fish up, or pointing toward the surface instead of the bottom, then you can direct the fight. With its head up, the fish is disoriented and can't see where to go (that is, it can't see a rock to slip under or a weedbed to dive for). If the fish can get its head down, you're in the position of reacting while the fish picks where it will take the fight.

Keeping the head up doesn't mean rearing back at all costs. Sometimes a little pressure to one side or the other will do the trick. You're in contact with the fish, and you just have to feel your way through the fight, responding to its twists and turns by pulling back, easing up, or changing direction — whatever it takes. Fighting a fish is mostly about feeling the movements of the fish and reacting to counter those moves.

Using current if it's there

A fish tends to run away from the pressure of a hook, line, and rod. If you have hooked your fish in moving water, try to position yourself downstream from the fish. That way, the fish fights not only you and your tackle, but the current, as well. This move may not always be possible, but when it is, do it, even if you have to back out of the water and walk downstream. When boat fishing, it may mean moving toward the stern of the boat. (Assuming the bow is pointed upstream.)

Reacting when the fish jumps

If your tussle with a fish ends suddenly when the fish takes to the air, it can mean only one thing — the fish has jumped free, and your fight is over. It may have broken the line or shaken the hook, but either way, it's off. In most such cases, I (Peter) bow when a fish jumps. When I *bow* to a fish, I literally bow. I bend from the waist, drop my rod tip, and extend my arms like a waiter offering a tray full of canapes. As soon as the fish falls back to the water, I come tight again. When a fish is airborne, it may reach a point in its trajectory when all of its weight and momentum snap against the line. Without the buoyancy of the water to act as a shock absorber, this is a very good time for knots to break under the added force of gravity. A hard-mouthed fish, like a tarpon, may not be very deeply hooked to begin with. The force of a jump may be all that is needed to dislodge a hook.

Handling a snagged fish

Where I (Greg) fish for flathead catfish, the fish live among hundreds of sunken trees. Although the trees make for great cover, it can be a nightmare to fight a big fish near all this timber. What happens with a hooked fish from time to time is that the fight will suddenly lurch to a halt — the fish will wrap my line around a log or limb, and stay put, content to wait it out. This can happen to you, too, any time you're fishing near weeds, docks, rocks, or other cover. (In other words, everywhere you should be fishing.) When this happens, you'll feel sick, but you have at least one trick to try. It may not work, but if a slow, steady pull won't free the fish, try giving it slack line. This is the only time you should give a hooked fish slack line, but giving the fish freedom from the pull will sometimes make it swim away from the snag and free itself.

Knowing how long to play a fish

You should always try to get a fish in as soon as possible, especially if you plan on releasing it. The longer a fish fights, the more lactic acid builds up in the fish's muscles, and the harder it is to revive. Releasing a fish that you have fought to the point of exhaustion makes no sense because the fish may well die anyway. Sometimes the fish can be revived (more on that in a bit), but not always. When it comes to being able to release a fish, a sprinting fight is better than a marathon.

In the ocean, ending the fight quickly is even more important (even if you are keeping the fish) because a long, splashy fight often attracts predators like sharks that will end the fight for you by taking a meal. This happened to me (Peter) in the Florida Keys with a tarpon that weighed more than 100 pounds. I fought hard, but I could have fought harder and followed my guide's advice and gotten the tarpon into the boat within ten minutes. Instead, I prolonged the fight, and my heart was broken because 200 yards out I saw a tremendous commotion and then felt my line grow slack as a huge shark devoured my tarpon.

The warmer the water is, the more stress the fish will endure during the fight. When fishing warm water during the peak of summer, try to land the fish after a short fight.

Landing, Netting, and Gaffing Fish

After you have fought a fish to the bank or boatside, your next task is to land or boat it. Most fish can be caught by a lone angler. A word of warning, though: Many, many big fish have gotten away at the last possible moment. More than a few anglers have suffered heartbreak as a trophy fish eluded the net or hand right at boat- or bankside. When I (Greg) hook a big fish, my first goal is to get it up where I can see it. My second goal is to get it in hand, and that goal requires attention to detail right up until the end.

This section gives you the lay of the land (or the water) for most fish that you can land by yourself. The larger the fish, the more the task calls for at least one helper. When fishing for big fish in salt- or freshwater, think about landing the fish before you hook it — do you have what you need to safely land a large fish? It's hard to operate both the rod and reel and net or gaff by yourself. (To say nothing about posing for and taking the obligatory photograph to come next.)

The right way to use a landing net

For trout and bass, some say that you definitely should net a hooked fish if you want to release it back into the water with the hope that it will live and reproduce. The theory assumes that the fish will be less exhausted when netted rather than landed by hand.

Having said that, I (Peter) can tell you that I rarely use a net when trout fishing (or when bass fishing, for that matter). At this stage of my angling career, I can get most fish within my grasp when they still have some life in them. With trout, I reach under the belly and lift up until I'm cradling the fish gently. Then I lift it out of the water. For bass, I grab the fish by the lower lip. If I'm fishing a lure with several treble hooks, I hold the line taut with my free hand and then come around with my rod hand to grasp the fish by the lower lip. If I have a really big fish, I use a net.

If you use a net, you or your partner should have the net positioned in front of the one doing the netting as the fight concludes. Keep it out of the water, though, until you intend to net the fish. This works better if other rods, tackle boxes, and so on have been cleared away. As you bring the fish closer to the net and netter, make sure the fish's head is up and the fish is not still totally *green,* or full of fight. (You don't want to fully exhaust a fish, but bringing it in too green will only result in chaos, and the fish will often get away.) Then, in one smooth motion, the netter should swoop the net down and around the fish, getting the fish through the center of the net, head-first. As shown in Figure 18-6, hold the rod tip high and swoop the net under the fish, head-first.

Never try to net a fish tail-first, and don't chase the fish through the water with the net. If the fish eludes the net on the first try, get the net clear of the water and fight the fish back to the bank- or boatside. When it approaches again, make another attempt to net the fish. Avoid letting the hook or hooks in the fish's mouth get tangled in the edge of the net.

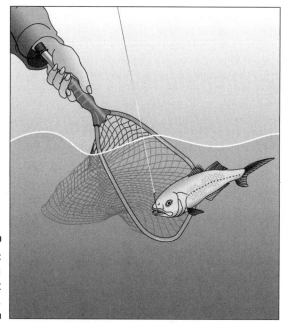

Figure 18-6:
The classic
landing net
position.

What about a gaff?

Certain things in life are designed so well that you take one look at them and you know what they are for. A *gaff* is one of them. It's really nothing more than a humongous hook on a long shaft. Used almost exclusively in saltwater, a gaff allows you to snag a hooked fish and bring it ashore or onboard. Think of it as a net that grabs hold. When you gaff a fish, most of the time you intend to keep it. This is not always true. For example, a lip gaff, not quite the heavy artillery of a standard gaff, is often used by tarpon fishermen who want to release their catch. But for most other cases, you gaff and kill.

Surf fishermen have short hand-held gaffs that are great for bluefish, but most gaffs are long-handled and are designed to be used while leaning over the side of a boat. With smaller fish (anything up to 30 pounds), you can probably do your own gaffing. Try to gaff the fish somewhere in the head, gill, or shoulder region.

When It's Time to Say Goodbye: Releasing Fish

Fishing, like hunting, can be a blood sport. But it's very different in one significant way. After you shoot a deer or bird, it's a goner — you can't release it back into the wild. A caught fish is different, in that it can always be returned. So you have a choice: Do you kill the fish, or do you let it go?

First, you need to ensure that it is legal to keep the fish. Know your state laws, and the rules governing the particular body of water you're fishing. Some places have size, bag (the number of fish in your possession), or slot limits (protecting the largest and smallest of a species), and some fish can't be killed at all. So, before you endanger the fish, it's your responsibility to know the laws. We cover licenses more completely in Chapter 2, and you can check your local laws by looking up your state's fish and wildlife department online or in the phone book.

If the fish is legally yours, so is the decision about the fish's fate. Don't let anybody tell you that you're immoral if you decide to kill fish. If you intend to eat them, killing them is okay with us. However, and this is a big however, if we all killed all the fish we caught, fishing would stink for all of us.

This is especially true of top predator gamefish like trout, bass, catfish, and walleye. They're the top predator in their environment, and the way nature has set things up, there are fewer top predators out there relative to animals lower down the food chain. Which means that if you take a bunch of trout out of a stream, the fishing quality in that stream will definitely decline. The same holds for ocean-going big game, like marlin and tuna. The world just doesn't have that many top predators left. Humans, the ultimate predator, need to kill other predators responsibly.

Besides, the smaller (but legal) fish of most species taste better than the old warriors. It's much better for the overall fish population if you take three 1-pound channel cats home to fry, as opposed to one 10-pounder. And you'll be happier too, as the meat of the smaller fish will be cleaner and fresher-tasting. Leave the biggest adult fish to breed and pass on the big-fish genes. Most bodies of water have many more juvenile fish of a species than elders, and taking these smaller fish often has no ill effect on the lake's health.

Taking quick action after landing a fish

If you decide to release a fish, or if you're required by law to release a fish, you must act quickly to allow the fish to survive its encounter with you. A fish can handle getting caught — there's no question catch-and-release fishing works. But certain species survive being caught better than others, and other conditions such as temperature and handling affect mortality rates.

Follow these tips to increase a fish's chances of surviving:

✔ **Leave the fish in the water as much as possible.**

✔ **Handle the fish as little as possible.**

✔ **Wet your hands or use a wet rag (if you have one handy) to hold the fish.** Theses technique causes less damage to its scales and protective coating.

✔ **Use forceps, pliers, or hook removers to remove the hook.** (Hook removers work especially well on hooks deep in the fish's mouth.)

✔ **If the hook is embedded very deep inside the fish's mouth or gullet, too deep for removal, cut the line, leaving the hook in the fish.** The hook may eventually rust out or work itself free, and the fish may be able to feed normally with the hook still in its mouth. By the way, artificials are usually not taken deep, and setting the hook quickly will help prevent swallowed hooks. And circle hooks often hook the fish's mouth, not its throat or stomach.

Sometimes, releasing the fish is relatively easy. You simply remove the hook, and the fish wiggles vigorously, which lets you know that it is ready to take off for freedom. Sometimes, the fish won't wait for you to release it. Instead, it will wriggle free as it nears the bank or boat and hightails it away.

Reviving an exhausted fish

If the fight has been especially long or strenuous, the fish comes in totally exhausted. You'll know this because the fish will float on its side or back, hardly moving. If you simply unhook and release an exhausted fish right away, you have a belly-up, soon-to-be-dead fish on your hands. Before you release, you need to revive.

A good rule of thumb to follow in figuring out if a fish needs reviving is this: If the fish lets you hold it and doesn't struggle, revive it. After all, any self-respecting wild animal will take off like greased lightning to escape the clutches of a strange creature. To a fish, a human is a strange creature.

If a fish is merely exhausted (and not bleeding or otherwise injured), it may spring back to life and be fine if it receives the proper care. Follow these steps to help ensure that a caught-and-released fish survives:

1. **If you're in heavy current, move to gentler current. Hold the fish gently and keep it under the surface of the water, pointing it upstream.**

   Cradle it from below if you can. If you cannot, hold it gently by its sides. You may grasp some mid-size fish (salmon and stripers, for example) by the tail. On lakes or in the ocean, however, current usually isn't a factor when reviving a fish.

2. **Move the fish backward and forward (mostly forward, if possible) so that its gills are forced to open and close.**

   When properly done, this technique delivers oxygen to a heavily oxygen-depleted fish. Reviving the fish so that it can swim under its own steam may take a few minutes, and sometimes up to an hour. It lets you know that it is ready to be released when it starts to wiggle.

3. **Release the fish.**

   It should swim slowly away. If it rolls over on its back and lays there, this is not a good sign. Bring the fish back under your control and continue to revive it.

If you can't revive the fish, take it home and eat it. Or give it to someone who will. Or leave it in the water, where it will be eaten by other fish, turtles, or other creatures of that habitat. Know that you did what you could to revive it.

Part V
After the Catch

"Someone should tell Phil he's sautéing three of my lures in that pan of onions and garlic."

In this part . . .

Because catch-and-release fishing is so popular, you'll find a bunch of advice on taking a good photograph of a trophy fish, and tips for releasing a fish safely back into the water. There's even material here covering the latest in fish mounts — fiberglass replicas that allow you to release the fish and still have a trophy on the wall. For those times when you're looking to catch and eat, you'll find step-by-step instructions for cleaning those fish you've caught and tasty recipes for cooking them.

Chapter 19

Photographing and Preserving Fish for Posterity

*T*homas Edison, when asked what went into the glamorous job of being an amazing inventor, replied, "99 percent perspiration, 1 percent inspiration." Sounds like fishing! You spend almost all your time trying to catch fish, and the actual amount of fish-on-the-line time seems very small by comparison. So how do you make the memories last?

Today's technology makes it possible to keep the memories of your fish alive and kicking — and the fish can be alive and swimming, too! Digital cameras range in price from expensive to very affordable, but even the least-expensive cameras take quality photographs. You can easily carry your camera along on fishing trips (we recommend placing it in a bag or waterproof container). Video cameras are compact, lightweight, and suitable to record fishing memories, too.

In the old days, a trophy fish ended up cooked or hanging on the wall. Today's anglers often release their biggest fish, but that doesn't mean they can't have wall mounts in their homes or offices. Fiberglass replicas, produced from photos and measurements of live trophy fish, allow you to have your fish and release it, too.

Catching a big fish is an amazing thing: it's a reward for hard work, a celebration, a gift. This chapter tells you how to make the most of the moment when it happens so that you can enjoy it for years to come.

Hurry Up and Take Your Time: Photographing Fish

Very few people are born with the natural ability to catch fish consistently, but most of us have a native talent to take lousy pictures. What makes photographing big fish difficult starts with this happy problem: You just caught a big fish, and you're shaking like a leaf! Compounding the issue is the fact that your subject is alive, and if you intend to return it to the water alive, you don't have a lot of time for a photo shoot.

The time to prepare for a great fish photo comes before the fish is hooked. Know where your camera is and how to use it. Check the batteries before each trip and make sure the lens is clear. Then, all you have to do is catch a fish worthy of a picture. I (Greg) take photos of many of the fish I catch. Why not? With digital cameras, the cost is nil. That way, all the photos become a log of sorts of the whole trip.

This section breaks down everything you need to have, do, or think about to photograph your catch in its best light.

Digital cameras: Perfect fishing partners

Your cellphone may take photographs, but that doesn't mean it's a real camera. A fishing magazine I (Greg) subscribe to recently explained that it can no longer print most reader-submitted fish photos, because most of them were taken with cellphones, and those photos often can't be enlarged enough to print in the magazine. (And we're not talking about a full-page spread.)

You want a quality photo of your big fish, so carry a real camera. Most are small, compact, and maybe even water-resistant. Keep the batteries fresh or freshly charged, and empty the photos onto your computer or other source from time to time to preserve them, should the camera be lost or damaged.

With digital cameras, not only can you see immediately how well you framed the shot, you can take a ton of photos. Do it. You never know which pictures will turn out. Shoot fast and often, and then release the fish. (Take photos of the release, too.)

One of the most effective tools for good picture taking is a wide-angle lens. Some point-and-shoot cameras have a wide-angle function included. With a wide angle, you can get closer to your subject, which makes the fish that the angler is holding up look a lot bigger in the foreground. You might think this is cheating, but it's not. All it does is ensure that the fish in the photo looks as big, as nice, and as exciting as the fish in your memory. Boaters take note — a wide-angle is the only effective way to get the boat _and_ the subject in the picture without having to leave the boat to get the shot.

More and more cameras now do more and more of the work, leaving less opportunity to mess up to the photographer. Of course, real photographic artists may want the ability to make their own choice of lenses, exposures, and so on. But for most of us, most of the time, all we want is the best picture with the least fuss. If this is your outlook, automatic everything works great. These are called "point and shoot" cameras.

Of course, as with everything else, there are more and less-expensive point and shoot cameras. If you want to spend a few extra bucks, look for the following features:

✔ Autofocus gets your subject looking sharp without a lot of unnecessary fiddling around while your fish tries to squirm out of your hands. Remember to point the camera at the _most important_ thing first because that is what it will focus on. Then lock the focus and finish composing your shot.

✔ A simple zoom function will give you more choices, especially close-up capability.

✔ In Chapter 6, I recommend polarized lenses for your sunglasses. For the same reason, a polarizing filter on a camera works well when taking pictures on the water. Not only does it cut down on glare, but it also enhances the richness of the colors in the scene. Also, a polarizing filter will let your camera see into the water to capture the look of a clear lake, or a glimpse of a trout feeding in a pool. This gives you a look into the world of the fish.

Lighting at all times

When you can, follow the basic rule of photography — position the sun over the photographer's shoulder so that it illuminates the subject. The angler holding the fish should look into the sun.

It's easy for me to tell you as a photographer to get the sun over your shoulder, but there are times when the sun doesn't want to go over your shoulder. You could be stuck on a riverbank looking into the sun. Or it might be high noon and the sun hangs directly overhead. In cases like this, a flash will fill in the shadows on your subject.

Because you often fish in low light periods, such as dusk and dawn, poor lighting hurts many fish shots. Get the subject into as much natural light as you can find, and use a flash to brighten the shot, regardless of the time of day. (This is another argument against relying on cellphone cameras, as not all of them have flashes.) The constant use of your camera's flash will brighten anglers' faces hidden under ball caps and any other shady spots.

Working with live subjects . . . or not

You must first decide if you are going to kill the fish. Part of the point of taking a good photograph is so that you can then release your fish but remember it always. If you don't want to kill the fish, there are tips in Chapter 18 for getting the fish free and back in the water in a minimum amount of time. If you decide to kill the fish, time isn't a crucial factor, although you don't want to prolong the death of your catch.

Whether you kill the fish or not, a good photograph will preserve your fish at its finest — right after you caught it, when it's colorful and vibrant. Photos taken hours after a fish's death — sometimes posed in the driveway or garage — don't do much to render the fish's world. In general, a fish looks best when you photograph it fresh out of the water. The wetness makes the colors pop and gives an overall sheen to the fish.

As long as you hold the fish in the water, facing upstream (if there is a current); the fish will survive a long, long time. When you want to snap a picture, lift the fish out of the water, supporting its body as you do so. (Remember, the fish's internal organs are normally supported by the buoyancy of water.) Always handle a fish with wet hands to protect the fish's natural slimecoat.

Another trick is keeping the fish in the landing net, with the net lowered into the water. This forms a temporary holding pen for the fish, and allows you to get ready for a good photograph. If your boat has a livewell, that's another option.

Hold 'em high: Posing fish for photographs

In your mind's eye, you remember everything about where you caught that big fish. You can see it vividly: the trees in the background, the mountains in the distance, the boat under you, your kid who said "I don't care about the fish, Daddy. I'm tired and I want to go home." Don't try to capture all this in a photograph. You'll end up with a picture where everything looks dinky. Instead, remember that anyone looking at your fish photos will respond to two things: the fish and the human. Concentrate on those two elements and have them occupy as much of the photo as you can, as you see in Figure 19-1.

Figure 19-1: Hold your catch high and pose with a smile on your face.

Hardly anyone takes photos the way they used to back in the early days of photography — all those stiff, unsmiling people staring into the lens with all the warmth and happiness of someone who has just swallowed a live toad. Today, we want some action, some facial expression (a smile is never wrong). We all appreciate photos with a little art to them, where the subjects don't look like early arrivals at an embalmer's convention.

The successful angler should always be the one holding the fish, although Greg's wife has been known to refuse to hold some of the "mean-looking" catfish she has landed. Hold the fish horizontally and across your body. This looks more natural because a fish seldom swims vertically. If you push the fish too far out in front of you, you look like you're trying to fool the camera, making the fish appear bigger than it is. But don't let the fish disappear against your body, either. (And while we're on this subject: a decent shirt makes a better background for a fish than say, a "Bikini Inspector" t-shirt from Spring Break, 2006.)

I (Peter) have a mess of pictures of me with fish. In all honesty, they're just a bunch of mug shots of a grinning goon. Happy, but pretty goofy. I much prefer pictures where the angler is caught in action, such as

✔ During the fight with the rod bent. This kind of photo tells a story, and people find it naturally interesting.

✔ When landing the fish, when the viewer gets to savor some of the anticipation and excitement of the moment.

✔ When releasing the fish. This presents the fish and the angler in the fish's environment. As with the fight, this photo expresses a story.

Taking measurements for bragging rights

They say a photo is worth a thousand words, and this time, they may be right. But when I (Greg) show someone a fish picture, they almost always ask for numbers, too. If possible, carry a scale designed to weigh fish. Because I fish for catfish, I have handheld scales that go up to 75 pounds. If you fish for bass, one that weighs up to 15 pounds will suit you well. You can choose from spring or digital scales. Digital scales rely on batteries, but spring scales are ready all the time. Some spring scales feature jaws that pinch the fish's mouth for you, making the fish both easier to weigh and hold. Scales of all kinds are available anywhere tackle is sold. I know, I know, fishermen are supposed to lie. But go ahead and weigh a fish on a good scale. You can always be the only one of us telling the truth.

If you don't have the room for a scale, you should carry a tape measure. With it, you can record the length and girth of your fish. Measure the girth by going around the fish right behind the pectoral fins. This will help the taxidermist or the artist making your fiberglass replica, and there are mathematic formulas out there for converting the length and girth of a fish into a weight. (Different species require different formulas.)

Come On, Everyone's Doing It: Making a Fish Videotape

I'm (Greg) a photograph guy. But then a few years ago my older brother started bringing his palm-sized video camera along on fishing trips. Suddenly a photograph of a caught fish wasn't enough. Now the whole fight had to be videotaped.

At first, like so many things my older brother does, this weirded me out. Wasn't video footage only for those Saturday morning fishing shows? Apparently not any longer. I must admit, though, he got some pretty exciting battles caught on tape (and that hilarious moment when I threw the head of a shad at our younger brother).

More than that, we also documented stretches of river, campsites where we stayed, and bald eagles flying around a nest. I still love the understated art of a photograph, but I see the value of a videotape, and maybe you will, too.

YouTube, here you come

As with digital photographs, when it comes to videotaping, the sharing of the images becomes the issue. Popular Web sites like YouTube have made it possible to post video clips online, where anyone can go and watch it. If you go on a deep-sea charter with five of your college buddies, an edited clip of the most exciting fish battles could be posted online, where everyone from the trip will have access.

Like photo-sharing sites, this allows you to place the clip in one place without having to mess with e-mailed files. As with photography, there is a skill and an art to taking good video. Editing is the key. Using either your camera's or computer's software, pare the trip down to the good parts. A fishing trip might be slow and contemplative, and that may be the best part of the whole trip. But a fishing video should probably be more action-packed. Adding good music helps.

Downsides to being your own videographer

It takes a second to capture a good photograph. You can pick up the camera, click a shot of your partner fighting a fish, and then get back to the business of readying the net and preparing to land the fish. If you're trying to videotape the whole struggle, leaping fish and all, you're not being very helpful to your partner. Videotaping works best if you have at least three people along on a trip. One works the camera while the other helps land the fish.

You might also need to think about your goals for fishing. Are you fishing merely to document the act of doing it? Are you hoping to get your clip discovered by Hollywood agents? Probably not. So don't get overly obsessed with recording the event.

You Want This Fish Forever: One for the Wall

For some anglers, a photograph or even a videotape is insufficient to memorialize a great fish. You might want a three-dimensional representation of your fish, and if you do, you have two options. You can kill and keep your fish, take it to a taxidermist, and have the fish *mounted,* or turned into a wall mount, or you can have a fiberglass replica made of your fish. The replica could be made to match your fish in appearance, size, and shape. With replicas, the fish does not have to be kept or killed, although the artist will want the measurements and good photographs.

Baitshops, diners, and hunting camps often have walls dotted with mounted fish. Nothing really portrays the actual size of a fish quite like a wall mount — either a real skin mount or a replica.

Caution: Taxidermist at work

If you truly want to keep your fish forever, and looking as close as possible to a living, breathing fish, then you need to take your fish to a taxidermist. A great taxidermist is an artist, and he or she will make your fish look as life-like as it did the day you caught it. The fish can also be posed on driftwood or other natural-looking backdrops.

A mounted fish doesn't rot — all the natural parts have either been pre-served or replaced with a foam filler. With care, a good mount should last for a long time. But, a mount isn't a real fish anymore, and eventually, the colors will fade and the fish will look like what it is — a shell of what it was when it was alive.

Ask around, and shop online or in the phone book for a good taxidermist. You'll want one fairly close to home; if you catch a big fish on vacation, you probably should choose a taxidermist closer to where you live, not visit. While you face the hassle of getting the fish home, you stand a better chance of knowing your taxidermist's reputation if you go local. You can also stay in better contact while the work is being done.

Taxidermy isn't cheap, due to the time and effort involved in the process. Taxidermists will often charge by the inch, so the bigger a fish is, the more it costs to have a mount made.

Know the laws: Keeping fish

If you intend to keep a fish for a wall mount, you must of course ensure the fish can be legally kept. Know the size limits for the body of water. Don't assume that just because the fish is big it's legal — some fish have seasons, and some bodies of water have *slot limits,* meaning that only fish within a cer-tain slot can be kept. (This protects the largest and the smallest of a species.)

Knowing the laws beforehand will prevent you from being in the awkward situation of having a big fish on the bank or in the boat with no idea of what you can legally do with it.

Honey, look what followed me home: Taking fish on the road

The better you handle your fish, the better chance your mount has of looking like the fish that you caught. Here are a few tips:

- ✔ **Photograph the fish as soon as you can.** Photos give your taxidermist the most accurate record of the appearance of your fish.

- ✔ **If possible, lay the fish out flat, put it in a sealed plastic bag (or at least one that has as much air as possible squeezed out of it), and immediately freeze the fish. Make sure the fins are in their natural position, not folded over or pinched in any way.**

- ✔ **If freezing is impossible, cover the fish with a wet cloth to preserve the sheen and colors of the skin and put the fish in your cooler, laying it as flat as possible.**

- ✔ **If you don't have a freezer or ice, try to keep the fish alive and in the water, tethering it with a stringer through the jaw.**

- ✔ **Write down where and when you caught the fish; what kind of bait, fly, or lure you used; your name, address, and phone number; and your fishing license number.** This information will help with conservation officers, customs officials, and your taxidermist. Although fish switching may not be as upsetting as having your baby switched in the maternity ward, it is nice to know that the beautiful fish hanging on the wall is definitely, positively the fish that you caught.

Fiberglass replicas: A win-win alternative

Due to the increased national drive for catch-and-release fishing, artists have begun making fish mounts not from real fish but from photographs and measurements of real fish. Instead of using the actual fish, a replica is made from fiberglass and painted to look like your trophy.

Check online and ask around in baitshops to see if anyone makes fiberglass replicas in your area. It's okay to have a replica made in another state, if that's necessary. You won't have to get the actual fish to the place, and the replica can be shipped to you.

Not that these are inexpensive, either, but a fiberglass replica does allow you to save the life of the fish. It's a win for you and a win for the fish. Not only does this allow someone else the pleasure of catching your trophy fish in the future, but you return that fish to its natural habitat and allow it to continue doing its thing — which includes making more baby fish. Trophy fish genes are what you want in your local waters. The more big fish reproduce, the more healthy, big-fish genes get passed on.

Fiberglass replicas look lifelike, and hold up well to time and elements. Like skin mounts, they can be positioned in a variety of poses and habitats. If you desire a replica, do what you were probably going to do anyway — measure your fish for length and girth, and take photographs of the fish from several angles. Then release it. I bet you both go home feeling better.

Chapter 20

Cleaning Fish for the Table

. . . .

In This Chapter

▶ Scaling, skinning, and gutting

▶ Filleting and steaking

▶ Storing your catch

. . . .

Cleaning fish isn't the most fun part of fishing. On a cold night, standing at the dock and filleting a mess of bluefish is a miserable, smelly job. But if you want to eat fish, you have to clean the fish (unless of course you're a parent, in which case we strongly suggest you have your kids clean the fish).

Remember, too, that something important is going on when you kill a fish to eat it. Our ancestors fished only so they could eat, so catching a few fish for the table is a grand old tradition. Give it the respect it deserves. With all the attention paid to catch-and-release fishing these days, some will try to make you feel guilty for killing even a single fish. Don't let them. On the other hand, remember that many fish such as trout and salmon are top predators, meaning they're at the top of the food chain. There are far fewer of them than there are herd animals, so it's far easier to fish out all the trout in a stream than all the minnows.

Fish are a renewable resource, and there's nothing morally wrong with keeping and eating legally caught fish. But you want to treat fish humanely, and you want those fish to taste the best they possibly can. And so this chapter covers all you ever wanted to know about readying a fish for cleaning, slicing it up, and freezing it for maximum freshness.

Taking Quick Action to Preserve Taste and Texture

Before you catch any fish, you should know whether you plan to keep any to eat. If your plan is to fish for food, have a cooler handy, or some method of keeping the fish alive, like a livewell or stringer. Then, when you catch a fish, place it in the livewell (see the later "Storing and transporting so your fish stay fresh" section for more on livewells), creel, or on the stringer. If you can't keep the fish alive, kill it quickly and humanely. For the sake of good eating, as well as being a nice person, you really should kill the fish right away. There are two big advantages to a quick kill if you want to eat the fish:

- ✔ It allows you to dress the fish at the peak of freshness. All those guts can affect the flavor of the fish if you leave them in there all day.

- ✔ As with tomatoes or peaches, bruised tissue is mealy. A dead fish will not flop around and bruise its flesh trying to escape.

The following sections explain how to kill a fish quickly — for its benefit and your own — and how to store and transport your fish properly so it will taste as fresh as possible on the dinner table.

Being a good executioner

I recommend that you buy yourself a small club called a *fish priest*. Then, when you have a fish you want to eat, you whack it over the head a couple of times. If you're out on the salt and you have brought in a bigger fish (up to 50 pounds or so), an old bowling pin serves wonderfully as a club.

Killing a fish with a club is not pleasant. But it shouldn't be a dramatic, drawn-out process, either. Hold a small fish firmly around the middle of its body, and use the priest to deliver a crisp blow to the top of its head. When killing a fish that's too large to hold with one hand, position the fish on the ground or floor of the boat. You might use your feet to keep the fish from moving around too much. Again, deliver a blow to the top of the fish's head with sufficient force to kill it. Don't tap the fish. Swing the club hard enough to kill it quickly and humanely.

Storing and transporting so your fish stay fresh

If there is anything that smells worse than bad fish, we don't want to know about it. Part of the reason that fish can turn so quickly is because they're so delicate. Handled with proper tender-loving care, a well-cooked fish is one of the freshest-tasting things you can eat. The late A.J. McClane, former editor of *Field & Stream,* once explained the smell of fresh fish by saying that all fish, when kept properly, will smell a little bit like a cucumber that you just sliced open. He's right.

When you go fishing, plan ahead if you intend to keep any fish to eat. Carry one of the following along to keep your selected fish fresh, cool, and sometimes even alive until it's time to head home:

- ✔ **Willow creel:** A *creel* is a lightweight basket made to be worn over the shoulder, and the willow creel is a classic for a reason. The weave of the willow branches allows air to circulate, which is what you want. If you use a willow creel, the accepted old-timey way to keep fish is to line the bottom of the creel with green grass and then to put a layer of grass between the layers of fish. This method is good for a few hours (no more) in hot weather. Creels work best when wading and pursuing fish like trout.

- ✔ **Canvas creel:** Less pricey than willow creels, these usually have a washable plastic liner inside a canvas outer bag. If you dip the creel in water and get it good and soaked, evaporation will help cool fish. As with the willow creel, the canvas creel is for the freshwater angler.

- ✔ **Cooler:** Open the cooler, put the dead fish in. Close the chest. Coolers work best if you don't have to carry them far. Don't forget to add ice before you begin fishing! The ice will keep better if you leave it in bags.

Some anglers carry large plastic bags, like one- or two-gallon size or larger, and place their catch into those bags each time they ice a fish. This barrier keeps the fish from sliming your cooler, and it makes counting easier!

- ✔ **Livewell:** A *livewell* is a compartment plumbed with pumps to circulate fresh water through the compartment. Many boats have livewells. In most cases, you can keep fish alive in one for hours, although the warmer the water is, the harder it is to keep fish lively. If you happen to catch your fish from very deep water, more than 30 feet deep, the pressure change from lake to livewell may also kill it.

- ✔ **Stringer:** A piece of string or rope with a loop on one end designed to pass through one gill of the fish. Another kind of stringer features a light metal chain with clips at intervals that can be hooked through the bottom jaws of fish. You can keep a mess of fish alive this way by attaching one end of the stringer to your boat or the bank and putting the other end (with all the fish on it) back in the water. This is more of a freshwater tactic. I don't recommend it in the ocean because big gamefish on the prowl will treat your stringer like a nice big gob of live bait.

Cleaning: A Good Meal Starts with the First Cut

Fish cleaning can be a kitchen-destroying operation: scales flying everywhere, drying and sticking to everything, and guts sliding off the counter and clogging up the sink. Speaking from long and tragic experience, we can tell you that part of the reason that many spouses secretly hope that their mates come home fishless is that they do not want to deal with the mess. Guess what? — it doesn't have to be that messy. Our advice to you is that whenever possible, you clean the fish *before* you bring it into the kitchen.

You don't clean every fish the same way, and some of the following steps will vary based on fish species and personal preference. We'll tell you how to gut a fish, for example, but if you're filleting your fish, you probably won't need to mess with gutting it first (provided the fish can be kept alive until the knife comes out). Similarly, scaling is a bit of a hassle, but you don't always have to do it. The next sections give you everything you need to know about cleaning a fish, from scaling and gutting to filleting and cutting up your very own fish steaks.

You need only one tool to *dress* (another term for cleaning) most fish: a good knife. Peter's favorite is the Dexter, an American-made carbon steel knife that retails for less than $30. It sharpens easily, holds an edge fairly well, and performs double duty for vegetable slicing, cheese slicing, and any other general chopping or slicing chore. Find it online or at any store that sells good knives. You may also try a Rapala J. Marttiini, which is a very thin Finnish fillet knife that also works well as an all-rounder — but in the end, the Dexter works the best. Its blade is thin and with a slight curve that works well for filleting tasks, and it has enough oomph to cut through the backbone of a larger fish when you are making steaks. Unfortunately, it doesn't come with a sheath or holder, but most anglers fashion a case out of two pieces of cardboard taped together. The size of fillet knife you need depends on the size of the fish you're cutting up. For panfish, a four-inch fillet knife will work fine. Bigger fish call for longer blades, but a longer knife is harder to handle. For most fish, a six- or seven-inch blade will work great. A good cutting board helps, too.

Scaling

You want to *scale* a fish, or remove all its scales, when you intend to cook a fish with the skin on. Although most fish have scales (catfish do not), not every fish needs to be scaled. The scales on a trout, for example, are so small that you don't have to worry about them. In fact, you wouldn't know there were any scales on a trout if someone like me hadn't told you. Here's how to scale a fish:

1. **Take some newspaper and lay out about four spreads.**

2. **Run the knife against the grain of the scale.**

   Your motion should be firm enough to remove the scales, but not so strong that they go flying all over the place. (***Note:*** You can buy a specialized fish scaler, which is a handheld contraption with serrated edges made for rubbing off scales. It's probably worth the small investment because your knife will stay sharper longer if you don't use it for scaling.)

3. **When you have finished scaling, lift the fish and peel back the top sheet of paper. Lay the fish down on the next (clean) sheet of newspaper and throw out the top sheet with the scales.**

4. **Rinse the fish.**

If you're going to fillet a fish and remove its skin, there's no need to scale it.

Gutting

If you need to kill a fish but can't clean it for quite a while, you need to gut, or *eviscerate,* the fish to prevent the body organs from tainting the taste of the meat. If the fish can be kept alive until an hour or so before cleaning, and if you intend to fillet them, you can fillet a fish without gutting it. If you intend to scale your fish, too, that should be done before gutting it. You gut a fish to get rid of the organs in the body cavity. These are filled with all kinds of gunk, including digestive juices. For this reason you want to exercise care in slitting open the belly. It's less messy and keeps the flesh fresher if you don't pierce the organs while gutting:

1. **With the blade pointed toward the head, pierce the stomach cavity and make a slit toward the head.**

   Try not to make too deep a cut, just enough to get through the top layer of skin and flesh.

2. **Now pointing the knife toward the tail, completely open the stomach cavity.**

3. **Reach in and pull out the guts.**

4. **Detach the guts with the knife, or simply pull away.**

5. **Wrap the guts in the top sheet of paper and discard.**

Skinning catfish

Catfish don't have scales, but they must be skinned. Skinning a cat might be trickier than scaling a normal fish, and you need a set of pliers in addition to your knife. To skin a catfish:

1. **Make a cut in the skin right behind the gills, from the backbone to the belly, on both sides.**

2. **Make a cut along the backbone, going around the dorsal fin.**

3. **Use the pliers to pull the skin back toward the tail.**

   They do make special *skinning pliers* for this, and if you eat a lot of catfish, go ahead a get a pair at any tackle shop.

   Remember: After the skin is removed, a catfish can be filleted, steaked, or gutted like any other fish.

Filleting

Filleting a fish — that is, removing just the meatiest parts of the fish as efficiently as possible — is the perfect choice for many species of fish, most of the time. The process takes a certain amount of skill and dexterity, but expending a little more effort at the cleaning stage is worth it because it means no bones at the eating stage. When you get the hang of filleting, you can zip through a pile of fish pretty quickly, and it gives you a sense of accomplishment that you can do something as well as the old-timers.

Don't worry too much if you don't get absolutely all the meat off the fish when you first start filleting. The idea at the beginning is to get *some*. If you remove the skin from the fillets, as recommended , you don't have to scale the fish first, because the scales will come off with the skin. You'll be left with two pieces of skinless, scaleless, boneless meat (one from each side of the fish). Obviously, if you like to eat the skin, you can fillet a fish without removing the skin. In that case, you would still scale the fish unless you like to eat scales, too. Figure 20-1 shows the basics of filleting a fish:

1. **Cut down to the backbone just behind the gills (see Figure 20-1a).**

2. **Hold the fish by the head or tail, with the fish's back toward you. With the knife blade pointing away from you and across the body of the fish, begin to cut along the backbone toward the tail or head (see Figure 20-1b). Use the backbone to guide your knife. Use the knife tip to work around the ribcage and organs. (If you have not gutted the fish. You don't need to if you're filleting it.) Don't cut all the way to the tail. Instead, leave about an inch of fillet attached to make removing the skin from the fillet easier.**

3. **Flip the fish over and do the same thing: Free the fillet by following along the backbone (see Figures 20-1c and 20-1d). This time, when your knife nears the tail, you can remove the tail (and the two fillets) by cutting through the backbone near the tail.**

   You now have a head, guts, and backbone ready for the trash. You also have a tail with two fillets, skin, and scales still attached.

4. **To take the skin off, begin by holding the fillet by the tail, skin side down. Hold the knife crosswise across the fillet and insert the knife between the skin and the flesh. While holding the skin, cut in the direction of where the head formerly was (see Figure 20-2).**

5. **Repeat Steps 4 through 6 for the other fillet. When done, you'll have the tail still connected to two pieces of skin, which you discard.**

Figure 20-1:
Try this technique for filleting fish.

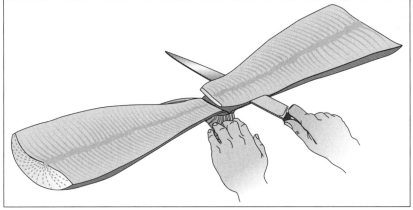

Figure 20-2:
Laying the skin flat on the cutting board, carefully work the knife against it to remove the fillet.

Cutting steaks

If you're cleaning a mess of particularly large fish, say, more than 20 pounds each, you may want to consider steaking them. I (Peter) am not a big fan of the current fashion at expensive and fashionable restaurants where one part of the meal is named after another: Fish Sorbet, Fruit Soup, Rack of Turnip. However, *fish steak* is an old and time-honored phrase. Many people don't go in for cooking fish steaks because they are too dry. My advice to you: Make thinner steaks, an inch or less. You can make fish steaks by using a wide-bladed chef's knife (like the kind chefs use on TV when they chop vegetables) or a Dexter knife (see the earlier "Cleaning: A Good Meal Starts with the First Cut" section for more detail on this tool). Just follow these steps (see Figure 20-3 for the visual):

1. **Scale the fish.**

   I explain how to scale a fish in the earlier "Scaling" section.

2. **Make a row of cuts crosswise along the fish, spacing them so they're the thickness of the steaks.**

3. **Cut down to the backbone, hitting the back of your knife with a stick to get through the bone, if needed.**

Figure 20-3:
Cutting a
fish into
steaks.

Freezing to Avoid an Oily, Fishy Taste

Frozen fish does not have the consistency of flesh that has never been frozen. The physics behind this are simple. Living cells are filled with water. Water expands when frozen, and this expansion breaks down tissue. However, if you are not going to eat fish right away — like within a day — then we recommend freezing. It keeps the fish tasting fresh. For example, many people say they don't like the taste of bluefish. It's too oily, they say, or too "fishy." What they are really referring to is the taste of fish oil that has come in contact with the air and turned rancid. Bluefish has a lot of oil, so unless you cook it on the day you catch it, it will have that oily, fishy taste. Freezing stops this process short and preserves the fresh taste. I usually freeze fish that I have filleted first. Wrap each fillet in wax paper. Store them in a plastic bag, keeping the fillets flat.

Vacuum sealers work great for fish headed to the freezer. If you don't have a vacuum sealer, place fillets in a freezer bag and fill the bag with water to help prevent freezer burn. Place only enough fillets for a meal in one bag, and label the outside of the bag with the date, kind of fish, and number of fillets. This will help you prevent waste because you can thaw only what you need at that time.

Chapter 21

Biting Back: Cooking and Eating Fish

*I*f people hadn't started eating fish a long time ago, I doubt that anyone would have had the bright idea of fishing for them just for the fun of it. Now, of course, you know that fighting a good fish thrills you, whether you keep the fish or throw it back. Still, cooking a fish over a fire next to the lake where you caught it will connect you to your ancestors in a way few things can. A well-prepared fish is one of the healthiest, tastiest meals you can eat.

Is It Done Yet?

Fish is either cooked, or it isn't. You seldom ask for a medium-cooked fish. When cooking fish, one minute the flesh looks milky and semi-transparent and resists cutting with a fork. Then, just like that, the flesh turns opaque and a fork will flake it easily: the fish is done.

Ten minutes to the inch

How do you know how long to cook fish? The best guestimate method I know was originally published by the Canadian Fisheries Board: Whether you boil, fry, poach, or broil, you should cook fish no longer than *ten minutes for each inch of thickness.* Measure the fish at its thickest part, and multiply it by ten minutes for each inch. The one exception is charcoal broiling. In this case, use the ten-minutes-to-the-inch rule as a rough guide. The intensity of the fire and the closeness of the fish to the fire will lengthen or, more often, shorten the cooking time.

The more experienced cooks among you will no doubt have reckoned that the Canadian Fish rule means the thin part of the fillet will be done before the fat part. You're right. However most fillets are pretty uniform in thickness, as are all steaks, so I usually don't worry about it.

A neat way to even up the thickness of fillets that have a long thin "tail" is simply to flip the tail over so that the thin end of the fillet is doubled up, which means it will respond to heating the same way that a thicker piece would. Thanks to chef Susan Spicer of Dayona in New Orleans for this tip.

Marinate with caution

Everybody likes marinated food. Garlic, salt, wine, soy sauce, lemon juice — all the classic marinating ingredients — sound so good. A duck or a cut of venison can sometimes be marinated for days to the benefit of the completed dish. Marinating gives flavor and/or tenderizes tough cuts of meat. Basically, there is no such thing as a tough cut of fish. So by all means, pile on the lemon juice, the white wine, the teriyaki sauce, but half an hour of marinating will give it more than enough flavor without giving your fish the consistency of a wet paper towel.

Fearless Frying

Crispy, crunchy, salty. Show me someone who doesn't like deep-fried fish and I will show you someone who is possibly an extraterrestrial. The big trick with frying is *hot oil.* You want the oil to be between 320 and 360 degrees. Use a thermometer and get it right. If the oil isn't hot enough, the coating will absorb a lot of grease, and you have yourself a potential stomach ache with some nice heartburn thrown in for good measure. If the oil gets too hot, you'll notice excessive smoke. With hot oil, the crust is crisp, light, and nongreasy. If you don't have a thermometer, drop a pinch of bread into the oil. With the oil temperature right, the bread should immediately sizzle and jump.

I cook a lot with olive oil these days, which takes a fair amount of heat before it smokes. You can also use canola or peanut oil:

- ✔ **Traditional Fried Fish:** The best fish frying recipe I know is also the first one I learned. I was in the Florida Keys and I had caught a nice grouper. The captain, whose name I forget, gave me this recipe, which I have used ever since. He also told me that the best cure for seasickness was to wrap both arms around an oak tree.

- ✔ **Reddened Blackfish:** Blackening, unless it's done right, is a perfect way to take good food and use it to fumigate your house with smoke. This alternative recipe results in a quick, clean, beautiful red-gold crust of powerful spices — without a smoky kitchen. You can use any fish for this recipe.

- ✔ **Crispy Fish with Asian Dipping Sauce:** Many anglers relish in the flavor and texture of crispy, freshly fried fish. This recipe is quick and easy to prepare, and you can make the dipping sauce in advance for even more convenience. Any white-fleshed fish works well in this recipe, and the fresher the better. (This recipe is courtesy of Chef Lucia Watson's *In-Fisherman Presents Cooking Freshwater Fish.*)

If you're new to the traditional fish fry and want to ease into it, look in your local grocery story for any of a variety of pre-packaged seasoning and breading products for fish.

Traditional Fried Fish

Prep time: 10 min   •   **Cook time:** 20 min   •   **Yield:** 4 servings

Ingredients	*Directions*
1 cup flour	**1** In a straight-sided cast-iron skillet, heat about an inch of oil to around 375 degrees. If you use a 10-inch skillet, you can fry two or three fillets per batch.
1 teaspoon salt	
1 teaspoon ground black pepper	**2** While the oil heats, combine flour with salt and pepper in a shallow dish. Put the buttermilk in another shallow dish, and the cornmeal in yet another.
1 cup buttermilk	
1 cup cornmeal	
8 fillets of white fish, trimmed to four inches in length	**3** Dredge the first two or three fillets (depending on the size of the pan) in the flour mixture. Shake off excess flour, dip the fillets in buttermilk, and dredge in cornmeal.
2 to 4 cups vegetable oil, depending on size of skillet	
	4 Carefully place the coated fillets in the heated oil and fry for about 2 minutes.
	5 Use tongs to turn the fish, and fry another 2 minutes. While the second side fries, set a cooling rack on top of paper towels.
	6 When done, the fish will float to the top of the hot oil. Remove the fillets to the cooling rack to drain.
	7 Repeat Steps 3 through 6 with the remaining fillets.

Per serving: Calories 492 (From Fat 104); Fat 12g (Saturated 2g); Cholesterol 174mg; Sodium 591mg; Carbohydrate 27g (Dietary Fiber 2g); Protein 66g.

Reddened Blackfish

Prep time: 10 min • **Cook time:** 10 min • **Yield:** 4 servings

Ingredients	*Directions*
1 teaspoon onion powder	*1* Rinse the fillets in cool water, pat dry, and set aside.
¾ teaspoon oregano	
¾ teaspoon thyme	*2* Combine the first nine ingredients (the seasonings) in a bowl and mix well.
1 teaspoon black pepper	
1 teaspoon white pepper	*3* In a pan, heat 2 tablespoons of oil over medium-high heat until hot but not smoking.
1 teaspoon cayenne pepper	
2 teaspoons salt	*4* While the oil is heating, dredge two fillets in seasoning.
4 teaspoons paprika	
1 teaspoon granulated garlic powder	*5* Fry the fillets for 2 to 3 minutes on each side.
2 tablespoons corn, peanut, or olive oil	*6* Repeat Steps 3 through 5 with the remaining fillets.
4 fillets of white-fleshed fish (redfish, blackfish, weakfish, snapper, dolphin, and so on)	*7* Remove the fillets from the heat, and serve with fresh lemon wedges.
Lemon wedges	

Per serving: Calories 290 (From Fat 91); Fat 10g (Saturated 1g); Cholesterol 80mg; Sodium 1,261mg; Carbohydrate 2g (Dietary Fiber 1g); Protein 45g.

Crispy Fish with Asian Dipping Sauce

Prep time: 10 min • **Cook time:** 8 min • **Yield:** 2 servings

Ingredients	*Directions*

Ingredients

4 to 6 cups corn, peanut, or olive oil

About 12 ounces of your fish of choice, small fillets cut into finger-sized strips

1 cup cornmeal

½ cup all-purpose flour

Pinch of salt

Pinch of pepper

Pinch of cayenne pepper

1 egg

1 tablespoon of water

Asian Dipping Sauce (see the following recipe)

Directions

1 Before starting the fish, prepare the following Asian Dipping Sauce so it's cooled and flavorful when the fish is done.

2 On the stovetop, heat 2 inches of oil in a deep, heavy pot to 375 degrees.

3 While the oil is heating, combine the flour, cornmeal, salt, pepper, and cayenne in a small dish.

4 In small bowl, lightly beat an egg with a tablespoon of water.

5 Dip the fish in the egg and water mixture; then dredge the fish in the cornmeal mixture.

6 In batches, carefully transfer the fillets to the hot oil and fry until just done and crispy, about 2 to 3 minutes until golden brown. The fish will float to the top of the oil when done. Use a slotted spoon to remove to a plate lined with paper towels to drain before serving with dipping sauce.

Asian Dipping Sauce

Prep time: 7 min • **Cook time:** 5 min • **Cool:** 15 min • **Yield:** 2 servings

Ingredients	Directions
6 tablespoons rice wine vinegar	***1*** In a small saucepan, boil the vinegar and sugar together over medium-high heat, stirring until the sugar dissolves. Remove from heat and set aside to cool.
3 tablespoons sugar	
1 tablespoon dark soy sauce	
1 jalapeño pepper, seeds removed and finely minced	***2*** When cooled, transfer vinegar mixture to a small bowl. Stir together with the other ingredients. Taste and adjust the seasoning.
2 tablespoons lime zest (grated lime peel)	
Juice of ½ lime	
1 small knob ginger, peeled and finely grated	
1 clove garlic, peeled and finely minced	
2 tablespoons fresh cilantro, chopped	

Per serving: Calories 475 (From Fat 148); Fat 17g (Saturated 2g); Cholesterol 80mg; Sodium 498mg; Carbohydrate 49g (Dietary Fiber 4g); Protein 32g.

Tip: An oil thermometer helps keep your eye on the oil in the pan so it stays in the range you want. Don't let the oil temp dip below 355 degrees or above 375 degrees. Keeping it in the range of 360 to 370 degrees while cooking is ideal for frying fish.

Tip: Serve with steamed white rice or Japanese soba (buckwheat) noodles, and toss with soy sauce and fresh cilantro if you like.

Poaching Allowed

If people know you are an angler and you get married, I guarantee one of your friends will give you a fish poacher, one of those long pots with a little rack inside to lift out the poached fish. It's a good thing to have, but I can honestly say I don't know anybody who ever bought a fish poacher on their own. You can poach fish without one, but a poacher sure makes the job a lot easier.

Poaching is a method of cooking fish that is well suited to delicate flesh (and most fish is pretty delicate). It allows the flavor and texture of the fish to come through. If the fish is absolutely fresh, you might want to serve it with nothing more than steamed potatoes:

- ✔ **Poached Fish:** After you've poached the fish, you can serve it hot or cold. For me, cold poached fish with some dill or mustard mayonnaise is pretty hard to beat.

- ✔ **Poached Whiting with Littleneck Clams:** In the wintertime, there isn't a whole lot of fishing going on in the northeastern U.S.; however, you will meet other die-hard anglers on the party boats that are usually the only game in town for anglers. I love to go out from the old fishing village at Sheepshead Bay in Brooklyn. An old Sicilian gave me this recipe for whiting on one of those 60-degree days that brings out the anglers and helps to lighten the sentence of February in New York.

Poached Fish

Prep time: 10 min • **Cook time:** 35 min • **Yield:** 4 servings

Ingredients	*Directions*
One 1½-pound fillet, such as salmon with the pinbones removed **Fish Stock Poaching Liquid (see the following recipe)**	*1* Place fish on poaching rack in poacher. If you don't have a poacher, any pan big enough to hold the fish will do.
	2 Cover fish with 2 to 3 inches of stock. It's okay if the tops of the fish aren't completely covered with the liquid.
	3 Bring to boil and then reduce to a very low simmer; cover.
	4 Simmer until the internal temperature of the thickest part of the fish reads 125 to 130 degrees on a meat thermometer — for example, 10 to 12 minutes for a 2-inch salmon fillet. When done, the fish should be opaque.
	5 When the fish is done, lift it out of the broth using the two handles on the poaching rack. If you don't have a poacher, stick a couple of slotted spatulas underneath the fish and gently lift it out so that it doesn't break apart.
	6 After removing the fish, increase the heat under the poaching liquid and rapidly boil, uncovered, for a few minutes. Drizzle a little of the reduced broth onto the fish to add a little more flavor.
	7 Garnish with parsley or dill, and serve with mustard sauce, homemade mayonnaise, salsa, or anything else with a little tang and taste to it that catches your fancy.

Fish Stock Poaching Liquid

4 cups water or dry white wine

Fish bones and head

1 carrot

1 onion

1 celery stalk

½ teaspoon salt

10 black peppercorns

Sprig of parsley

1 Combine all ingredients in a medium-size pot and simmer 20 minutes, covered.

2 Strain and save the liquid; discard the solids.

Per serving: Calories 215 (From Fat 58); Fat 6g (Saturated 1g); Cholesterol 97mg; Sodium 124mg; Carbohydrate 0g (Dietary Fiber 0g); Protein 37g.

Tip: Experiment because fish prepared this way is kind of like chicken: It picks up the flavor of whatever you serve it with. Also, poached fish is great cold.

Poached Whiting with Littleneck Clams

Prep time: 7 min • **Cook time:** 10–12 min • **Yield:** 4 servings

Ingredients	*Directions*
4 whole, gutted whitings (heads on, tails intact) **1 dozen littleneck clams, scrubbed** **1 clove garlic, peeled** **½ cup white wine** **¼ cup chopped parsley**	*1* Place fish in a large pot or Dutch oven and surround them with clams. Add garlic. Pour in wine and bring to simmer. *2* When the liquid begins to simmer, cover the pot and continue the low simmer for 10 to 12 minutes. The clams will steam open and add their broth to the cooking liquid. *3* Transfer the fish to a wide, flat bowl with a few clams. Pour broth in the bowl and top with chopped parsley. To serve, peel back the skin and serve portions of fish each with some clams, broth, and crusty bread to soak up the tasty broth.

Per serving: Calories 75 (From Fat 10); Fat 1g (Saturated 0g); Cholesterol 50mg; Sodium 81mg; Carbohydrate 0g (Dietary Fiber 0g); Protein 15g.

Firing Up the Grill

Salty, crusty, and peppery. Grilling fish is an easy way to get the taste of broiled fish you love from a restaurant without the dried-out taste and texture that tends to accompany broiling fish at home. (Your broiler most likely isn't as hot as one of those gas-powered top-broilers found in restaurants.)

For basic grilled fish, just brush your fish fillets with some olive oil, sprinkle both sides with salt and pepper, and slap 'em on a hot grill for 10 minutes per inch of thickness. Add a clean, untreated, water-soaked cedar plank to the equation — just brush it with a little cooking oil and lay the fish on top of it — for a smoky flavor. (Soak the plank in water for at least an hour to prevent burning. If you notice that it catches fire while grilling, spray it with water.)

If you're looking for something a bit more pulled together with more flavors, the following recipe for Islamorada Grilled Speckled Trout is both simple and delicious. Islamorada, in the Florida Keys, is one of the best fishing-friendly towns in the United States. The best dining, or at least my (Peter's) favorite, has always been at Manny & Isa's, a simple roadhouse run by a Guatemalan couple. This dish gets its zip from my version of Manny & Isa's tomato mint sauce. Topped off with frizzled onions or leeks, it looks like a real restaurant dish. As with many of these recipes, any white-fleshed fish will do if you can't get specks or weakfish.

If you barbecue, fish fillets tend to break apart and fall through the slots on the grill. However, there is a product that came out on the market in the last few years that has virtually revolutionized my fish-grilling life. It's cheap, uncomplicated, and it works, which are three unusual things to find in a new product these days. It's called a Griffo Grill, and the simple original version (which I haven't seen lately) is nothing more than heavy window screening that you lay on top of your grill. Flipping is no longer an anxious game of waiting and seeing if the fish is going to fall apart. The recent, more jazzed up version is a piece of enameled steel with pea-size holes. The principle is the same in both models: Little holes to let the radiant heat through are small enough to keep fish flakes from falling off.

Islamorada Grilled Speckled Trout

Prep time: 10 min • **Cook time:** 16 min • **Yield:** 4 servings

Ingredients	Directions
Two 1-pound or four 8-ounce speckled trout fillets, skinned	*1* Prepare the Islamorada Salsa according to the following recipe, and cover the pan to keep it warm while you grill the fish.
2 tablespoons olive oil	
Salt	*2* Brush your grill with olive oil and heat. Brush fillets with olive oil; add salt and pepper to taste.
Pepper	
Islamorada Salsa (see the following recipe)	*3* Lay the fillets on the grill over hot coals. When you see the edges start to get white (or opaque), after roughly 2 to 3 minutes depending on the thickness of the fillets, flip the fish and let it cook another 2 to 3 minutes.
¼ cup white wine or lemon juice (or both)	
	4 Pour the salsa over the cooked fillets, and return the salsa pan to the stove top.
	5 Increase the heat under the salsa pan to medium-high and deglaze the pan with wine and/or lemon juice. (Pour the liquid in the pan and stir it as it boils down). Pour over fish, and serve.

Islamorada Salsa

1 chili pepper, diced	*1* Sauté chili pepper for 1 minute in hot olive oil. Then add garlic and shallots for another minute.
2 teaspoons olive oil	
2 cloves garlic, diced	*2* Add chopped tomatoes and simmer for a few minutes until most of the liquid has evaporated. Stir in mint before serving.
1 shallot or scallion, diced	
2 ripe tomatoes, peeled, seeded, and chopped	
¼ cup chopped fresh mint	

Per serving: Calories 381 (From Fat 176); Fat 20g (Saturated 4g); Cholesterol 121mg; Sodium 250mg; Carbohydrate 9g (Dietary Fiber 1g); Protein 42g.

More Favorite Fish Recipes

The following recipes aren't the only ones by a long shot, but they are a really good spectrum of techniques. After you've mastered these, experiment to your heart's content:

- **Great South Bay Roast Striper:** No turkey or standing rib roast ever arrived at the table to more oohs and aahs than the Great South Bay Roast Striper that follows: a large striper stuffed with minced local shell-fish. This meal — or rather, the idea for the meal — began as I (Peter) was visiting my friend Neil Ganek's take-out shop (Petite Crevette or The Little Shrimp) on Atlantic Avenue in Brooklyn.

- **Door County Fish Boil:** Door County is a very long and thin peninsula that sticks out into Lake Michigan just above Green Bay, Wisconsin. Generations of commercial fishermen have made their living hauling their catch out of the rich lake waters. This recipe, which I have modi-fied for the home cook, originated in a shore dinner that the fishing boat captains used to make for their crews and families.

- **Halibut Stew with Red Wine Sauce:** They say that red wine is for meat and white wine is for fish. This recipe is yet another reason I want to meet that famous "they" because, as you will see when you taste this marvelous recipe, "they" don't know what "they" are talking about. Thanks for this dish go to my good friend and cooking buddy Bryan Miller, author of *Cooking For Dummies* and the former restaurant critic of *The New York Times*.

- **Hearty Fish Chowder:** This is a recipe that works with mild-tasting fish, such as walleye, crappies, white bass, bluegills, and perch. Striper would also be excellent, as would smaller largemouth bass. You can also use frozen fish for convenience. (This recipe is courtesy of Chef Lucia Watson's *In-Fisherman Presents Cooking Freshwater Fish.*)

- **Fish Salad Sandwich:** This is a wonderful sandwich spread to take with you when fishing. For this particular mix of ingredients, a mild-flavored white-fleshed fish works best. Walleye's a favorite, but crap-pies, bass, bluegills, and perch are fine. Properly frozen fish also work well in a salad like this. (This recipe is courtesy of Chef Lucia Watson's *In-Fisherman Presents Cooking Freshwater Fish.*)

Great South Bay Roast Striper

Prep time: 35 min • **Cook time:** 1 hr • **Yield:** 8 servings

Ingredients	*Directions*
1 striped bass, 6 to 8 pounds	*1* Remove the skeleton by slitting the fish along the backbone. Then cut and separate the two fillets from the spine. Snip the backbone, and remove the skeleton.
¼ cup olive oil	
Juice of 2 lemons	
Juice of 2 limes	
Basil, rosemary, thyme (to taste)	*2* Cut open the stomach from the top and remove the innards.
1 teaspoon crushed red pepper flakes (optional)	*3* Drizzle about half the olive oil in a 9x13 baking pan. Stuff the bass with the shellfish stuffing and place in the pan. Sprinkle with the remaining olive oil and lemon juice.
Shellfish Stuffing (see the following recipe)	
	4 Add herbs, red pepper flakes, and lime juice to pan.
	5 Roast at 375 degrees for approximately 1 hour. If desired, baste periodically with pan juices for a moister roast.
	6 Serve on a big platter, cutting the bass crosswise.

Shellfish Stuffing

1½ cups scallops (around 1-inch in diameter)

1 dozen oysters, shucked

1 dozen littleneck clams, shucked

1½ cups crab meat, picked through for cartilage and shell

1 shallot, diced

2 cloves garlic, minced

2 teaspoons butter or oil

3 egg whites

1 cup bread crumbs

1 tablespoon Dijon mustard

2 tablespoons applejack (or brandy)

1 Dice the shellfish and place in large bowl.

2 Heat butter or oil in small skillet. Sauté the shallot and garlic until soft and add to the shellfish.

3 In large bowl, combine the shellfish mixture with egg whites, bread crumbs, mustard, and applejack.

Per serving: Calories 358 (From Fat 113); Fat 13g (Saturated 2g); Cholesterol 171mg; Sodium 412mg; Carbohydrate 14g (Dietary Fiber 1g); Protein 45g.

Door County Fish Boil

Prep time: 10 min • **Cook time:** 25 min • **Yield:** 4–6 servings

Ingredients	Directions
2 quarts water	**1** Combine water and salt in a large stock pot. Add potatoes and onions to the salted water. Partially cover the pot and bring to a boil over high heat; cook for 15 minutes until the potatoes are almost tender when pierced with a fork.
2 tablespoons kosher salt	
2 lbs medium red potatoes, scrubbed and cut in half	
4 white fish steaks, ½ pound each	**2** Arrange the fish in a single layer on top of the vegetables. (Don't worry if the fish isn't entirely covered by the water.) Lower heat to moderate and cook until the whitefish flakes easily (about 10 minutes).
8 small onions, peeled	
Black pepper to taste	**3** Using a slotted spoon or large slotted fish fork, transfer the whitefish to a large, warm platter. Spoon the potatoes and onions around the fish. Sprinkle with parsley and black pepper to taste. Serve with melted butter and lemon wedges alongside.
2 tablespoons chopped parsley	

Per serving: Calories 568 (From Fat 128); Fat 14g (Saturated 2g); Cholesterol 140mg; Sodium 592mg; Carbohydrate 57g (Dietary Fiber 6g); Protein 51g.

Vary It!: This recipe also works well with striped bass.

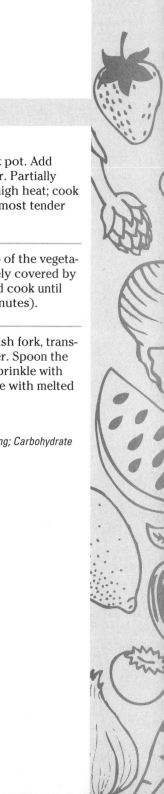

Halibut Stew with Red Wine Sauce

Prep time: 7 min • **Cook time:** 35 min • **Yield:** 4 servings

Ingredients

2 tablespoons butter

½ pound small mushrooms; if large, cut into quarters

½ cup finely chopped onion

¼ cup finely chopped shallots

¼ cup finely chopped carrots

¼ cup finely chopped celery

1 teaspoon finely chopped garlic

2 teaspoons chopped fresh thyme or 1 teaspoon dried

2 tablespoons flour

1½ cups dry red wine

1 cup fresh fish broth (see the poaching recipe) or bottled clam juice

1 bay leaf

2 whole cloves

1½ pounds halibut fillets, cut into ½-inch cubes

Salt and freshly ground pepper to taste

2 tablespoons cognac

2 tablespoons finely chopped parsley

Directions

1 Heat the butter in a saucepan and add the mushrooms, onion, shallots, carrots, celery, garlic, and thyme. Stir until the onion is wilted, about 7 minutes over medium heat.

2 Add the flour and stir as the mixture cooks for 1 minute. Add the wine, fish broth, bay leaf, and cloves, stirring with a wire whisk. Bring to a boil. Simmer, uncovered, for 20 minutes and reduce liquid to about 1¾ cups.

3 Add the fish, salt, and pepper, stirring gently so that the fish is coated with the sauce. Simmer for about 5 minutes and add the cognac. Remove the cloves and bay leaf. Sprinkle with parsley and serve.

Per serving: Calories 277 (From Fat 82); Fat 9g (Saturated 4g); Cholesterol 70mg; Sodium 381mg; Carbohydrate 11g (Dietary Fiber 2g); Protein 38g.

Hearty Fish Chowder

Prep time: 15 min • **Cook time:** 40 min • **Yield:** 4–8 servings

Ingredients	*Directions*
4 ounces bacon	*1* In a large, heavy soup pot, fry the bacon over medium heat until crisp. Remove the bacon to a paper towel-lined plate to drain.
1 large onion, chopped	
1 stalk celery, chopped	
¼ cup unbleached all-purpose flour	*2* In the pot with the bacon fat, sauté the onion and celery over medium heat until soft. While the vegetables cook, chop the bacon and set aside.
2 medium potatoes, peeled and diced	
2 cups low-sodium canned chicken broth	*3* Sprinkle the flour over the onion and celery; stir and cook for about 3 to 4 minutes.
1 bay leaf	*4* To the soup pot, add the potatoes, chicken stock, bay leaf, and a sprinkle of salt and pepper, and bring the mixture to a boil. Immediately reduce the heat and simmer uncovered until the potatoes are soft, about 20 minutes.
Salt and pepper to taste	
2 cups whole milk	
½ red bell pepper, cored, seeded, and chopped	
½ green bell pepper, cored, seeded, and chopped	*5* Add the milk, bell peppers, corn, and fish to the chowder mixture, and simmer for 8 to 10 minutes, taking care not to let it boil. Adjust the seasoning to taste, adding salt and pepper, and perhaps a dash of hot sauce or a splash of wine if desired.
3 cups whole corn kernels (frozen or fresh cut from 4 to 5 ears)	
1½ pounds fish, such as haddock, cut into 1-inch pieces	*6* Just before serving, sprinkle with the bacon and herbs.
Salt and pepper to taste	
Fresh chives, basil, or parsley, chopped, to equal about 1 tablespoon (use one herb or a combination)	

Per serving: Calories 478 (From Fat 107); Fat 12g (Saturated 5g); Cholesterol 125mg; Sodium 539mg; Carbohydrate 50g (Dietary Fiber 6g); Protein 47g.

Vary It!: Use the best of your own local fresh ingredients in this chowder, given the season. For example, try garden squash and a pinch of sage in the fall. In winter, try a splash of heavy cream and white beans. In the spring and summer, replace the corn and peppers with 1-inch pieces of asparagus and wild mushrooms. For a slightly different taste, add 1 cup white wine along with the broth. And for a less thick chowder, increase the milk to 3 cups.

Fish Salad Sandwich

Prep time: 5 min • **Cook time:** None • **Yield:** 2–4 sandwiches

Ingredients	*Directions*
Two 8-ounce fish fillets, cooked and flaked	*1* In a large bowl, mix all ingredients together. Layer on toasted bread, adding sliced tomato, lettuce, and onion as desired.
1 rib celery, diced	
1 small onion, diced	
½ cup mayonnaise	
2 sweet pickles, chopped	
Squeeze of lemon juice	
Salt and pepper to taste	
Sandwich fixings as desired (bread, tomato slices, onion slices, lettuce)	

Per serving: Calories 741 (From Fat 432); Fat 48g (Saturated 7g); Cholesterol 139mg; Sodium 1,196mg; Carbohydrate 34g (Dietary Fiber 2g); Protein 43g.

Part VI
The Part of Tens

The 5th Wave   By Rich Tennant

In this part . . .

In the grand For Dummies tradition, this part contains quick reference chapters of our top ten lists. You get the scoop on ten tips we learned the hard way, as well as ten tips to get kids involved in fishing. Fishing is one of the best family activities available, and it's important to show others what you've learned!

Chapter 22

Ten Fishing Lessons You Don't Have to Learn the Hard Way

*T*hroughout this book, we stress the need to pay attention while fishing. We say a lot about experience, and how there really is no substitute for it. All things in fishing — from casting to netting a big fish — get easier the more you do them. Although true, this advice assumes you're learning on your own. Fish with an experienced angler, though, and you can learn a lot about what to do, and even what not to do. This shortens the learning curve. Here are ten things one or both of us learned the hard way.

Avoid Making Bad Vibes

The fish's lateral line enables it to sense vibrations. When a fish picks up vibrations, it pays attention: Is a predator nearby? A scared fish flees; it doesn't bite. Whether you're wading or walking the bank, walk quietly. Rubber boots are good for this.

In a boat, avoid dropping anything against the hull — that's like hitting a bass drum underwater. Put rubber mats over the floor of your boat to dampen vibrations. People often warn against talking while fishing, but your feet are what really get you into trouble.

Know Gimmick Lures When You See Them

Giving someone a lure shaped like a can of beer might be a funny gag gift, but most lures that require a battery to power their flashing red eyes or special fish call are a waste of money. Stick with proven lures like those we cover in Chapter 13, and learn to fish them well.

Cast No Shadow

Like vibrations, shadows falling on the water's surface often trigger a fleeing instinct in fish. On bright sunny days, and even moonlit nights, avoid letting your shadow hit the water. Stay low and keep the sun in front of you and the element of surprise is yours.

Choose Clothing That Blends In

That Aerosmith concert t-shirt may be your lucky shirt, but if it's too garish, it might not be your luckiest fishing shirt. Wear comfortable clothes while fishing, and try to blend into the background. When wading, dark earth tones will blend into the bank better than day-glo orange. While boating, dark clothes stand out against the sky more than light colors. So think like a hunter while fishing — try to disappear against whatever background the fish sees.

Reuse Home Items

I (Greg) am an admitted gear hound. I love acquiring new stuff to make my fishing life easier. But I've learned that a lot of the best items for fishing weren't made for fishing. Kitchen containers and pill bottles make great waterproof units for medicine, sunglasses, cellphones, you name it. Leather carpenter bags make great sinker carriers. Golf towels work for fish slime. Those funny foam pool noodles can be made into large livebait bobbers. A piece of foam pipe insulation makes a great tool for holding pre-rigged leaders. (Just pop the loop or swivel in the split, wrap the line around the insulation, and sink the hook into the soft foam.) I look for fishing gear wherever I go.

Pick a Bait Cooler

If you fish with bait at all, you need a way to carry it and keep it cool. Coolers come in every shape and size. Buy one that fits the kind of bait you use and label it as your bait cooler. Use it for bait and only bait. Trust me, it makes life easier.

After a day's fishing, rinse out your bait cooler and set it — with the lid open — in the sun to remove most of the odors.

Seek Out Advice

We hope this book helps you learn how to fish. But there's a lot to cover — the fishing world is vast — and your particular kind of fishing will lead you to more questions we didn't think to answer. Don't be the stubborn guy who refuses to stop and ask for directions. Most anglers will gladly help a fellow angler. If you see others fishing with success on your home waters, respectfully ask them for advice. Just don't interrupt their fishing!

Keep a Fishing Journal

I (Greg) am in the business of assigning homework, so I know it's no fun. But this isn't homework, even though it involves taking notes. Record data about every fishing trip you take: the weather, water conditions, fish caught, and lures used. Over time, this fishing journal becomes an invaluable source of information. If you had great luck fishing Bischoff Reservoir in March 2010 jigging soft plastic crawfish, odds are good March 2011 will offer the same results.

Be Open to Multispecies Angling

Don't be a fish snob. We all have our favorites, but there are so many kinds of fish out there! Branch out and fish for everything. That way, regardless of the season, you'll have something to pursue. And you'll find that the more you understand about different species of fish, the more you understand all fish.

Greg's a big fan of *In-Fisherman* magazine in particular, which comes out eight times a year and features articles about every kind of fish you might pursue in freshwater, including often-ignored species like alligator gar and carp.

Take Someone Along for the Trip

I (Greg) like to fish alone a lot of the time. Gives me time to think, ponder, blah blah blah. I'm also a terrible singer, but the kingfishers on the riverbank never complain. Preserve your private time because it's one of the greatest gifts of angling. Still, bring a non-angler along once in a while. Introducing more people to the sport you love benefits us all in the long run. The more anglers there are, the more of us there are who are concerned about the resources and habitat fishing requires. When it comes to tasks like spotting polluters or poachers, the more watchdogs on the water, the better. Plus, why keep such a great thing to yourself?

Chapter 23

Ten Ways to Get Kids Involved in Fishing

● ●

In This Chapter

▶ Picking the best catch for kids

▶ Keeping it fun

▶ Making competition friendly

▶ Showing kids the other worlds of fishing

● ●

Almost everyone has a fishing memory from childhood. Usually, a grandparent or a parent takes a child fishing, antics ensue, and 20 years later the child is an adult with a treasured fishing memory. People see fishing as something often done with kids, but, like so many things involving kids, it's easier said than done. And if it's done improperly, no one will want to repeat the experience.

Kids need to be introduced to fishing the right way. Fishing trips should be fun for all involved. (To that end, whenever you take little ones fishing, make sure you pack plenty of food and drink. No one has fun fishing when they're hungry or thirsty.) And while you might not be able to catch fish because you're busy watching the youngsters, some fish should be caught. Although there are some risks — there's no kid-friendly hook — fishing can be one of the best ways to get youngsters outdoors. There's no better way to interest kids in biology than to take them somewhere where they can get their feet wet. Fishing is a wonderful way to introduce kids to the natural world and all it entails. After all, in 20 years, no one wants to tell the story about the wonderful childhood memory of playing videogames.

Tap into Bluegill Mania

Bluegills are the universal "first fish." Because they live in almost every retention pond in America, bluegills are widespread, and they happen to be willing to bite almost every day. They also school and seem to be attracted to fishing activity. Find a dock or sunny cove and cast bits of earthworm or wax worms on small hooks. Bluegills love taking baits suspended under floats, which give kids something to watch, and these small fish tussle quite hard when hooked. Catching one bluegill seldom spooks the others in the area, either. Just watch the sharp dorsal spines after you land them.

Make Bait Fun

Livebait fishing works for kids because it works for the fish. Bait works, and if fish are around, they'll take it.

Make the act of gathering natural bait part of the adventure. Gathering worms, setting minnow traps, and catching grasshoppers or crayfish might be more enjoyable to kids than the act of fishing. Let it be.

The trick is handling the life and death issues connected to livebait. Gage your child's reaction and respond accordingly. You might need to release one bait for every one you use. Usually, though, kids handle this part better than we think they will.

Get Gear That Works

Fishing poles with cartoon characters work great to get kids excited about fishing, but a short rod makes it tough to set the hook. (If you don't believe me, try fishing with one yourself.) You want kids to actually catch fish, not just see them bite. Experiment with circle hooks, which eliminate the need to set the hook (you just hold the rod steady until the fish hooks itself), and whether you use circle or J hooks, cast sharp, small hooks that penetrate quickly. And think about replacing that short cartoon rod with one about 5 feet long. It's harder to handle, but easier to hook fish with.

Combine Fishing and Tubing

Whether you own a boat or are looking to rent or borrow one for a day of fishing with kids, keep in mind that although some kids might be slow to take to fishing, almost all kids like playing in the water. I (Greg) can tow a two-seater tube with my deep-V, and I'm constantly amazed at how much all kids enjoy tubing, no matter how fast or slow the boat goes. Why not spend a day combining tubing and fishing? You can fish for a while in a secluded cove, and when patience wanes, drop the tube overboard for a bit. I've never met a kid who didn't smile while riding a tube.

Give Out Fish Awards

When the kids are involved in fishing, there's nothing wrong with a little friendly competition. For more than ten years, my family has held an annual Fish Awards night. We display a slideshow of fishing photos from the past year and give trophies for the largest fish of several species. We have fried fish, hush puppies, and door prizes. It's like our Academy Awards. The kids love it. The adults love it. We do this in the winter, and it stokes the fishing fires for the coming season.

Canoe into the Local Wilderness

For kids old enough to be comfortable in a canoe, there's no better way to spend a Saturday than to canoe a quiet stretch of the local stream. Even near major metropolitan areas, small rivers and streams tend to remain wild because building is often prohibited in the floodplain. You'll be amazed at the wildlife you can spot, and you should catch some really nice fish, too. Boredom is seldom an issue because you're always able to paddle on down the river.

Chum Up Carp

Check your local laws, but most states allow you to *chum* for fish. This practice involves placing an attractant in an area to lure fish. For sharks, chum consists of blood and ground-up fish. For carp, it involves a handful of canned sweet corn. Heat a can of corn in a saucepan over the stove, adding a bit of maple syrup and Kool-Aid (any flavor will do — carp aren't that picky). When you get to the lake or stream, toss a handful of corn as far out as you can. Then bait a hook with several kernels of corn and cast into the same area. Hold on! Carp come to the corn, and then feed ravenously. Carp fight hard, so don't let them pull the rod into the water!

Try Fish Camping

Fishing and camping go together like football and tailgating. Too often, fishing time is defined by the trip there and the departure. Setting up camp near a likely fishing spot removes the pressure. Like Nick Adams in "Big Two-Hearted River," you can relax and enjoy the fishing. For kids, a campsite means a campfire, marshmallows, flashlights, tents, and snuggly sleeping bags. Camping while fishing makes the fishing part of the adventure — not the whole adventure itself.

Crank Up Tourney Time

It's quite possible that kids are too competitive these days. Still, catching fish naturally leads to some good-natured competition. Who caught the most fish? The biggest? We see nothing wrong with a little tournament action for an afternoon's fishing session. After all, unlike sports such as soccer, fishing might favor the quiet, contemplative kids that care less about active sports. Fishing is a great equalizer in that way. Bass pros compete for million dollar purses — we recommend prizes like a new tackle box or a fishing hat.

Go Night Fishing

Night fishing is more challenging, potentially risky, and more frustrating than daytime fishing. Seems like the exact opposite of what a kid needs. True, but night fishing is also absolutely enchanting. The world, quite literally, changes. Exposing experienced kids to night fishing is like opening the door to another world.

You should not attempt to take a kid night fishing until you're an expert yourself, but being outside at night is something a kid never forgets.

Index

C

• •

• *E* •

• S •